The Beloved Apostle?

The Beloved Apostle?

The Transformation of the Apostle John
into the Fourth Evangelist

Michael J. Kok

CASCADE *Books* • Eugene, Oregon

THE BELOVED APOSTLE?
The Transformation of the Apostle John into the Fourth Evangelist

Copyright © 2017 Michael J. Kok. All rights reserved. Except for brief quotations in critical publications or reviews, no part of this book may be reproduced in any manner without prior written permission from the publisher. Write: Permissions, Wipf and Stock Publishers, 199 W. 8th Ave., Suite 3, Eugene, OR 97401.

Cascade Books
An Imprint of Wipf and Stock Publishers
199 W. 8th Ave., Suite 3
Eugene, OR 97401

www.wipfandstock.com

PAPERBACK ISBN: 978-1-5326-1021-9
HARDCOVER ISBN: 978-1-5326-1023-3
EBOOK ISBN: 978-1-5326-1022-6

Cataloguing-in-Publication data:

Names: Kok, Michael J.

Title: The beloved apostle? : the transformation of the Apostle John into the Fourth Evangelist / by Michael J. Kok.

Description: Eugene, OR: Cascade Books, 2017 | Includes bibliographical references and index.

Identifiers: ISBN 978-1-5326-1021-9 (paperback) | ISBN 978-1-5326-1023-3 (hardcover) | ISBN 978-1-5326-1022-6 (ebook)

Subjects: LCSH: John, the Apostle, Saint. | Beloved Disciple. | Bible. John—Criticism, interpretation, etc. | Christian literature, Early—History and criticism.

Classification: LCC BS2615.2 K5 2017 (print) | LCC BS2615.2 (ebook)

Manufactured in the U.S.A.   11/01/17

To my parents, John and Valerie Kok, for all of their unconditional love and support and for the example that they have set for me as beloved disciples of Jesus.

Contents

Acknowledgments | ix
*Introduction: The Reception
  of the Beloved Disciple* | xi

CHAPTER 1 **The Beloved Son of Zebedee?** | 1
The Case for the Traditional View | 2
The Case against the Traditional View | 10
The Literary Function of the Beloved Disciple | 19
Conclusion: An Elite Judean Disciple | 28

CHAPTER 2 **The Beloved Evangelist?** | 30
Inconclusive Textual and Stylistic Arguments | 31
Inconclusive Thematic Arguments | 35
The Anachronism of Authorial
Self-Representation | 43
The Anachronism of Peter's Crucifixion | 50
Conclusion: The Contribution of the
Johannine Epilogue | 56

CHAPTER 3 **Would the Real John Please Stand Up?** | 58
Papias and the Elder John | 59
Papias and the Evangelist John | 73
Justin Martyr and the Seer John | 80
Irenaeus and the Apostle John | 90

Contents

Conclusion: The Construction of
the Ephesian John | 101

CHAPTER 4   **Why Does the Authorship of the Fourth Gospel Matter?** | 103
What Does an Author Do? | 104
The Criterion of Apostolicity | 109
The Gospel according to Cerinthus? | 114
Conclusion: The Authorial Function | 126

CONCLUSION: **The Historical and Theological Implications** | 127

Bibliography | 131
Author Index | 143
Ancient Document Index | 151

Acknowledgments

AFTER REVISING MY PHD dissertation for publication under the title *The Gospel on the Margins: The Reception of Mark in the Second Century*, I realized that, with regards to my brief excurses on the Elder John and on the *Rezeptionsgeschichte* ("reception history") of John's Gospel, I was just scratching the surface. A full monograph was needed on the construction of the traditions about Saint John of Ephesus. I initially contemplated pursuing postdoctoral studies and am grateful to the Professors Adele Reinhartz, Judith Lieu, and Catrin H. Williams for critically examining my research proposal on what the scribal addition of the Johannine Epilogue to the text of the Fourth Gospel reveals about the reception of the text in the second century CE. I also gained valuable feedback after presenting on the same topic for the Canadian Society of Biblical Studies hosted at the University of Calgary in May 2016.

There are a number of people to whom I owe a debt a gratitude for the completion of the project. Professor Christopher W Skinner has been a huge help in offering me publishing advice, permitting me to put his name down as an academic reference, and reading through the rough versions of a few chapters. A number of scholars provided constructive criticisms after reading the drafts of select chapters, or emailed me various scholarly publications that I was not able to get a hold of. These scholars include Jonathan Kruschwitz, James Barker, Jonathan Bernier, Stephen Carlson, Michael Bird, Hannah M. Strømmen, Willi Braun, and Matthew Ferguson. At any point where I failed to listen to their corrections and recommendations, the blame should fall entirely

Acknowledgments

on me for my own stubbornness. Sarah Hussell, who runs a proofreading service called *Proof-Ed*, formatted my bibliography and appendices. Finally, thanks to the team at Cascade Books for all of their editorial assistance in preparing this book for publication.

Introduction

The Reception of the Beloved Disciple

THERE ARE MANY RIDDLES in "the Gospel according to John" (*to euangelion kata Iōannēn*),¹ but the mystery surrounding the "disciple whom Jesus loved" may be the most vexing of them all.² Did Jesus really have a disciple whom he cherished above all the rest, someone who was seated beside him at the Last Supper (John 13:23-25) and adopted into his own family (19:25-27)? Considering the standing of this character in the narrative world of the Fourth Gospel, it is all the more bewildering that the narrator opts to never disclose his or her name.³ Contrary to the Fourth Gospel's reticence to remove the shroud of anonymity, the academic and popular quest to unveil the beloved disciple's name has become a veritable cottage industry. James H. Charlesworth exhaustively surveyed twenty-two conjectures about the beloved disciple's

---

1. Since the identity of the evangelist is the subject matter under dispute, I will henceforth refer to the "Gospel according to John" as the Fourth Gospel.

2. Beck ("Anonymity and Identity," 221) complains that the character's purposeful anonymity is subverted when scholars resort to titles like "Beloved Disciple" or abbreviations like "BD." I plan to continue to use "beloved disciple" as a convenient shorthand, but I will keep it in lowercase letters to clarify that it is not a title.

3. After this point, I will stick to masculine pronouns for the beloved disciple since this accords with the text of the Fourth Gospel and with the adoption of the beloved disciple as a "son" (*huios*) in John 19:26. Note, however, the rebuttal of Esther de Boer (*Gospel of Mary*, 184-85) that women could fulfill the obligation of sonship (cf. Ruth 4:15) and pious women could be treated like honorary males in some ancient Christian texts.

INTRODUCTION

identity,[4] some plausible and others wildly improbable, before settling on his own fairly novel hypothesis.[5]

Irenaeus, the bishop of Lugdunum in Roman Gaul (modern-day Lyon in France) in the last quarter of the second century, was equally confident that he could peer behind the screen of the beloved disciple's anonymity. He professed that the disciple who leaned on the Lord's chest at his final meal was none other than the Apostle John who published his Gospel during his stay in Ephesus (*Adv. Haer.* 3.1.1; Eusebius, *Hist. Eccl.* 5.8.4). This judgment was repeated by the theologians Clement of Alexandria (in Eusebius, *Hist. Eccl.* 6.14.7), Origen of Alexandria (in *Hist. Eccl.* 6.25.6), Tertullian of Carthage (*Marc.* 4.5), and Eusebius of Caesarea (*Hist. Eccl.* 3.23.1) from the late second to the fourth century CE. The Fourth Gospel differs from the other three "Synoptic" Gospels in some striking ways, so the Christian intellectuals in the Patristic era either labored to harmonize their divergent details or settled on Clement's assessment that the evangelist John supplemented the "bodily facts" in the Synoptic Gospels with a more spiritually profound rendition of the life of Jesus Christ (in *Hist. Eccl.* 6.14.7). The Muratorian Canon, a vulgar Latin translation of a Greek original traditionally dated to the end of the second century and named after its discoverer Ludovico Antonio Muratori (1672-1750),[6]

---

4. Charlesworth, *Beloved Disciple*, 128-223. Charlesworth scrutinizes numerous candidates from the New Testament texts (e.g., John the son of Zebedee, John the Elder, Matthias, Apollos, Paul, Judas Iscariot, Andrew, Philip, Nathaniel, Lazarus, John Mark, Judas, the rich young ruler, and one of the anonymous disciples in John 21:2). He scours the parallels in the Hebrew Bible and even in Buddhist and Hindu literature. Finally, he reviews the scholars who remain indecisive about the historical identity of Jesus' privileged disciple or who regard him as a narrative fiction or cipher for the Johannine church or the prophetic office. For other surveys, see Kügler, *Der Jünger*, 438-48; Grassi, *Secret Identity*, 5-10, 11-18; Culpepper, *Life of a Legend*, 72-84. A few options not covered in the above works include Jesus' brother James (cf. Tabor, *The Jesus Dynasty*, 5, 81, 91, 165, 206-7, 258) and Mary Magdalene (cf. de Boer, *Gospel of Mary*, 178-190).

5. Charlesworth, *Beloved Disciple*, 225-86. Charlesworth's hypothesis that the beloved disciple was the Apostle Thomas had been earlier advanced by Schenke, "Function and Background," 123-25.

6. For a helpful overview of the academic debate over the contents, dating,

INTRODUCTION

fleshed out the circumstances that impelled John to write after much fasting and meditation (lines 9-16).

At the beginning of the second century, Papias, the bishop of Hierapolis, propagated intriguing tidbits about the evangelists Mark and Matthew (in *Hist. Eccl.* 3.39.15-16). Papias was a rare exception as the quotations or allusions to the New Testament Gospels were normally unattributed around his time. The noun *euangelion* ("gospel") connoted the oral proclamation of the "good news" about Jesus' lordship well into the second century.[7] Justin, a philosopher who was surnamed "the martyr" after he was sentenced to death by the urban prefect Q. Junius Rusticus between 162 and 168 CE, styled the plural *euangelia* or "Gospels" (*1 Apol.* 66.3; *Dial.* 10.2; 100.1) at his disposal as the "memoirs of the apostles" (*apomnēmoneumata tōn apostolōn*) collectively (*1 Apol.* 66.1-3; 67.3; *Dial.* 100.4; 101.3; 102.5; 103.6, 8; 104.1; 105.1, 5, 6; 106.1, 4; 101.7). Theophilus, the Patriarch of Antioch (ca. 169-183 CE), preceded Irenaeus in prizing the magisterial opening prologue of the Fourth Gospel as the masterwork of "John" in his *Apology to Autolycus* (2.22).[8] As one of the "spirit-bearing persons" (*pneumatophoroi*), John's literary production was every bit as spiritually inspired as the Hebrew prophets before him in the eyes of Theophilus (cf. *Autol.* 2.9; 3.12).[9] The lateness of combining the titular usage of *euangelion* with an identifiable evangelist should be factored against Martin Hengel's thesis that the standard gospel titles were imputed to the gospels as soon as multiple copies

---

and provenance of the Muratorian Canon, see Schnabel, "Muratorian Fragment," 231-64. Although a few scholars have re-dated this fragment to the fourth century, the reference to the composition of the *Shepherd of Hermas* in the Roman episcopacy of Pius (ca. 138-155 CE) that was near to the date of the fragment's author leans towards the late second century.

7. Koester, *Ancient Christian Gospels*, 14-20. Kelhoffer's study ("'How Soon a Book' Revisited," 1-34) is an important corrective to Koester's analysis on the titular usage of *euangelion* in the *Didache* and *2 Clement*, but neither writer quotes the first canonical Gospel under its standard title "the Gospel according to Matthew."

8. Koester, *Ancient Christian Gospels*, 27, n.1.

9. Nagel, *Rezeption*, 59; Hill, *Johannine Corpus*, 79.

INTRODUCTION

of them were stored at Christian scriptoria in major centers like Antioch, Ephesus, and Rome.[10] A better explanation for the prevailing gospel titles is that they were formulated when the fourfold gospel canon began to be disseminated in the second half of the second century; the fundamental principle was that there was a singular *euangelion* or proclamation of "good news" heralded "according to" the vantage points of four worthy emissaries.

There was an audience for the Fourth Gospel among theologians outside of Irenaeus's comfort zone. The apocryphal *Acts of John* centered on John's fantastic recollections about Jesus, such as what it felt like to rest his head against the Lord's chest when they were dining at the table (89.5-6; cf. John 13:23-25), and his missionary adventures in Asia Minor that lasted until he was peacefully buried in Ephesus. The star protégés in the so-called "Gnostic" school of Valentinus-Ptolemy (cf. Irenaeus, *Adv. Haer.* 1.8.5; Epiphanius, *Pan.* 33.3.6), Theodotus (cf. Clement of Alexandria, *Ex. Theod.* 7.3; 35.1; 41.3), and Heracleon (cf. Origen, *Comm. Jo.* 6.3.3)—recognized the "disciple" or "apostle" John's handiwork in the Fourth Gospel. In an older academic synthesis, Ptolemy's authorial attribution of the Fourth Gospel to the "disciple John" went hand-in-hand with the positive estimation of the Fourth Gospel among "Gnostic" thinkers like the Valentinians before more mainstream Christians began to appreciate its theological merits.[11] It is Michael Lattke's allegation that "the early

---

10. See Hengel, *Four Gospels*; Hengel, *Frage*, 204-9. It may be that anonymous writings were imputed a title in libraries and bookshops, but Gregory (*Luke and Acts*, 51) plausibly suggests that the opening verses of the New Testament gospels may have once functioned as their titles.

11. See Bauer, *Orthodoxy and Heresy*, 205-6; Sanders, *Fourth Gospel*, 45-46, 47-66; Barrett, *John*, 113-14; Hillmer, "Second Century," 79-80, 172; Lindars, *John*, 28; Haenchen, *John*, 1.18-19; Schnackenburg, *St. John*, 1.192-95; Campenhausen, *Christian Bible*, 141, 168; Brown, *Community*, 145-54; Wiles, *Spiritual Gospel*, 7, 96-111; Pollard, *Johannine Christology*, 25; Koester, *Ancient Christian Gospels*, 245-46; Culpepper, *Life of a Legend*, 114-18; Lattke, "Gnostic Jesus of John," 149-53; Zumstein, *Kreative Erinnerung*, 4-5; Sloyan, "Gnostic Adoption," 125, 128-29; DeConick, "Catholic-Gnostic Debate," 152-59. There is an extensive review of the so-called "Orthodox Johannophobia Paradigm" in Hill, *Johannine Corpus*, 13-55.

INTRODUCTION

Catholic church snatched John away from the growing Gnostic movement and canonized it by redaction and the formation of Ephesian legends."[12] This academic paradigm was too one-sided. Recent scholarly re-appraisals of the second-century textual and iconographic data point to livelier intra-custody battles over the ownership of the Fourth Gospel among multiple heterogenous Christian communities.[13]

Since Ptolemy unreflexively transmitted the ascription of the Fourth Gospel to the "disciple John" without explanation or apology, he probably did not invent it. How much earlier it pre-dated Ptolemy is an unsolved problem. For example, the wealthy ship-owner Marcion of Sinope was driven to "rescue" a kernel of Christian dogma after he stripped it of its Jewish bearings, canonizing a collection of edited Pauline Epistles and a version of a Gospel that may have approximated the text of Luke, and was purportedly excommunicated from the churches in Rome around 144 CE. From Tertullian's standpoint in the beginning of the third century, Marcion was emboldened to malign the apostolic gospels by the precedent set by Paul's rebuke of the "Jerusalem Pillars" Peter, James, and John in Galatians 2:13–14 (*Marc.* 4.3). For Leon Morris, this is proof that the association of the Fourth Gospel with "John" was current in mid-second-century Rome.[14] Yet Tertullian was active after the fourfold gospel canon was firmly in place and it may have been his hindsight bias that misjudged Marcion's appropriation of a local gospel text whose authorship he never spelled out as an overt rejection of the apostolicity of the Gospels of Matthew, Mark, and John. The debate over the status of the Fourth Gospel for Justin Martyr will be scrutinized in chapter 3. If the Fourth Gospel was excluded from Justin's "memoirs of

12. Lattke, "Gnostic Jesus of John," 151.
13. For criticisms of the older paradigm, see Braun, *Jean le théologien*, 69–300; Hengel, *Johannine Question*, 3–22; Hengel, *Frage*, 9–95; Nagel, *Rezeption*; Hill, *Johannine Corpus*, 75–476; Rasimus, "Valentinian Exegesis," 145–56; Keefer, *Branches*, 21–95. I think that Hill (*Johannine Corpus*, 205–92) swings the pendulum too far in the opposite direction by sidelining the "Gnostic" reception of the Fourth Gospel as late, superficial, or hostile.
14. Morris, *John*, 19.

INTRODUCTION

the apostles," then the belief about Johannine authorship probably originated sometime between Justin and Ptolemy when the fourfold gospel canon was taking shape.

The traditional authorship is re-affirmed in plenty of modern commentaries on the Fourth Gospel.[15] Even critical commentators like Raymond Brown and Rudolf Schnackenburg were initially persuaded that John, the son of Zebedee, was the beloved disciple, though they differentiated the Apostle John from the actual author(s) of the text.[16] Similarly, C. K. Barrett postulated that the Apostle John trained an apprentice living in Asia Minor, a bold thinker steeped in Jewish and Hellenistic culture, and the evangelist acclaimed his apostolic mentor as the beloved disciple.[17] Although Martin Hengel demurs from this longstanding consensus in his contention that another presbyter named John was the head of the Johannine School in Asia Minor and was gradually mistaken for the Apostle John, he partially blames the editors of the Fourth Gospel for the confusion. According to Hengel, the editors of the Fourth Gospel fashioned a composite character or a "dual face" (*Doppelantlitz*), merging the Apostle John from Galilee with the Elder John who originally hailed from Judea.[18] Quite a number of prestigious scholars are convinced that the data from the Fourth

---

15. For a sample of commentaries, see Westcott, *St. John*, ix–lxvii; Hoskyns, *Fourth Gospel*, 86–95, 560; Carson, *John*, 68–81; Morris, *John*, 4–25; Ridderbos, *John*, 2–3, 672–83; Blomberg, *Historical Reliability*, 22–41; Keener, *John*, 81–139; Elowsky, *John 1–10*, xxiv–xvii; Köstenberger, *John*, 6–8.

16. See Brown, *John I–XII*, lxxxviii–xcvii; Schnackenburg, *St. John*, 1.75–104. It should be noted that both Brown and Schnackenburg changed their minds. Their later position was that this disciple was an anonymous follower from Jerusalem and not a member of the Twelve. See Brown, *Community*, 31–34; Schnackenburg, *St. John*, 3.383–87.

17. Barrett, *St. John*, 133–134.

18. Hengel, *Johannine Question*, 124–132; Hengel, *Frage*, 317–18. Other scholars simplify Hengel's thesis by identifying the beloved disciple strictly with the Elder John and removing the Apostle John from the equation altogether. See Bauckham, *Eyewitnesses*, 384–471; Bauckham, *Beloved Disciple*, 33–91; Thompson, *John*, 18; Von Wahlde, *Gospel and Letters*, 3.416–34. See also Charlesworth's review of this position in *Beloved Disciple*, 215–17.

INTRODUCTION

Gospel itself clears up, in whole or in part, why it was ascribed to one of the foremost representatives of the twelve apostles.

Be that as it may, many historical critics have long since jettisoned the Patristic accounts about the evangelists and substituted elaborate reconstructions of hypothetical literary sources and "gospel communities" in their place.[19] The incongruity between the ancient *Communis opinio* and modern academic trends about the formation of the gospel tradition is deserving of a critical inquiry in its own right. New Testament researchers may cross-examine the Patristic witnesses to figure out what light they might have shed on the authorship, date, and provenance of the canonical gospels. If their testimony does not stand up to historical-critical scrutiny it is often discarded as if it had no further value. This monograph will underline the huge impact that the second-century traditions had on the Christian reception of the Fourth Gospel.

The Outline of the Argument

It is one thing to rethink how the Christian *intelligentsia* in the Patristic period re-arranged the scattered pieces from discrete Christian texts in the first few centuries to arrive at a clearer picture of the person behind the persona of the beloved disciple. It is another matter to illuminate the ideological agendas at play as they puzzled out the identity of the beloved disciple. The aim of this study is not to swap the older Patristic edifice with one more innovative and provisional hypothesis about the source(s) or evolutionary history of the Fourth Gospel. Rather, the claims and counterclaims about the apostolicity of the Fourth Gospel will be contextualized in light of the pressing concerns facing second-century Christians.

The first three chapters concentrate on the "how" question, as in how the unidentified beloved disciple morphed into

---

19. For a paradigmatic source-critical commentary on the Fourth Gospel, see Bultmann, *John*, 6–7, 10–11. For a few recent source-critical commentaries, see Waetjen, *Two Editions*; Von Wahlde, *Gospel and Letters*, 1.50–55. For an influential reconstruction of the evolving Johannine community, see Brown, *Community*, 22–24.

INTRODUCTION

the apostolic, evangelist John. Chapter 1 will inspect the typical exegetical moves that enabled the equation of the beloved disciple with a member of the Twelve who started out as a Galilean fisherman (Mark 1:19-20 par) before becoming a founding "pillar" of the messianists headquartered in the Jerusalem church (Gal 2:9; 1 Cor 15:5; Acts 1:13-26). Without recourse to external textual data supplied from outside of the story world created by the Fourth Gospel, John, the son of Zebedee, would have never been a plausible choice. Apart from the epilogue at the end of the book (cf. 21:7, 20-24), the isolated vignettes about the beloved disciple or the "other disciple" in John 13:23-25; 18:15-16; 19:26-27, 35; and 20:3-10 can be assembled into a portrait of an upper-class resident of Jerusalem or its environs who hosted the Paschal meal for Jesus and whose loyalty was not deterred by Jesus' arrest and crucifixion.

Chapter 2 will look at how the editorial addition of an epilogue enhanced the reputation of the beloved disciple from a literary character who had an instrumental task to perform in the Passion Narrative to the creative inspiration behind the entire Fourth Gospel. The Fourth Gospel itself came to be treasured as the beloved disciple's permanent and abiding legacy. The text was then brought into ecumenical dialogue with centrist Christians who memorialized the Apostle Peter as their venerable founding figure and martyr. John 21:25 may thus constitute the oldest authorial tradition about the fourth evangelist. It predated the prevailing Patristic traditions about the Fourth Gospel for, while it transformed the beloved disciple into a gospel writer, it kept the beloved disciple distinct from the "sons of Zebedee" in John 21:2.

Once it was set in stone that John, the son of Zebedee, was the beloved disciple, Chapter 3 will canvass the Patristic contributions to the budding hagiography about the Apostle John in the second century CE. How did an apostle dwelling in Judea end up as a resident of Ephesus and the patron saint of the Christians in Asia Minor? Why was he identified as the prophet who was banished to the island of Patmos during the reign of the Roman emperor Domitian (ca. 81-96 CE) in Irenaeus's *Against Heresies*

INTRODUCTION

5.30.3? How plausible is it that someone who had walked with the historical Jesus as a young man was active in the reign of Trajan (ca. 98–117 CE), the second emperor of the durable Nerva-Antonine dynasty? Why are their conflicting social memories about whether he met a peaceful or a violent fate at the end to his life? This chapter will answer *how* the legends about the evangelist evolved over a century.

Chapter 4 will lay down the methodological groundwork for "why" the question of Johannine authorship mattered in the past and continues to matter in the present. It will be an overview about how authorship has been conceptualized in both the ancient and modern worlds. The aims of the "authorial function" are to authenticate a written work and to regulate between permissible and forbidden renderings of the author's intended meaning. Irrespective of the socio-historical circumstances that the fourth evangelist may have been molded by or may have reacted against, the ecclesiastical traditions about the fourth evangelist were what shaped the import of the Fourth Gospel on Christian communities down through the centuries. They were indispensable in clinching the Fourth Gospel's preservation and canonization. If they have been deconstructed by modern critical scholarship, the conclusion of this monograph will reflect on the potential consequences of discarding the witness of the Patristic age for readers who pick up the Fourth Gospel for academic or devotional purposes today.

1

The Beloved Son of Zebedee?

THE ENIGMATIC BELOVED DISCIPLE has piqued the curiosity of laypersons and academics alike. Some commentators restrict the exegetical analysis to the verses that explicitly designate a disciple in such a manner (John 13:23–25; 19:26–27; 20:2–10; 21:7, 20–24),[1] while others broaden the scope of the investigation to encompass additional references to an anonymous character (1:35–40; 18:15–16; 19:35; 21:2).[2] Redaction critics often consign the beloved disciple to a secondary or tertiary layer imposed upon older strata of tradition embedded in the Fourth Gospel.[3] Literary critics have delved into the characterization of the beloved disciple as the archetypical devotee.[4] In spite of this increasing methodological sophistication, the historic stance that the beloved disciple was the

---

1. See Lindars, *John*, 31–32; Michaels, *John*, 17.

2. Grassi, *Secret Identity*, 65–71, 107–14, presses a maximalist case by not only including these verses, but also bringing passages such as the child (*paidarion*) who brings his loaves to Jesus (6:9) and the "youth" (*neaniskos*) at Gethsemane and the empty tomb (Mark 14:51–52; 16:5–7) into the scope of his investigation.

3. Barrett, *St. John*, 116; Thyen, "Entwicklungen," 267, 274–92; Haenchen, *John*, 1.236–37; Kügler, *Der Jünger*, 419–20, 434; Culpepper, *Life of a Legend*, 72; Theobald, "Der Jünger," 501–13; Von Wahlde, *Gospel and Letters*, 1.235, 330–31; Dunderberg, *Beloved Disciple in Conflict*, 117; Skinner, *John and Thomas*, 127.

4. Some important studies on the literary characterization of this figure include Collins, *These Things Have Been Written*, 42–45; Skinner, *John and Thomas*, 125–37; Resseguie, "Ideal Point of View," 537–49; Beck, "Anonymity and Identity," 221–39; Bennema, *Encountering Jesus*, 299–316.

The Beloved Apostle?

Apostle John has proven to be a remarkably enduring position.[5] The pros and cons of this age-old authorial tradition thus deserve a fresh hearing.

The Case for the Traditional View

First, we must consider B. F. Westcott's celebrated apologetic for the traditional authorship of the Fourth Gospel. Westcott progressively whittled down the candidates who could have been the evangelist—the evangelist must be a Jew, a native of Palestine, an eyewitness of Jesus, and a seminal leader among the twelve apostles—until he reached the verdict that the Apostle John alone satisfies all of these conditions.[6] The first two criteria are relatively uncontroversial. Part of Westcott's justification for the last two criteria is that the "narrative is marked by minute details of persons, and time, and number, and place and manner, which cannot but have come from a direct personal experience."[7] Granted, the topographical precision and descriptive flourishes could have also stemmed from prior written sources, from personal sojourns to locales where Jesus was believed to have visited, or from efforts to create verisimilitude for the story.[8] It is not inconceivable that the evangelist corresponded with informants from the region who had interacted with Jesus in some capacity. Whether the evangelist was a direct eyewitness, and more so an apostle, depends on the wider exegetical considerations pertaining to the beloved disciple.

If the Apostle John was disguised behind this moniker, this might account for the otherwise inexplicable fact that he does not

---

5. See the overview in the introduction. For a historical survey, see Hoskyns, *Fourth Gospel*, 21–47; Charlesworth, *Beloved Disciple*, 197–215. See also the literature listed in Bauckham, *Eyewitnesses*, 413n.2.

6. Westcott, *St. John*, x–lii. Westcott's case is endorsed by Hoskyns, *Fourth Gospel*, 41–42; Carson, *John*, 71; Morris, *John*, 5, 8–12; Blomberg, *Historical Reliability*, 27–28; Keener, *John*, 89; Köstenberger and Snout, "Witness, Author, Apostle," 227.

7. Westcott, *St. John*, xxxix.

8. Barrett, *John*, 123; Casey, *Is John's Gospel True?*, 173–74.

THE BELOVED SON OF ZEBEDEE?

appear under his own name in the Fourth Gospel apart from a fleeting cameo in John 21:2. Moreover, when a "John" is named in the text, the referent is always the prophet who urged the people to undergo a baptism of repentance, but his name is never qualified with the sobriquet *ho baptistēs* ("the baptizer"). If the original consumers of the text were acquainted with the evangelist John on a personal basis, then they were not at risk of confusing the prophet John who prepared the groundwork for Jesus' announcement of goods news before he was beheaded by the tetrarch Herod Antipas with the evangelist John.[9] This second contention is a little weaker; the reason the prophet John is not qualified as the "baptizer" in the Fourth Gospel may be due to how the evangelist rendered the baptizing practices of Jesus' disciples as supplanting the rite of Jesus' predecessor (John 3:22–4:1).[10]

Zebedee's children, James and John, may also be missing because the Fourth Gospel generally did not cover any of the incidents from the Synoptic Gospels where they were singled out. An exception is in the fishing excursion in the Johannine epilogue that is noticeably similar to Luke 5:1–11, and "those from Zebedee" (*hoi tou Zebadaiou*) are among the cast of characters (John 21:2). This opaque reference in John 21:2 may not disqualify the Apostle John from the running for the coveted role of the beloved disciple, for his name was conspicuously skipped over.[11] J. Ramsay Michaels does not number the beloved disciple among the group of seven in John 21:2, but supposes that he was silently watching the scene in the background until verse 4, just

---

9. Westcott, *St. John*, xlvi–xlvii; Schnackenburg, *St. John*, 98; Carson, *John*, 72; Morris, *John*, 7–8; Ridderbos, *John*, 675–76; Blomberg, *Historical Reliability*, 30; Keener, *John*, 90–91; Köstenberger and Snout, "Witness, Author, Apostle," 228.

10. Casey, *Is John's Gospel True?*, 175.

11. Westcott, *St. John*, xlvi; Carson, *John*, 72; Morris, *John*, 6; Blomberg, *Historical Reliability*, 29, 274; Keener, *John*, 90–91; Waetjen, *Two Editions*, 26–27; Köstenberger and Snout, "Witness, Author, Apostle," 229. Charlesworth (*Beloved Disciple*, 7) is technically correct that John 21:2 does not specify the number of "those from Zebedee," but James and John are likely the ones in mind in order for there to be seven disciples.

The Beloved Apostle?

as he stood apart from the women huddled near the cross in John 19:25.[12] Yet the beloved disciple should not be excluded from the total of seven disciples since that number symbolizes completeness or perfection. The epilogue leaves few options—either the beloved disciple was one of Zebedee's two boys or one of the two nameless disciples—if we stick to the criterion of anonymity. Whenever this epilogue was appended to the Fourth Gospel, it furnished the last word on the beloved disciple from the publishers of the final edition of the text. For Herman C. Waetjen, the epilogue belonged to a second edition of the text and made the identification of the Apostle John as the beloved disciple tenable, situating him in a Galilean fishing milieu.[13]

An implicit clue might be in the anonymous adherent of the baptizing movement who, alongside Andrew, overheard the baptizer magnify Jesus as the "lamb of God" (John 1:35–40). First, if one correlates the Johannine call narrative with its Synoptic counterparts featuring two sets of brothers, Andrew and Peter followed by James and John (Mark 1:15–20 par), then the former pair of brothers is accounted for in John 1:35–42, while the unnamed disciple may be one half of the latter pair.[14] Second, there may be subtle hints that Andrew's associate was the beloved disciple.[15] Andrew

---

12. Michaels, *John*, 15, 1029.

13. Waetjen, *Two Editions*, 26–27. Waetjen theories that the second edition of the Fourth Gospel shifted the identification of the beloved disciple from Lazarus in the first edition.

14. Westcott, *St. John*, xlvii, 49; Hoskyns, *Fourth Gospel*, 180; Carson, *John*, 154; Morris, *John*, 136; Ridderbos, *John*, 84; Köstenberger, *John*, 76, 76n.69; Köstenberger and Snout, "Witness, Author, Apostle," 213, 214. Barrett (*St. John*, 117, 182) notes that if the original reading at 1:41 is taken to be that Andrew "first" (*prōtos*) found his brother Peter, this might suggest that the anonymous disciple then went out to find his brother too. However, there is a text-critical issue regarding whether the original reading was *prōton, prōtos*, or *prōi* and Barrett leans towards *prōton*, meaning that Andrew searched for his brother Peter "first" before he did anything else. See also the text-critical discussion in Quast, *Community in Crisis*, 34–35.

15. The following reasons are compiled from Westcott, *St. John*, 49; Hoskyns, *Fourth Gospel*, 180; Cullmann, *Johannine Circle*, 72; Thyen, "Entwicklungen," 274–75; Morris, *John*, 136; Beasley-Murray, *John*, 26; Brown, *Community*, 32; Quast, *Community in Crisis*, 31; Hengel, *Frage*, 217; Grassi,

is usually paired with Philip (cf. John 6:5-9; 12:20-22), but Philip did not meet Jesus until the next day and the name of Andrew's companion may have been concealed to keep it a secret. If this was to imply that he was the beloved disciple, it would vouch for his qualifications as one who stayed by Jesus' side "from the beginning" (15:27; 16:4; cf. Luke 1:2; Acts 1:21-22) and comprehended that Jesus was the sacrificed paschal lamb (19:29, 33-35). There may also be an inclusio revolving around the verbs "follow" (*akoloutheō*) and "remain" (*menō*) in John 1:37-39 and 21:20-22.

Even some commentators who accept the Fourth Gospel's traditional authorship may be hesitant to admit John 1:35-40 into the evidence since there is no indication that this anonymous disciple was "loved" by Jesus.[16] It is not until the Last Supper that the beloved disciple was explicitly at the forefront of the action. When Jesus uttered a baffling warning that someone at the table was plotting to betray him, Peter gestured to the beloved disciple to glean more information from Jesus (13:23-25). The beloved disciple covertly leaned back to Jesus to ask about the traitor, but it is unclear if Peter was able to eavesdrop on the ensuing conversation between the two of them. Unlike Leonardo da Vinci's renowned painting of the Last Supper where the Twelve sit upright on one side of a table, the disciples were reclining on their left side as they ate the meal in a typical Roman triclinium or U-shaped pattern. The beloved disciple had to be to Jesus' immediate right in order to lean his head back towards Jesus' chest. Scholars debate whether the spot of highest honor was to the left or right of the host of the meal.[17]

Secret Identity, 54; Schnelle, *Antidocetic Christology*, 18-19; Charlesworth, *Beloved Disciple*, 326-36; Witherington, *John's Wisdom*, 70; Ridderbos, John, 83-84; Moloney, *John*, 7, 59-60; Bauckham, *Eyewitnesses*, 127-29, 389-93; Theobald, "Der Jünger," 499, 503; Bauckham, *Beloved Disciple*, 85; Köstenberger, *John*, 76, 76n.69; Resseguie, "Ideal Point of View," 548; Beck, "Anonymity and Identity," 226; Bennema, *Encountering Jesus*, 300-301.

16. See Schnackenburg, *St. John*, 1.310-11; Blomberg, *Historical Reliability*, 30-31, 81; Keener, *John*, 1.468. Other scholars lean towards identifying this disciple as John, but admit that this inference cannot be proven (see Barrett, *St. John*, 182; Brown, *John I—XII*, xciv, 73; Carson, *John*, 154; Ridderbos, *John*, 84).

17. Some scholars note that the host was more vulnerable on his or her left

The Beloved Apostle?

According to the Synoptic parallels (cf. Matt 26:20; Mark 14:17; Luke 22:14), the Twelve dined with Jesus on this solemn occasion and the compliment that they were "chosen" from the beginning (John 13:18; 15:16, 19, 27; 16:4; cf. 6:70) may be fitting praise.[18] Turning again to the pages of the Synoptic Gospels, Peter, James, and John formed an inner circle of Jesus' confidants within the Twelve (cf. Mark 1:29; 5:37; 9:2; 13:3; 14:33 par). By the process of elimination, James was slain by the sword during the reign of Herod Agrippa I between 41 and 44 CE, so he would not have sparked a rumor that he would live forever (Acts 12:2; cf. John 21:23).[19] The beloved disciple did not just take precedence over Peter at the Last Supper; he did what Peter failed to do in staying loyal to Jesus to the bitter end and preceded Peter in the acceptance of Jesus' post-mortem victory over the grave (John 18:15–16; 19:25–27, 35; 20:2–9). The beloved disciple may have been a figurehead of considerable stature in the early church to be a credible competitor for Peter. Peter and John were co-preachers in Jerusalem (Acts 3:1, 3, 4, 11; 4:1, 6, 13, 19; 8:14, 17, 25) and

---

side, so that was the position of highest honor. See Barrett, *St. John*, 436, 447; Haenchen, *John*, 2.110; Brown, *John XIII—XXI*, 574; Morris, *John*, 625–26. Others judge it improbable that the beloved disciple would not be in the position of highest honor on the right side of Jesus. See Lindars, *John*, 458; Ridderbos, *John*, 469; Keener, *John*, 1.916; Blomberg, *Historical Reliability*, 193n283. Von Wahlde (*Gospel and Letters*, 2.606) agrees with the former group about the honorable position on the left side in conventional seating arrangements, but deems the notion that the disciples were seated according to an honor system that ranked them from the greatest to the least to be inconsistent with Jesus' social ethic.

18. Westcott, *St. John*, xlvi; Barrett, *John*, 116; Carson, *John*, 71, 73, 472; Charlesworth, *Beloved Disciple*, 122–25; Morris, *John*, 6, 555n52; Ridderbos, *John*, 675; Blomberg, *Historical Reliability*, 29; Keener, *John*, 84, 90; Köstenberger, *John*, 6; Köstenberger and Snout, "Witness, Author, Apostle," 228. Lindars (*John*, 457) agrees that the fourth evangelist was suggesting that the beloved disciple was among the Twelve, yet his anonymity ensures that he was not identifiable with any particular person but was an idealized and representative apostle.

19. Westcott, *St. John*, xlvi–xlvi, lxx; Hoskyns, *Fourth Gospel*, 180; Carson, *John*, 72; Morris, *John*, 7; Blomberg, *Historical Reliability*, 29–30; Keener, *John*, 85–86, 90; Köstenberger, *John*, 7; Köstenberger and Snout, "Witness, Author, Apostle," 228.

The Beloved Son of Zebedee?

John was one of the three men exalted by the Jerusalem messianic congregation as one of their foundational "pillars" (Gal 2:9). The next mention of "another disciple" (*allos mathētēs*), which may be an alternate guise for the beloved disciple, is in John 18:15–16. This disciple was "known" (*gnōstos*) to the high priest and entreated the gatekeeper to permit Peter to enter into the high priest's courtyard. The adjective *gnōstos* connotes much more than vague familiarity and may intimate that they had had some sort of friendship (cf. LXX 2 Kgs 10:11; Pss 55:14 [55:13]; 66:13; Luke 2:42, 44).[20] It is hard to envisage how a Galilean fisherman wielded this kind of social capital. Still, some scholars aver that Zebedee was a person of means to afford a boat and hired servants (Mark 1:19–20 par) and that his sons hauled fish through the Fish Gate to sell in landlocked Jerusalem (cf. Neh 3:3; Zeph 1:10).[21] Such rationalizations were championed as early as 400 CE by Nonnus of Panopolis and by an alleged citation from the Jewish Gospel used by the Nazoraeans in the late Medieval *Historia passionis Domini*. Alternatively, some Patristic or Medieval Christians ventured that John acquired wealth by selling his property in Galilee (e.g., Hippolytus of Thebes or Epiphanius the Monk) or was born into a priestly lineage (e.g., Polycrates of Ephesus or the *Acts of John by pseudo-Prochorus* [Vatican Gr. 654, fol. 88v]).[22]

---

20. Barrett, *St. John*, 525–26; Brown, *John XIII—XXI*, 822; Quast, *Community in Crisis*, 79; Morris, *John* 665–66n.35, Grassi, *Secret Identity*, 56, 64; Carson, *John*, 581; Beasley-Murray, *John*, 317; Köstenberger, *John*, 514, 514n16. Contra Ridderbos's view that the high priest had some vague and passing familiarity with this disciple who was only really known to a servant in the courtyard (*John*, 581).

21. Brown, *John I—XII*, xcvii; Brown, *John XIII—XXI*, 823; Morris, *John*, 666n.37; Carson, *John*, 74–75, 582; Blomberg, *Historical Reliability*, 35, 233, 233n.335; Köstenberger, *John*, 513, 513n14. It should be noted that commentators such as Brown, Morris, and Blomberg admit their uncertainty regarding whether the anonymous disciple in 18:15–16 should be equated with the beloved disciple.

22. For an overview of the reception history of John 18:15–16, see Culpepper, *Life of a Legend*, 61–62. For a sample of Patristic commentary on John 18:15–16, see also Elowski, *John 11—21*, 276–77.

The Beloved Apostle?

These fanciful speculations may be unnecessary if the high priest's "friend" was a clandestine disciple whose affiliation with Jesus was disavowed in public (cf. John 12:42) and, hence, could not be an exemplar of discipleship.[23] He may have merely been a minor character who helped Peter slip into the courtyard and then vanished from the scene. Charlesworth goes further in reasoning that this "disciple" was the treacherous Judas who was in league with the high priest, marched with the soldiers arresting Jesus into the courtyard, and placed Peter's life in grave danger by escorting him into enemy territory.[24] If that is the case, the beloved disciple did not resurface in the narrative until John 19:26-27.

John 19:26-27 is one of the most tender moments in the Fourth Gospel as Jesus' dying breaths were spent on arranging for the beloved disciple to care for his mother after he was gone (19:25-27). By combining the names of the women attested at Golgotha in the New Testament Gospels, one last clue may come to light. Mark 15:40 lists Mary Magdalene, Mary the mother of James and Joses (cf. Mark 6:3), and Salome. Matthew 27:56 lists Mary Magdalene, Mary the mother of James and Joseph, and the mother of the sons of Zebedee (cf. Matt 20:20). John 19:25 lists the mother of Jesus, the sister of Jesus' mother, Mary "of Clopas," and Mary Magdalene. Through an ingenious act of harmonization, Salome, Zebedee's wife, and Jesus' aunt can be fused into one person. Such a procedure would transform Jesus and John into cousins.[25] Normally, it was the surviving kin of the deceased who should have fulfilled the duty of looking after Jesus' widowed mother.[26] If

---

23. See Bultmann, *John*, 483; Schnackenburg, *St. John*, 3.235; Lindars, *John*, 32, 548; Kügler, *Der Jünger*, 425-27; Charlesworth, *Beloved Disciple*, 336-59; Michaels, *John*, 18, 898; Keener, *John*, 2.1091.

24. Charlesworth, *Beloved Disciple*, 341-59; cf. Brodie, *John*, 529.

25. Westcott, *St. John*, xlvii; Hoskyns, *Fourth Gospel*, 530; Carson, *John*, 616; Morris, *John*, 717; Ridderbos, *John*, 611; Blomberg, *Historical Reliability*, 35; Köstenberger, *John*, 548.

26. This is a key point in James D. Tabor's argument that Jesus' brother James was the beloved disciple, but I am not convinced by his dismissal of John 7:5 with its negative characterization of Jesus' brothers as a late interpolation (cf. *Jesus Dynasty*, 165).

The Beloved Son of Zebedee?

Jesus' siblings did not step up to the plate, his cousin could have shouldered this burden. Predictably, other exegetes are dismissive of the move to smooth over the divergent names across discrete Gospels as methodologically suspect, especially when there are no direct statements in the New Testament that the Apostle John was Jesus' relative.[27]

When puzzling out the secret identity of the beloved disciple, New Testament scholars have obtained several missing pieces from the texts of Matthew, Mark, and Luke-Acts. It is true that Clement, the erudite pedagogue in a catechetical school in Alexandria, figured that the evangelist John's intent was to supplement the "bodily facts" (*ta sōmatika*) of the Synoptic record with deeper "spiritual" (*pneumatikon*) levels of meaning (in *Hist. Eccl.* 6.14.5, 7). Although a majority of twentieth-century researchers were inclined to the Fourth Gospel's literary independence from the Synoptic Gospels, the pendulum of scholarly opinion seems to be swinging back to the Fourth Gospel's dependence on one or more of the Synoptic Gospels.[28] If that is destined to be the new scholarly consensus, which remains to be seen, then the evangelist has purposefully omitted the calling of the first disciples from their fishing boats and nets, the commissioning of the twelve apostles and their exclusive privilege as guests at the Last Supper, and the special triumvirate of Peter, James, and John. Therefore, to ascertain the identity or function of the beloved disciple, we must stay within the boundaries constructed in the Fourth Gospel's narrative world. It was the promulgation of the fourfold gospel canon that facilitated the cross-referencing between the Johannine and Synoptic Gospels and enabled the candidacy of the Apostle John for the office of the beloved disciple. Since John 21:24 ascribed the

---

27. See Brown, *John I—XII*, 904–6; Schackenburg, *St. John*, 3.277; Barrett, *St. John*, 551–52; Beasley-Murray, *John*, 348; Kügler, *Der Jünger*, 442.

28. For the history of research in this question, see Smith, *John among the Gospels*; Gregory, *Reception of Luke and Acts*, 55–69; Barker, *John's Use of Matthew*, 1–15. One of the advances of Barker's discussion is that he theorizes why the fourth evangelist did not strictly repeat, but imitated and re-interpreted his Synoptic sources, by paralleling his literary procedure with the rhetorical technique of *oppositio in imitando* (*John's Use of Matthew*, 35).

Fourth Gospel to the beloved disciple, John was then identified as the fourth evangelist.

The Case against the Traditional View

In his influential article, Pierson Parker rattled off twenty-one objections against the Johannine origins of the Fourth Gospel.[29] This is a convenient starting point for weighing the merits of the antique consensus. Parker is incredulous that John, a wrathful "son of thunder" (Mark 3:17) who was bitter towards Samaritans (Luke 9:54, but cf. Acts 8:14-25) and ambitious for power at the advent of Jesus' eschatological empire (Mark 10:35-41), crafted a tranquil, meditative masterpiece that had a realized eschatology and a friendly disposition toward Samaritans.[30] Such psychologizing of an ancient figure is dubious.[31] We may not have enough information to piece together John's psychological profile for Parker's complaints that the fourth evangelist "blotted out" John's personality and temperament to stick or carry any argumentative force. None of the evangelists were interested in the internalized motivations or dispositions of their flat minor characters when they pontificated on a range of topics which were to be illuminated by Jesus.

Another well-worn objection is that it would be the height of hubris to esteem oneself to be Jesus' disciple par excellence, while the admirers of this disciple could have bestowed the phrase "whom Jesus loved" upon him.[32] It is not unimaginable that John was mindful of the depths of Jesus' feelings of goodwill towards him; there was no presumption that no one else could be the re-

---

29. Parker, "Son of Zebedee," 35-43; cf. Grassi, *Secret Identity*, 7-9; Charlesworth, *Beloved Disciple*, xi-xii, 212-13.

30. Ibid., 37, 39, 40; cf. Grassi, *Secret Identity*, 103-106. Carson (*John*, 74) and Blomberg (*Historical Reliability*, 32-33) simply suppose that John was transformed or matured over time.

31. Schnackenburg, *St. John*, 1.92.

32. Barrett, *St. John*, 117, 125; Schnackenburg, *St. John*, 3.381-382; Lindars, *John*, 32; Thyen, "Entwicklungen," 294; Beasley-Murray, *John*, lxx; von Wahlde, *Gospel and Letters*, 3.413.

The Beloved Son of Zebedee?

cipient of Jesus' love (cf. John 13:1, 34; 15:9) and a mystic like Paul was also conscious of the self-sacrificial love that the Son of God had for him individually (Gal 2:20).[33] If an editor tacked on the phrase "whom Jesus loved" to a collection of verses that previously had the "other disciple" (cf. John 18:15–16; 20:3–4, 8), this would not rule out that the "other disciple" had a hand in significantly shaping the main contours of the Fourth Gospel.[34] Although the beloved disciple exceeds Peter in his level of intuition or devotion, other New Testament writings consistently ranked John in second or third place beneath Peter as the spokesperson for the apostles.[35] John, however, may have had quite a different self-estimate.

Parker broaches the more practical issue of whether a Galilean fisher was able to craft this elegant Greek composition.[36] This is not a stumbling block for commentators who have a certain conception of the Hellenization of Galilee, the allegedly higher rates of literacy among the first-century Palestinian Jewish population than was the norm in the wider Mediterranean, or the economic means of Zebedee to pay for his children's education (cf. Mark 1:19–20).[37] For the sake of argument, let us entertain the premises that Zebedee's children might have grown up in a functionally bilingual household and that John might have honed his literary skills over decades of ministering in metropolitan cities like Jerusalem and Ephesus.[38] This theory does not mesh well with the denigration of

---

33. Westcott, *St. John*, xlix, li; Carson, *John*, 76–77; Morris, *John*, 8; Blomberg, *Historical Reliability*, 33–34; Köstenberger, *John*, 6–7n14, 7n15.

34. Cullmann, *Johannine Circle*, 73; Brown, *John XIII—XXI*, 983; Moloney, *John*, 7; Witherington, *John's Wisdom*, 17; Blomberg, *Historical Reliability*, 32.

35. Parker, "Son of Zebedee," 40–41.

36. Ibid., 37–39.

37. Westcott, *St. John*, li; Schnackenburg, *St. John*, 94; Brown, *John XIII—XXI*, 823; Carson, *John*, 73–74, 75, 79; Blomberg, *Historical Reliability*, 33–34. For lower estimates of the literacy rates in first century Palestine, see Hezser, *Jewish Literacy*; Ehrman, *Forgery and Counter-forgery*, 242–46.

38. Barrett (*John*, 132n2) complains that there are too many hypotheticals concerning how John might have lived to old age, drew on sources in addition to his own eyewitness recollections, became fluent in Greek, and learned how to compose literature in a new idiom that extensively engaged with Greek thought forms.

The Beloved Apostle?

Peter and John as illiterate commoners by the Jewish scribal class in Acts 4:13. The religious establishment may have disdained Peter and John as theologically unschooled amateurs (*idiōtai*),[39] but the term *agrammatos* or "without letters" had the connotations of illiteracy too.[40] Dictating to a secretary who translated John's speech into the Gospel's distinctive idiolect was not a realistic option.[41] The textual corroboration for an amanuensis refining an author's literary style, much less contributing significantly to the content of a book, is scarce and generally confined to the aristocratic *literati*.[42]

Switching to the internal data within the Fourth Gospel itself, we have to deal with the criterion of anonymity. This principle seems to exclude every named character in the Fourth Gospel from qualifying for the role of the beloved disciple, for it would be inconsistent to divulge the name of this character in some passages and withhold it as a carefully guarded secret in others.[43] If we stopped reading before the twenty-first chapter, the Apostle John would be a serious contender since his name was omitted from John 1:1 to 20:31. Yet the precedent of anonymity tips the scales towards the beloved disciple being one of the two nameless individuals rather than "those of Zebedee" in John 21:2.[44] The epilogue may have drawn on a pre-formed memory about an astonishing catch

---

39. Westcott, *St. John*, lxviii; Schnackenburg, *St. John*, 94; Brown, *John XIII–XXI*, 823; Carson, *John*, 73; Blomberg, *Historical Reliability*, 33–34.

40. Adams, "Peter's Literacy," 132–33.

41. Contra Blomberg, *Historical Reliability*, 28n.28, 282; Keener, *John*, 83.

42. On this point, see Ehrman, *Forgery*, 418–22.

43. See Brown, *John I—XII*, xciii–xciv, xcv; Schnackenburg, *St. John*, 3.385; Lindars, *John*, 33; Michaels, *John*, 15, 24; Keener, *John*, 1.86; Von Wahlde, *John*, 3.428; Thompson, *John*, 241; Bennema, *Encountering Jesus*, 309. Charlesworth (*Beloved Disciple*, xv, 429) insists that there is a progression in the Fourth Gospel from veiled anonymity to full disclosure, but Beck ("Anonymity and Identity," 223) objects that the plethora of scholarly suggestions demonstrates the lack of transparency regarding the identification of the beloved disciple.

44. See Hanchen, *John*, 2.222; Schnackenburg, *St. John*, 3.384; Cullmann, *Johannine Circle*, 76; Lindars, *John*, 33; Kügler, *Der Jünger*, 443; Hengel, *Frage*, 314–317; Culpepper, *Johannine Circle*, 76; Casey, *Is John's Gospel True?*, 162; Maloney, *John*, 548; Bauckham, *Eyewitnesses*, 415; Bauckham, *Beloved Disciple*, 77–78; Von Wahlde, *Gospel and Letters*, 3.413; Thompson, *John*, 18.

The Beloved Son of Zebedee?

of fish involving disciples such as Peter, James, and John (cf. Luke 5:10) and implanted the beloved disciple into the middle of it.[45] If the Johannine epilogue was not original to the Fourth Gospel, which I will argue at length in my next chapter, it may not be legitimate to hang too much on John 21:1–25 for discerning who the writer of John 1:1–20:31 may have envisaged the beloved disciple to be. At the very least, the Johannine epilogue is a window into a very early stage in the reception history of the Fourth Gospel when the beloved disciple was not yet equated with the Apostle John.

The exegesis of the passages adduced in the previous section may fall apart on closer inspection. To start with John 1:35–40, it is far from evident that the Apostle John was the anonymous disciple. The obstacle to harmonizing the Markan and Johannine narratives about the calling of the first disciples is that they have little in common apart from the names of a few of the main participants.[46] The Johannine Jesus gained a couple of students after their former charismatic leader trumpeted Jesus as the "lamb" who would atone for the sins of the world, motivating them to chase after Jesus and lodge with him that day. The Markan Jesus happened upon two sets of brothers tending their fishing nets or tossing them into the sea and summoned them to start fishing for people. Without the addition of the Johannine epilogue, one would not get the impression that these disciples had an occupation in the fishing industry by reading the Fourth Gospel in isolation from the Synoptic Gospels.[47] These separate call narratives may be somewhat complementary, since it is reasonable that the disciples would have had some prior exposure to Jesus before complying with his absolute command to participate in his kingdom program,[48] but that would apply to Andrew and Simon at best. The narrator does not disclose

---

45. Culpepper, *Life of a Legend*, 56. There will be further discussion on this in chapter 2.

46. Barrett, *St. John*, 179; Culpepper, *Life of a Legend*, 59; Bauckham, *Beloved Disciple*, 76.

47. Parker, "Son of Zebedee," 37.

48. Blomberg, *Historical Reliability*, 80; Köstenberger, *John*, 73.

that the anonymous disciple had a brother to definitively match him up with either John or James.

John 1:35–40 may also have nothing to do with the beloved disciple.[49] The hallmarks of the beloved disciple—he was loved by Jesus and had a competitive rivalry with Peter—are not observable in this section. While Jesus would not have a strong emotional attachment to the beloved disciple at their first encounter, the Fourth Gospel does not hesitate to brand Judas as a "devil" and foreshadow his betrayal at an earlier point in the plot (John 6:70–71; 12:4). Not all of the disciples at the Last Supper were recruited by Jesus when John was baptizing in the wilderness, so the language of being with Jesus "from the beginning" in John 15:27 and 16:4 may have less to do with the commencement of Jesus' ministry than with the pre-existent choice of his elect from eternity past. The most valuable trait of the aspiring disciple, whenever he or she is initiated into the fellowship of believers, is to abide in Jesus' love by obeying his commands (13:34–35; 14:15, 23–24; 15:2–10, 12–17). Two disciples were listening in when Jesus was magnified as the "lamb" (1:35–36), so they could have repeated it to the rest of the disciples. This mystifying designation may have been incomprehensible to them until the beloved disciple realized its meaning when he witnessed how Jesus expired (19:35). Using similar logic, Charlesworth is adamant that the beloved disciple who saw the soldier stab Jesus with a spear in John 19:34 must be Thomas given his knowledge of the wound in Jesus' side in 20:25,[50] but this is another instance of a narrative gap where the narrator took for granted that the news about what transpired had spread to the disciples without narrating it. Finally, the names, vocabulary, and themes from the previous chapters were interwoven into the epilogue by a talented editor to bring the Fourth Gospel to a satisfying close. The re-employment of the verbs "following" and

---

49. Haenchen, *John*, 1.158; Schnackenburg, *St. John*, 1.310–11; Lindars, *John*, 114; Kügler, *Der Jünger*, 424–27; Michaels, *John*, 18, 121; Culpepper, *Life of a Legend*, 59; Keener, *John*, 468; Skinner, *John and Thomas*, 126–27; Von Wahlde, *Gospel and Letters*, 2.60; 3.424.

50. Charlesworth, *Beloved Disciple*, 227–233, 422–23.

"remaining" does not demand the common identity of the anonymous disciple in John 1:35-40 and the beloved disciple in John 21:20-24, but rather than such actions epitomize all true followers of Jesus from the start of Jesus' mission to the post-Easter epoch.

The first incontestable reference to the beloved disciple is at the Last Supper. Were there invitees on the guest list in addition to the Twelve for this occasion? The constituency of "the Twelve" (*hoi dōdeka*) is never fully defined in the rare allusions to them in John 6:67, 70, 71 and 20:24 and the Fourth Gospel does not affirm that there were no other participants in the Last Supper.[51] Even in the Synoptic Gospels, Jesus and his Galilean entourage presumably required someone in Jerusalem to make his or her accommodations available to them. The beloved disciple could have hosted the meal and, if he enforced the customary seating arrangements, Jesus was seated in the place of highest honor to his left.[52] The trio of Peter, James, and John is not singled out. In fact, with the exception of the Johannine appendix, every single Synoptic scene in which they play a major role is overlooked in the Fourth Gospel (cf. Mark 1:29-31; 5:37-43; 9:2-9; 13:3-4; 14:33)![53] It is not that John's historical involvement in Jesus' ministry can be reduced to a few incidents and there may be reasonable motives for the Fourth Gospel's omissions: Jesus' divine glory is displayed through plural "signs" (*sēmeia*) rather than through the Transfiguration, the resuscitation of Lazarus is substituted for that of Jairus's daughter, and the mental anguish of Jesus is conveyed to the crowd in John 12:27 rather than in a private prayer in the garden of Gethsemane.[54] Neither the Twelve nor the Three, however, loom large

---

51. Cullmann, *Johannine Circle*, 75-76; Beasley-Murray, *John*, lxx; Michaels, *John*, 13-14; Quast, *Community in Crisis*, 23, 68; Witherington, *John's Wisdom*, 14; Culpepper, *Life of a Legend*, 74; Bauckham, *Beloved Disciple*, 13-14; Von Wahlde, *John*, 3.413.

52. Michaels, *John*, 23-24; Witherington, *John's Wisdom*, 14; Bauckham, *Beloved Disciple*, 15n15.

53. Parker, "Son of Zebedee," 37, 39, 40, 41, 43, 44; Lindars, *John*, 33; Witherington, *John's Wisdom*, 14-15; Culpepper, *Life of a Legend*, 56, 76.

54. Schnackenburg, *St. John*, 1.93; Morris, *John*, 13; Blomberg, *Historical Reliability*, 30n19; Keener, *John*, 90.

in the Fourth Gospel. Since the beloved disciple is set over against Peter, the representative of the Twelve (cf. 6:67-69), he may be an outsider to their ranks.[55]

When we turn our attention to "another disciple" (*allos mathētēs*), the one who assisted Peter with getting into the courtyard in John 18:15-16, there are solid reasons to tag him as the beloved disciple.[56] There are linguistic and thematic links with the discourse about the good shepherd who surrenders his life for his sheep in John 10:1-18. The "gatekeeper" (*thyrōros*) opened the "door" (*thyra*) for the sheep to pass through the "gate" (*aulē*), but the ravenous wolves threatened to scatter the sheep. The disciple who arrived at the courtyard first robbed Peter of his glory of being the only male disciple to follow Jesus up to this point in the Synoptic Gospels and, thus, had a competitive edge over Peter. He was faithful to Jesus every step of the way from the courtyard to the cross, while Peter, frightened that the company of servants warming themselves near the fire would expose him to the wolves, severed his ties with Jesus by denying him three times (18:17, 25-27). John 20:2-4, 8 uses the phrase "the other disciple" (*ho allos mathētēs*) and verse 2 qualifies that this is the one "whom Jesus loved." There was a scribal interpolation of an article in 18:15 to line up the wording closer to 20:2, but this can be factored in as

---

55. Cullmann, *Johannine Circle*, 72, 75-76; Schnackenburg, *St. John*, 3.381; Brown, *Community*, 33-34; Quast, *Community in Crisis*, 24.

56. The following reasons are compiled from Westcott, *St. John*, 18, 357; Hoskyns, *Fourth Gospel*, 513; Cullmann, *Johannine Circle*, 72; Thyen, "Entwicklungen," 281; Brown, *John XIII—XXI*, 822, 841; Beasley-Murray, *John*, 324; Haenchen, *John*, 2.167; Collins, *These Things Have Been Written*, 42; Hengel, *Johannine Question*, 78-79; Hengel, *Frage*, 216, 216n30, 308; Quast, *Community in Crisis*, 77-81; Grassi, *Secret Identity*, 56, 64; Schnelle, *Antidocetic Christology*, 17; Witherington, *John's Wisdom*, 288; Culpepper, *Life of a Legend*, 62-63; Moloney, *John*, 487, 521; Waetjen, *Two Editions*, 19-20, 382; Theobald, "Der Jünger," 496-98, 500; Bauckham, *Testimony*, 78, 86; Ridderbos, *John*, 580; Köstenberger, *John*, 513, 513n.13; Skinner, *John and Thomas*, 128; Von Wahlde, *Gospel and Letters*, 2.757; Resseguie, "Ideal Point of View," 541-43; Beck, "Anonymity and Identity," 228; Bennema, *Encountering Jesus*, 301, 307; Thompson, *John*, 368. A strong, extensive case for this position is offered in Neirynck, "The 'Other Disciple,'" 113-41.

The Beloved Son of Zebedee?

evident that ancient readers perceived the beloved disciple to be in this verse.

On the other hand, if Judas was the one who led Peter into the courtyard in John 18:15-16, it seems strange that the evangelist retained the descriptor "disciple" for this defector and bothered to conceal his name. It seems doubly odd that Peter casually tailed behind the turncoat Judas accompanying the band of soldiers back to the courtyard, especially after Peter physically assaulted a servant within the arresting party![57] There is no parenthetical digression about this disciple suppressing his allegiance to Jesus to earn human praise (cf. 12:42-43) nor was he faulted for his prior association with the high priest; the brief notice that he was "known" to the high priest was an expedient device to rationalize why he was able to sway the gatekeeper to open the gate for Peter. Perhaps the high priest was so preoccupied with the trial that he was oblivious that one of Jesus' exceptional disciples was in the immediate vicinity, fulfilling Jesus' promise in John 18:9 that no one who had been given to him would be harmed.

John 18:15-16 is the Achilles' heel for the Johannine origins of the Fourth Gospel. It is unbelievable that a Galilean fisherman fraternized with the upper echelons of society. The assumption that Zebedee was a middle class entrepreneur may be built upon a modern capitalist market economy rather than an ancient peasant embedded economy; K. C. Hanson illuminates the plight of Galilean fishing families and hired laborers who toiled at subsistence levels while elite local brokers profited from controlling the rights to the harbors and fishing leases.[58] Zebedee and Yonah formed a fishing cooperative in Mark 1:16-20, but their fishing boat may not be indicative of the resources at their disposal. Hanson opines, "First, given the evidence of the Hellenistic and Roman-era fishing industries, it is at least *possible* that the boats were actually owned by the brokers and used by the cooperative . . . Even if the families owned boats, this would say no more about them than it would

---

57. Culpepper, *Life of a Legend*, 58.

58. See Hanson, "Galilean Fishing Economy," 99-111. Contra Keener, *John*, 2.1223-24.

about a peasant farmer who owned a yoke of oxen or a flock of sheep."[59] This is substantiated by how the Sanhedrin scorned Peter and John as uneducated peasants in Acts 4:13 and Peter's rustic Galilean accent may have betrayed his affiliation with Jesus (cf. Mark 14:70; Matt 26:69; Luke 22:59) while the beloved disciple slipped by unnoticed.[60] Within the narrative of the Fourth Gospel, we could construct the profile of the beloved disciple as an upper-class, cultured citizen of Judea.[61]

The evangelist's admiration of a Judean disciple may be complemented by the Fourth Gospel's concentration on Jesus' repeated sojourns to Jerusalem to the near exclusion of his travels through Galilee and its topographic precision concerning the sites in Judea and Samaria.[62] As one on the Galilean "pillars" who relocated to Jerusalem (Gal 2:9), the Apostle John had decades to become accustomed to his new surroundings before the Fourth Gospel was published.[63] Yet all of the instances where the beloved disciple was active in the ministry of Jesus, excluding 1:35–40 as a red herring and 21:1–24 as a later postscript, are confined to Jerusalem (13:23–25; 18:15–16; 19:25–27, 35; 20:2–9). Is it believable that the Apostle John would not recap the day when he dropped his kinship obligations and occupation to pursue a radically itinerant lifestyle, or a single memory of his personal involvement in Jesus' activities throughout rural Galilee, if he had anything to do with the Fourth Gospel? With regards to the identity of the beloved

---

59. Ibid., 105.

60. Parker, "Son of Zebedee," 44; Haenchen, *John*, 2.167; Beasley-Murray, *John*, lxxii; Witherington, *John's Wisdom*, 288; Grassi, *Secret Identity*, 56, 64; Culpepper, *Life of a Legend*, 62.

61. See Schnackenburg, *St. John*, 3.381; Cullmann, *Johannine Circle*, 78; Parker, "Son of Zebedee," 41, 44; Beasley-Murray, *John*, lxx–lxxv; Quast, *Community in Crisis*, 17; Hengel, *Johannine Question*, 76–80, 124–26; Hengel, *Frage*, 306–9; Brown, *Community*, 34; Grassi, *Secret Identity*, 115; Witherington, *John's Wisdom*, 14–15; Culpepper, *Life of a Legend*, 62, 64, 75, 84; Bauckham, *Eyewitnesses*, 412; Bauckham, *Beloved Disciple*, 76; Bernier, *Aposynagōgos*, 147–48; Thompson, *John*, 18. This would also be supported by the scholars who identify the beloved disciple as Lazarus or John Mark.

62. Parker, "Son of Zebedee," 36, 41, 42.

63. Carson, *John*, 73; Blomberg, *Historical Reliability*, 34.

disciple, Richard Bauckham has forthrightly admonished scholars that "John the son of Zebedee is a phantom that needs to be finally and completely exorcised."[64]

The Literary Function of the Beloved Disciple

There may be multiple rationales for masking the beloved disciple's identity. Perhaps naming him was superfluous since he was well-known to his fan club and his anonymity more easily facilitated their identification with him.[65] Perhaps he was a personal hero of the Johannine Christ congregations, but a nonentity for Christians outside of their tightly-knit social boundaries and disclosing his name might subject their high estimation of him as Jesus' rightful successor to derision.[66] Perhaps the theological implication is that there was no other name that was worth shouting from the rooftops aside from that of Jesus, the incarnate one.[67] Since no amount of discordant scholarly theories are going to recover the name of the beloved disciple, we should move on to more profitable questions about his literary function.

Isolating the vignettes on the beloved disciple in the Fourth Gospel—the prediction of Judas's betrayal, the denials of Peter, the crucifixion of Jesus, and the discovery of the empty tomb—I concur with Rudolf Schnackenburg and Marianne Meye Thompson that his purpose was to establish the veracity of key events in the Passion story.[68] A resident of Jerusalem who crossed paths with Jesus during his final hours in it city before his crucifixion could have served the evangelist's aims. This entails that the beloved disciple was not a purely fictional device interjected into the episodes paralleled in the Synoptic Gospels to legitimize the Johannine

---

64. Bauckham, *Testimony*, 75.

65. Bennema, *Encountering Jesus*, 310.

66. See, for instance, Schnackenburg, *St. John*, 3.384; Quast, *Community in Crisis*, 17–21; Brown, *Community*, 82–83; Bennema, *Encountering Jesus*, 310.

67. Beck, "Anonymity and Identity," 223–24.

68. Schnackenburg, *St. John*, 3.378–79; Thompson, *John*, 19.

community's interpretive spin on them.⁶⁹ A character fabricated out of whole cloth would be useless for authenticating the historicity of Jesus' Passion and the beloved disciple is no more idealized than Peter as his literary foil.⁷⁰ Ismo Dunderberg broadens his analysis to other beloved disciples in Christian literature such as Mary Magdalene (*Gos. Phil.* 62.32—64.9; *Gos. Mary* 10.1–6; 18.14–15) or Jesus' brother James (*2 Apoc. Jas.* 56.16–23).⁷¹ This does not substantiate the non-historicity of the Johannine beloved disciple. The *Gospel of Philip*, the *Gospel of Mary*, and the *Second Apocalypse of James* converted known historical figures within the Christ movement into mouthpieces for the ideological stances epitomized in the documents. In the same way, the Fourth Gospel imputes Johannine insights back to a real Judean disciple.

The term "witness" (*martyria*) with all of its Johannine undertones should not be diminished to mere physical sight; I do not dissent from Andrew Lincoln's findings that witnessing was primarily a matter of testifying to Jesus' glorious status as it was visualized through the lens of faith.⁷² A lawsuit metaphor pervades the evangelist's conception of testimony, but this does not preclude the value of autopsy for the defendant's case.⁷³ There are literal and metaphorical dimensions to the beloved disciple's observations. For example, Jesus was not just satisfying the obligations of familial piety when he granted the beloved disciple custody over his

---

69. Contra Kügler, *Der Jünger*, 478–88; Schenke, "Function and Background," 116; Neirynck, "John 21," 334–36; Casey, *Is John's Gospel True?*, 159; Dunderberg, *Beloved Disciple in Conflict*, 117, 131–32.

70. Cullmann, *Beloved Disciple*, 74; Schnackenburg, *St. John*, 1.100, 3.378; Haenchen, *John*, 2.237–38; Brown, *John I—XII*, xcv; Brown, *Community*, 31–32; Lindars, *John*, 34; Quast, *Community in Crisis*, 16; Grassi, *Secret Identity*, 17–18; Blomberg, *Historical Reliability*, 36n27; Bennema, *Encountering Jesus*, 309; Von Wahlde, *Gospel and Letters*, 3.323.

71. Dunderberg, *Beloved Disciple in Conflict*, 177–87. See also Meyer, "Beloved Disciples," 80–89.

72. Lincoln, "Fourth Gospel as Witness," 7–10

73. See the critique in Bauckham, *Eyewitnesses*, 385–86, 410–11. Lincoln ("Fourth Gospel as Witness," 12) acknowledges that John 19:35 might be an exception to the purely metaphorical or confessional use of *martyria*.

THE BELOVED SON OF ZEBEDEE?

mother (19:25-27).[74] And the flow of blood and water from Jesus when he was pierced with a lance was not just a medical sign confirming that he had expired (19:35). These verses are permeated with theological symbolism.

Jesus' mother anticipated the abundance of the messianic era back in John 2:3-4, but that "hour" did not arrive until Jesus was lifted up on the cross (13:1; 17:1; 19:27) and a new family of faith was forged in its wake.[75] A few scholars presume that the beloved disciple exited the stage with Jesus' mother at this point as John 19:35 does not specify who "that one" (*ekeinos*) was who beheld the spear thrust into Jesus.[76] This is a wooden reading of the "hour" of Jesus' glorification that had commenced in John 13:1. With the exception of the beloved disciple, there were no males attending the crucifixion whom the Fourth Gospel paints as sympathetic to Jesus, and the evangelist built up the reliability of the beloved disciple to assure the reader about the truthfulness of his testimony (19:35; cf. 20:30-31). The "blood and water" may allude to the sacraments of the Eucharist and baptism,[77] illustrate the living water

---

74. Contra Westcott, *St. John*, 313; Haenchen, *John*, 2.193; Carson, *John*, 616; Morris, *John*, 717-18, 718n67; Köstenberger, *John*, 549, 549n47; Michaels, *John*, 959; Von Wahlde, *Gospel and Letters*, 2.806. This seems to be a Protestant overreaction against how this scene has influenced the Mariology of Catholic exegetes. Brown (*John XIII—XI*, 924-27), a Roman Catholic scholar, may push too far in the other direction in linking Jesus' mother with Eve as the mother of a new humanity and Lady Zion as the embodiment of faithful Israel.

75. Hoskyns, *Fourth Gospel*, 530; Barrett, *St. John*, 552; Schnackenburg, *St. John*, 3.278-29; Lindars, *John*, 579-80; Quast, *Community in Crisis*, 94-95; Witherington, *John's Wisdom*, 310; Schnell, *Antidocetic*, 16; Zumstein, *Kreative Erinnerung*, 261-62, 311; Ridderbos, *John*, 613-14; Culpepper, *Life of a Legend*, 63; Moloney, *John*, 504; Theobald, "Der Jünger," 506-7; Keener, *John*, 2.1145; Skinner, *John and Thomas*, 129; Resseguie, "Ideal Point of View," 543; Bennema, *Encountering Jesus*, 300; Thompson, *John*, 400.

76. Lindars, *John*, 589; Casey, *Is John's Gospel True?*, 158-59; Michaels, *John*, 18, 960, 970-74.

77. Hoskyns, *Fourth Gospel*, 533; Bultmann, *John*, 678; Brown, *John XIII—XI*, 913; Kügler, *Der Jünger*, 287-88; Schnelle, *Antidocetic Christology*, 209-10; Casey, *Is John's Gospel True?*, 158; Charlesworth, *Beloved Disciple*, 66; Zumstein, *Kreative Erinnerung*, 233, 269; Maloney, *John*, 5056, 509.

streaming out from the cross (cf. 7:38),[78] or reinforce that Jesus literally died against "docetist" disavowals of his full humanity.[79] An irreducible element of sight was needed to verify Jesus' crucifixion in real time and space before all of these theological implications could be teased out.

Some scholars render the beloved disciple as a cipher for the Johannine community whom Jesus loved as his own (13:1). For Maurice Casey, this community fathomed that Jesus had control over his fate (13:23-25), inherited everything that belonged to Jesus (19:25-27), and trusted in the risen Lord without requiring tangible proof (20:2-9) or worrying over the delay of the Lord's return (21:23).[80] This is close to Rudolf Bultmann's reading of the beloved disciple in John 13:23-25, 19:25-27, and 20:2-9 as a symbol for "Gentile Christianity" surpassing the "Jewish Christianity" embodied by Peter and Jesus' mother.[81] Bultmann theorized that the beloved disciple was historicized by an ecclesiastical redactor who interpolated the parenthetical interjection in John 19:35 and stuck on the epilogue after 20:31,[82] but his argument would be falsified if 19:35 was original to the evangelist and 21:24 was

---

78. Hoskyns, *Fourth Gospel*, 533; Barrett, *St. John*, 556-57; Schnackenburg, *St. John*, 3.294; Brown, *John XIII—XI*, 949-50; Lindars, *John*, 586-87; Grassi, *Secret Identity*, 60-61; Kügler, *Der Jünger*, 288; Carson, *John*, 624; Charlesworth, *Beloved Disciple*, 66; Morris, *John*, 724; Witherington, *John's Wisdom*, 311; Morris, *John*, 725; Lincoln, "Fourth Gospel as Witness," 14-15; Waetjen, *Two Editions*, 405. Köstenberger, *John*, 552; Keener, *John*, 2.1153; Von Wahlde, *Gospel and Letters*, 2.819; Resseguie, "Ideal Point of View," 544; Thompson, *John*, 404.

79. Barrett, *St. John*, 556; Haenchen, *John*, 2.195; Lindars, *John*, 586, 589; Thyen, "Enwicklungen," 288; Quast, *Community in Crisis*, 96-97; Schnelle, *Antidocetic Christology*, 209-10; Beasley-Murray, *John*, 356-57; Carson, *John*, 623-24; Charlesworth, *Beloved Disciple*, 65; Witherington, *John's Wisdom*, 311; Morris, *John*, 724; Culpepper, *Life of a Legend*, 65; Zumstein, *Kreative Erinnerung*, 268; Köstenberger, *John*, 552n67; Michaels, *John*, 974; Thompson, *John*, 403-4.

80. Casey, *Is John's Gospel True?*, 159-64.

81. Bultmann, *John*, 484, 673, 685.

82. Ibid., 11, 483-84, 679.

The Beloved Son of Zebedee?

a redactional imitation of it.[83] Bauckham pinpoints the flaw in reducing the beloved disciple to a paradigmatic or representative function, for his unique privileges of eating with Jesus, welcoming Jesus' mother into his house, and attesting to Jesus' folded linen clothes in the tomb cannot be replicated by future Christians.[84] It is a more natural reading to take the beloved disciple to have been a historical individual who socialized with the high priest Caiaphas, the Apostle Peter, and the mother of Jesus.

Finally, the correction in John 21:23 to the fallacious belief that the beloved disciple was exempt from the human propensity to die weighs in favor of his historicity.[85] Joachim Kügler neutralizes this point by arguing that apocalyptic eschatology was a late addition to Johannine theology, so there was no foothold for the falsehood that the beloved disciple would survive until Jesus' *parousia* ("coming") to gain any traction within the Johannine community and thus 21:23 was nothing more than a literary fiction.[86] Screening out the futurist eschatology from the Fourth Gospel as redactional is debatable (e.g., 5:25, 28–29; 6:39–40, 44, 54; 14:3). Dunderberg retorts that fictional characters in fables die too and that John 21:23 may just be a parenetic saying that no follower of Jesus is guaranteed a form of immortality that precludes natural death.[87] The incentive to discourage older eschatological expectations that some of Jesus' contemporaries might not taste death (cf. Mark 9:1; 1 Thess 4:15–17) was precisely that they were dying off.

83. See my argument against this view in Chapter 2.

84. Bauckham, *Beloved Disciple*, 83; cf. Dunderberg, *Beloved Disciple in Conflict*, 128–32.

85. See, for example, Cullmann, *Johannine Circle*, 71, 75; Haenchen, *John*, 2.228, 233; Schnackenburg, *St. John*, 3.376–77, 379; Brown, *John XIII—XXI*, 1119; Thyen, "Entwicklungen," 269; Brown, *Community*, 31; Quast, *Community in Crisis*, 17; Hengel, *Frage*, 214n.27, 218; Grassi, *Secret Identity*, 9–10; Beasley-Murray, *John*, lxxi; Charlesworth, *Beloved Disciple*, 45, 141–42; Moloney, *John*, 8, 561; Culpepper, *Life of a Legend*, 70, 72, 84; Lincoln, "Fourth Gospel as Witness," 22; Bauckham, *Beloved Disciple*, 80; Von Wahlde, *Gospel and Letters*, 3.426.

86. Kügler, *Der Jünger*, 483–84.

87. Dunderberg, *Beloved Disciple in Conflict*, 122–28. See further discussion on this point in chapter 2.

If the beloved disciple was, at minimum, a historical person who had been a part of that first generation, it would strengthen the point that no one, not even Jesus' best friend, would get any assurances that they would have front row seats for Jesus' "Second Coming." Jesus is not beholden to our apocalyptic calendars.

One last historical-critical issue that must be squarely faced is that the beloved disciple is ignored in the Synoptic Gospels and seems like almost an afterthought within the narrative of the Fourth Gospel. John 13:23–25 and 20:2–10 are cases in point. When Peter motioned to the beloved disciple to ask Jesus about the double agent in their midst, Jesus replied that he would pass a morsel of bread to the traitor (13:23–27). Why did Peter beseech the beloved disciple to act as a mediator between him and Jesus rather than talk to Jesus directly (cf. 6:68; 13:6–10, 36–38), why did the beloved disciple not mediate anything back to Peter, and why was everyone at the table (including the beloved disciple?) blissfully unaware of Judas's treachery when he snuck out after taking the bread from Jesus' hands (13:28–29)? Omitting the dialogue with the beloved disciple altogether might smooth over these tensions.[88] For Barrett, John 13:23–28 is secondary to the Synoptics and merged the Markan account of the Twelve's obliviousness (Mark 14:18–21) with the Matthean account of the public exposure of Judas's scheme (Matt 26:21–25).[89] As for John 20:1–10, Mary Magdalene alerted the disciples that Jesus' corpse had gone missing (20:1), but the beloved disciple was applauded for coming to faith in Jesus' resurrection before her (20:8). Why did Peter's examination of the folded grave clothes in the tomb and the beloved disciple's renewed faith have no noticeable impact upon her (20:2–10)? She was inconsolable until two angelic visitors sitting in the tomb where they had not been previously spoke to her

---

88. Thyen, "Entwicklungen," 276–80; Haenchen, *John*, 2.110–12; Theobald, "Der Jünger," 504–5. If this was a redactional creation, there is a heightening of the supernatural element in the account as Judas becomes demonically possessed upon his ingestion of the morsel of bread and an increasing emphasis on the unmasking of the traitor, perhaps reflecting the redactor's contemporary anxiety concerning the defectors from the Johannine community.

89. Barrett, *St. John*, 116,

(20:11).⁹⁰ Turning to the parallel in Luke 24:12, Peter alone was described as racing to the grave site and marvelling at the linen clothes lying there.

In all probability, traditional and editorial material was interwoven throughout the Fourth Gospel. There is a degree of subjectivity, however, in untangling this web. If we skip right from John 13:22 to 13:27b, bypassing the explanation that Jesus gave to the beloved disciple about why he handed a piece of bread to Judas (13:26–27a), the bewilderment of the disciples about Judas's hasty withdrawal from the table becomes comprehensible. We may not have to resort to such a drastic surgical excision if John 13:28 was deleted as an editorial aside, though it would be odd for a redactor to add a clarification that may have inadvertently made the beloved disciple look daft after Jesus transparently signalled to him who would betray him.⁹¹ Both procedures require a clumsy redactor who did not carefully edit the source text, so it may be better to grapple with the chapter as it stands as a literary whole. The beloved disciple leaned back to Jesus to discretely whisper his question to him, so John 13:28 may pertain to the rest of the disciples who did not hear Jesus' chat with the beloved disciple above the noise around the table and were in the dark about why Jesus advised Judas to put his plans into motion. The beloved disciple did not alert Peter so as not to interfere with Jesus' divinely-ordained fate.⁹² John 20:1, 11–18 and 20:2–10 may have conjoined two discrete memories about a Christophany to Mary Magdalene and the rigorous inspection of the tomb. A common tradition probably underlies John 20:2–10 and Luke 24:12,⁹³ but

90. See Schnackenburg, *St. John*, 302–5; Thyen, "Entwicklungen," 288–90; Theobald, "Der Jünger," 509–11; Von Wahlde, *Gospel and Letters*, 843.

91. See Bultmann, *John*, 480; Schnackenburg, *St. John*, 2.14.

92. Casey, *Is John's Gospel True?*, 160.

93. The authenticity of Luke 24:12 has been debated by text critics. According to Westcott and Hort's theory of "Western Non-Interpolations," the Western text correctly preserved the shorter reading and Luke 24:12 was interpolated to either prepare for Luke 24:24 or to stress the bodily nature of Jesus' resurrection against Docetism. On the other hand, this theory relies on generally inferior manuscripts, verse 12 seems to be the natural antecedent

the reference to "some" (*tines*) of the disciples who checked out the grave site in Luke 24:24 is a transparent sign that Peter was not, in fact, alone.[94] The beloved disciple could have been among these unspecified plural visitors.

Without a doubt, the Synoptic Gospels have no concept of an exceptional disciple who was elevated above the Twelve, but I see no indication that the beloved disciple was not an original and essential aspect of the story that the fourth evangelist wished to tell. The fourth evangelist may have exaggerated the prestige of a Jerusalem resident who opened up his accommodations for Jesus to celebrate the Passover and had some contact with the high priest. Some stories about him may have been generated to impress theological truths on the readers. For example, it was Jesus' siblings rather than the beloved disciple who were the custodians for his mother in Acts 1:14,[95] but this does not change the moral of John 19:26–27 that Jesus redefined kinship around the family of faith (cf. Mark 3:33–35 par). Finally, the beloved disciple embodied the narrator's ideal point of view and the ideological norms and values that the readers ought to emulate.[96]

A defining trait of the beloved disciple was his perceptiveness. The image of him resting his head "on the bosom" (*en tō kolpō*) of Jesus in John 13:23 corresponds to the inclination of the pre-existent *logos* or "Word" "towards the bosom" (*eis ton kolpon*) of the Father in heaven (1:18).[97] In Christopher Skinner's literary-

---

for verse 24, and the omission of Luke 24:12 could be explained by a scribe who was not able to square Peter's continued skepticism in that verse with the report that the Lord "has appeared to Simon" in verse 34. The theory of "Western Non-Interpolations" is discussed in Metzger, *Textual Commentary*, 164–66. The authenticity of Luke 24:12 is defended by Metzger, *Textual Commentary*, 157–58 and Quast, *Communities in Crisis*, 102–4.

94. Brown, *John XIII—XXI*, 1000–1001; Lindars, *John*, 600; Beasley-Murray, *John*, 368; Carson, *John*, 636; Blomberg, *Historical Reliability*, 261; Michaels, *John*, 989–90, 999n.19.

95. Barrett, *St. John*, 116, 552; Haenchen, *John*, 2.193.

96. Resseguie, "Ideal Point of View," 537–38, 548.

97. The vast majority of commentators on the Fourth Gospel pick up on this echo. A significant recent exception is Urban C. Von Wahlde (*Gospel and Letters*, 2.606) who thinks that the evangelist was just painting a picture of the

critical study of the Fourth Gospel, the Johannine characters are positively or negatively evaluated based on their comprehension of the themes in the Prologue,[98] so the beloved disciple's close fellowship with Jesus was nearly equivalent to that between Jesus and his heavenly Father.

The question is whether the beloved disciple's perspicacity has been idealized to the point of perfection. Cornelis Bennema notes two instances of the beloved disciple's fallible perception in John 13:28 and 20:9.[99] Yet I argued above that the beloved disciple was not one of the uninformed table guests in John 13:28. It is also explicit that the beloved disciple "believed" (*episteusen*) in the absolute sense at the sight of the empty tomb in John 20:8. It would be trite to notify the reader that he trusted Mary that the corpse was stolen, so most commentators agree that he had a full-fledged Easter faith.[100] Bearing in mind the gloss that "they [Peter and the beloved disciple] had not yet known the scripture" (20:9), the beloved disciple's faith could have been rooted in experiential rather than exegetical knowledge. Redaction critics may maneuver to eliminate 20:9 as an editorial insertion[101] or as a residue of a lost source where the plural referred back to Peter and Mary,[102] but this fails to deal with the text as it stands. Charlesworth translates *episteusen* in John 20:8 as an inceptive aorist, meaning that the beloved disciple was barely starting to believe until more documentation came to light.[103] His rudimentary belief may have been that Jesus was translated to heaven (cf. 14:28; 16:28), but his faith in

---

beloved disciple's physical proximity to Jesus in order to quietly whisper to him and that there is no intentional parallel to John 1:18.

98. Skinner, *John and Thomas*, 37-40. See also Skinner, *Reading John*, 96-122.

99. Bennema, *Encountering Jesus*, 309.

100. See the survey of scholars who support this view in Charlesworth, *Beloved Disciple*, 73-76.

101. Bultmann, *John*, 685.

102. Schnackenburg, *St. John*, 3.306, 313.

103. Charlesworth, *Beloved Disciple*, 81, 95.

Jesus' bodily resurrection may have not been fully formed.[104] I am more persuaded by Urban C. Von Wahlde that the pluperfect tense of *ēdeisan* ("they had known") refers to a completed action in the past time; John 20:9 seeks to explicate why Peter and the beloved disciple were dumbfounded by what Mary told them and rushed to the unoccupied tomb because the scriptural prophecies about the resurrection had not yet entered into their thinking.[105] Upon their arrival at the tomb, the beloved disciple's mind was opened to the reality of the resurrection and, having served his literary purpose, retires to his home (20:8–10). Peter would not be won over to Easter faith without a glimpse of Jesus' reanimated body.

The love that Jesus had for the beloved disciple was not like his sentimental feelings for Lazarus, Mary, and Martha (11:5, 36). Abiding in Jesus' love in the fullest Johannine sense is premised on obedience to his commandments (14:21; 15:10, 14).[106] Accordingly, loyalty is the second essential trait of the beloved disciple. His fidelity to Jesus did not waver when Jesus was on trial before the priestly interrogators or condemned as guilty by the Roman governor. While the rest hid in shame, the beloved disciple boldly stood at the foot of the cross. The readers cannot exactly mimic what the beloved disciple said and did in Jesus' lifetime, but they can exhibit the same level of commitment to the crucified one within their own social contexts. It is the beloved disciple's anonymity that invites the reader's identification with him.[107]

Conclusion: An Elite Judean Disciple

Although not all of Pierson Parker's critiques against the traditional authorship of the Fourth Gospel hit the mark, his summation of the state of the evidence that the Apostle John was an "unlettered fisherman from the north country" and the beloved

104. Ibid., 80–81; cf. Witherington, *John's Wisdom*, 325; Michaels, *John*, 992; Thompson, *John*, 412.

105. Von Wahlde, *Gospel and Letters*, 839, 844.

106. Ibid., 425, 427.

107. Lincoln, "Fourth Gospel as Witness," 23.

The Beloved Son of Zebedee?

disciple was a "cultured citizen of Jerusalem" and a "familiar visitor at the high priest's court" is on point.[108] The Patristic testimony is irreconcilable with the internal data from the Fourth Gospel. The beloved disciple may have once been an unexceptional Judean associate of Jesus, but the fourth evangelist raised him on a pedestal so that he could perform two literary functions. He was a highly competent "witness" to Jesus' Passion, with both the literal connotations of physical sight and the metaphorical connotations of spiritual insight, and set the standard of discipleship that future believers should emulate. In the end, though, the verses about the beloved disciple (13:23–25; 18:15–16; 19:26–27, 35; 20:2–10) are few in number and consist of a minor subplot in the latter half of the Fourth Gospel. He was not present for the great bulk of the narrative, so how he was transformed into the source of the whole Fourth Gospel in the epilogue (21:24) will be the subject matter under investigation in the next chapter.

108. Parker, "Son of Zebedee," 43.

2

The Beloved Evangelist?

THE FOURTH GOSPEL HAS an omniscient narrator who is cognizant of all the internal thoughts and feelings of the characters in the story world. At a few junctures, this narrator intrudes in on the action to issue a direct plea to the reader in the second person. John 19:35 has the affirmation that "the one who has seen" (*ho heōrakōs*) Jesus' crucifixion "has testified" (*memartyrēken*) to it and knows that his "testimony" (*martyria*) is "true" (*alēthinē*). This ought to evoke faith in the implied reader. John 21:24 duplicated the terminology of 19:35 and heightened the rhetoric.[1] It is explicit that the "disciple" (*mathētēs*) was both "the one who is testifying" (*ho martyrōn*) and "the one who has written" (*ho grapsas*) these things and that his "testimony" (*martyria*) is "true" (*alēthēs*). If the narration of the beloved disciple in the third person ostensibly intimated that he was distinct from the implied author in 19:35,[2] the surprise in 21:24 is that the beloved disciple and the implied author were one and the same person. The disclosure that the beloved disciple was the fount of the whole tradition seems utterly unexpected in light of the character's absence from everything that happened before John 13:23.[3]

1. See Schnelle, *Antidocetic Christology*, 15.

2. It is true that ancient historians like Thucydides (*Hist.* 1.1.1; 2.70.4; 4.104.4 5.26.1) referred to themselves in the third-person when they were participants in the narrated events (see Jackson, "Ancient Self-Referential Conventions," 24–30; Keener, *John*, 1.111; Bauckham, *Eyewitnesses*, 393), but it seems strange that there was no hint that the beloved disciple was anything other than a flat character in the drama until the second to last verse.

3. Lincoln, "Fourth Gospel as Witness," 16.

Therefore, I disagree with Rudolf Bultmann's view that 19:35 and 21:1-25 were editorial supplements from the same ecclesiastical redactor.[4] Likewise, I am not persuaded that every verse about the beloved disciple was part of a uniform redactional layer.[5] There is a genuinely new twist about the beloved disciple in the so-called "Johannine epilogue" that one might not have anticipated from his intermittent appearances in the Fourth Gospel beforehand. If the epilogue is not by the same hand as the evangelist, it is nonetheless the product of an inspired editor whom I will call the "redactor" and is a valuable window into the obstacles that the proponents of the Fourth Gospel's theological vision had to overcome in the early second century. The epilogue served an authenticating seal for the Fourth Gospel, certifying that it was written down by an unreservedly reputable authority figure and advocating for the truth of its testimony for a wider Christian readership that venerated Peter as their figurehead and martyr.

Inconclusive Textual and Stylistic Arguments

In the heyday of source, form, and redaction criticism in the twentieth century, the postulation that John 20:31 was originally the last verse of the Fourth Gospel and that 21:1-25 was a later addendum was a mainstay of critical scholarship. Indeed, Dwight Moody Smith accentuated how the critical consensus on the Johannine epilogue was "the key and cornerstone for any redactional theory."[6] This was not just the bias of modernist critics operating with a hermeneutic of suspicion. In 1641, the Dutch jurist Hugo Grotius was not bothered by the prospect that an Ephesian bishop appended a postscript to the Fourth Gospel.[7] Nonetheless, as literary and canonical critical approaches began to flourish in the New Testament guild, the sway of the older source critical theories

4. Bultmann, *John*, 11, 483-84.
5. Contra Thyen, "Entwicklungen," 267-68, 295-96; Von Wahlde, *Gospel and Letters*, 1.235, 329-31; 3.429; Theobald, "Der Jünger," 498-513.
6. Smith, *Bultmann's Literary Theory*, 234.
7. See Baum, "The Original Epilogue," 242.

began to wane and an increasing minority of New Testament scholars reaffirmed that the epilogue was an integral component of the literary structure and design of the Fourth Gospel.[8]

The first concession that must be granted is that the external support for a manuscript that broke off after John 20:31 is scarce to non-existent. Michael Lattke quotes the theologian Tertullian (ca. 155–240 CE) on the "conclusion" (*clausula*) of the Fourth Gospel in the purpose clause of John 20:31 in his polemical tract *Against Praxeas* 25.4.[9] Lattke disagrees that Tertullian's remarks elsewhere that there was a misguided expectation that the Apostle John would live until the coming of the Lord (*An.* 50.5) and that Peter was "girded" (*cingitur*) when he was fastened to a cross (*Scorp.* 15.3) exhibited literary contact with John 21:18–24, for Tertullian may have been cognizant of oral legends about John's unusually long lifespan and Peter's crucifixion.[10] There is a greater probability that Tertullian was influenced by the Johannine epilogue's illumination of Jesus' opaque aphorisms. Deprived of the redactor's own interpretive spin in verses 19a and 22b, it is not obvious that the imagery of an frail Peter stretching out his arms to be girded up by another signified the kind of death that he would undergo or that the beloved disciple had not been literally destined "to remain" (*menein*) in the flesh until Jesus returned.

The unanimity of the textual witnesses for the authenticity of the Johannine epilogue has also been disrupted by the recent discovery of a fourth-century Sahidic papyrus leaf catalogued in the Bodleian Library in Oxford (MS. Copt.e.150P). It has John 20:19–31 inscribed on it with some extra space after the last verse so that it apparently did not carry on to the succeeding verse in 21:1, but the fragmentary state of the manuscript deters some text-critics from factoring it in as evidence for the existence of a copy of the Fourth Gospel without its epilogue.[11] Compare this to

---

8. For a full list of scholars, see Gaventa, "Archive of Excess," 249–50n.8; Bauckham, *Beloved Disciple*, 272n.3; Baum, "Original Epilogue," 229–30.

9. Lattke, "Buchschluß," 288–90.

10. Ibid., 291.

11. This manuscript was catalogued in Schenke, "Johannes 20,19–31,"

the divided manuscript and Patristic attestation for the so-called *pericope adulterae* in John 7:53–8:11 and the longer ending in Mark 16:9–20.[12]

In the *pericope adulterae*, Jesus protected an adulteress about to be stoned by an angry mob, reminding her self-righteous accusers about their own sins. Alas, irrespective of its enormous popularity, the evidence is overwhelming that it was secondarily interpolated into John 7:53–8:11 in the vast majority of the manuscripts where it is present, though a minority of late witnesses relocate it to other spots in the third or fourth canonical gospels.[13] It is unattested in a manuscript of the Fourth Gospel before Codex Bezae in the fifth century CE, it diverges linguistically and stylistically from the fourth evangelist's typical style, and it interrupts the narrative sequence from John 7:52 to 8:12. An unadorned memory that Jesus pardoned a woman charged with imprecise transgressions seems to have been orally transmitted over centuries and the details were embellished with each retelling (cf. Papias, in Eusebius, *Hist. Eccl.* 3.39.17; *Did. Apost.* 7; Didymus the Blind, *Comm. Eccl.* 223.6–13). Likewise, a scribe who was dissatisfied with how the women fled from the angel at the tomb in terror in Mark 16:8 augmented it with condensed adaptations of the resurrection appearances narrated in John 20:11–23 and Luke 24:13–51. Mark's longer ending has a wealth of manuscript and Patristic support, but it is omitted in the major fourth-century biblical codices Vaticanus and Sinaiticus along with some other ancient witnesses and doubts were voiced about its authenticity since antiquity (cf. Eusebius, *Quaest. ad Marinum* I.1–II.1; Jerome, *Ep. 120, To Hedibia*).[14]

The nonexistence of any manuscripts that incontrovertibly stopped at John 20:31 is noticeable and could be construed in one

---

893–904. See the cautionary, preliminary assessment by the text critic P. J. Williams, "The John Manuscript 'Without John 21'" online (http://evangelicaltextualcriticism.blogspot.ca/2006/09/john-manuscript-without-john-21.html).

12. This same point is made by Porter, "Ending," 72–73.

13. There is an overview of the textual data in Metzger, *Textual Commentary*, 187–89.

14. There is an overview of the textual data in ibid., 102–6.

of two ways. For some scholars, it validates the unity of all twenty-one chapters of the Fourth Gospel. For others, there was a short gap between the Fourth Gospel's publication for a circumscribed readership among the Johannine community and its broader circulation among Christians in general for the epilogue to have been affixed to the text and to not leave a trace in the manuscripts. David Trobisch's theory that the Johannine epilogue was one of the last additions to the scriptural "books" (cf. John 21:25) that comprise the canonical edition of the New Testament,[15] influencing every succeeding copyist of the Fourth Gospel to follow suit in reproducing it as far as we are aware, is less probable.

This debate will have to be adjudicated on the basis of internal criteria such as language, style, and theology. The hitch is that the specialists are split over whether John 21:1–25 deviates enough from the linguistic and stylistic traits of John 1—20 to be statistically relevant.[16] The simple sentence structure, the omission of conjunctions or connective particles between clauses (i.e., asyndeton), the use of the Greek conjunction *oun* ("therefore," "then") to advance the plot, and the re-occurrence of favorite expressions like the double amen (i.e., "truly, truly") formula is paralleled in the prior twenty chapters. There are threads binding 21:1–25 to what preceded it such as the names of Nathanael, with the added

15. Trobisch, *First Edition*, 97–100. See also Chris Keith's judgment that the "books" that 21:24 has in mind were the other Gospels that were eventually canonized, though, in contrast to Trobisch, Keith's leaning is that the epilogue was part of the evangelist's original draft (cf. "Competitive Textualization," 321–37).

16. Rudolf Bultmann (*John*, 700–701), Charles Barrett (*John*, 576), and Ernst Haenchen (*John*, 1.89; 2.229) enumerate the unique vocabulary and stylistic traits of the chapter. Armin Baum ("Original Epilogue," 244–46) judges that the syntactical evidence leans in favor of the evangelist's authorship of chapter 21, but the semantic evidence from his review of 21:1–14 leans in favor of a second hand. Eugene Ruckstuhl ("Johannes 21," 327–53), D. A. Carson (*John*, 665–66), Craig Keener (*John*, 2.1219, 1219n4), and Stanley Porter ("Ending," 58–62), on the other hand, offer reasonable grammatical or literary explanations for the minor changes in vocabulary or style. They endeavor to show that the variations are statistically negligible when compared to other sections of the Fourth Gospel and do not overturn the case for the stylistic unity of all twenty-one chapters.

The Beloved Evangelist?

specification about his hometown (21:2; cf. 1:45-49), and Thomas who bore the nickname *Didymos* or "twin" (21:2; cf. 11:16; 20:24). Several of the twenty-eight *hapax legomena* or the words that are used only once in the chapter are interconnected with its peculiar content: the chapter has the solitary example of the disciples embarking on a fishing outing in the Fourth Gospel and has a pastoral conversation between Jesus and Peter about shepherding.[17] *Paidia* ("children") and *adelphoi* ("brothers") are terms of endearment that are not found in John 1—20, though Jesus comforted his *teknia* ("children") in John 13:33, and there are further minor syntactical differences such as in the selection of prepositions. Leading twentieth-century Johannine commentators like C. K. Barrett and Raymond Brown, each of whom assigned the epilogue to the redactor, admitted that the stylistic arguments were inadequate for settling on a final verdict about this matter.[18]

Inconclusive Thematic Arguments

Many scholars are at a loss about why an afterword was desirable after John 20:30-31.[19] Willi Braun appraises these verses as con-

17. Bultmann (*John*, 700-701) and Barrett (*John*, 576) list *aigialos* ("beach"); *alieuein* ("to fish"); *apobainein* ("to get out"); *aristan* ("to eat"); *arnion* ("lamb"); *boskein* ("to feed"); *gēraskein* ("to grow old"); *gymnos* ("naked"); *diktyon* ("fishing net"); *ekteinein* ("to stretch out"); *exetazein* ("to investigate"); *ependytēs* ("outer garment"); *epistrephein* ("to turn around"); *zōnnynai* ("to fasten"); *ischyein* ("to be able"); *ichthys* ("fish"); *makran* ("far"); *neōteros* ("younger"); *oiesthai* ("to suppose"); *pēchys* ("cubit"); *poimainein* ("to shepherd"); *probation* ("sheep"); *prosphagion* ("broiled fish"); *prōia* ("morning"); *syrein* ("to drag"); *tolman* ("to dare"); and *triton* ("third"). Porter ("Ending" 60) discards *epistrephein* since this is just a prefixed form of the lexeme *strephein* (cf. John 1:38; 12:40; 20:14) and *tolman* since this occurs no more frequently in the Gospels of Matthew and Luke.

18. Barrett, *John*, 577; Brown, *John XIII—XXI*, 1088.

19. Westcott, *St. John*, 359; Bultmann, *John*, 700; Barrett, *John*, 575; Brown, *John XIII—XXI*, 1057, 1078; Lindars, *John*, 617; Schnackenburg, *St. John*, 3.337, 339-40, 343, 350; Haenchen, *John*, 2.212; Braun, "Resisting John," 66, 68; Moloney, *John*, 545; Beasley-Murray, *John*, 388, 395; Schnelle, *Antidocetic Christology*, 13; Casey, *Is John's Gospel True?*, 154; Zumstein, *Kreative Erinnerung*, 299-300; Weatjen, John, 424-26; Skinner, *John and Thomas*, 133n144;

stituting the formal and teleological closure to the Fourth Gospel and its Christological climax.[20] The text would have been finished on a high point: the "signs" (*sēmeia*) documented in this book were more than sufficient to compel readers to put their trust in Jesus' divine sonship and inherit the life attainable through him. These "signs" were not restricted to the manifestations of the risen one in 20:14–17, 19–23, and 26–29,[21] for the evangelist began numbering the signs in 2:11 and 4:54. For Bauckham, John 20:30–31 wrapped up the book of Jesus' "signs," but the epilogue peered beyond the horizon of Jesus' lifetime to the "miracle" of the disciples' fruitful missionary project after Easter and it is "these things" (*tauta*) that are the epilogue's central theme (21:24).[22] For some scholars, the Fourth Gospel seems incomplete without blessing the disciples' evangelism campaign to the nations (cf. Matt 28:16–20; Luke 24:50–53).[23] Since their missionary assignment was foreshadowed in John 20:22–23 when Jesus conferred the Spirit on them and authorized them to forgive sins, though, it is questionable whether a second commissioning of them was compulsory.[24]

John 20:30–31 may be an appropriate closing statement, but Craig Keener accumulates examples from classical literature where an ostensible conclusion is followed up by ancillary, anti-climactic illustrations or commentary.[25] John 20:30–31 may not be an iso-

---

Thompson, *John*, 431.

20. Braun, "Resisting John," 68.

21. Contra Hoskyns, *Fourth Gospel*, 550; Minear, "Original Function of John 21," 87–90; Ellis, "Authenticity of John 21," 20–21; Breck, "Appendix," 29; Michaels, *John*, 1021–23.

22. Bauckham, *Eyewitnesses*, 365–68; Bauckham, *Beloved Disciple*, 27.

23. Hoskyns, *Fourth Gospel*, 550; Morris, *John*, 758.

24. See Brown, *John XII—XXI*, 1078; Barrett, *John*, 576; Quast, *Community in Crisis*, 127–28. Carson (*John*, 651–55) may nitpick when he writes that 20:22 does not explicitly say that Jesus breathed on the disciples nor that they received the Holy Spirit at that very moment. Carson's ultimate goal is to harmonize John 20:22–23 with the advent of the Spirit at the festival of Pentecost in Acts 2:1–4.

25. Keener, *John*, 2.1213, 1213n3. For a few of his examples, Aeschines's speech *Against Timarchus* followed up a summary statement (177) with a further indictment against Timarchus's moral flaws, Polybius supplemented

lated example within the Fourth Gospel itself where the narration does not cease after a summary statement (John 12:36; 14:31; cf. 1 John 5:13; Rev 22:5).[26] Moreover, the Fourth Gospel might be purposefully framed by a prologue and an epilogue,[27] but the abstract theological ruminations about the pre-cosmogonic state of the *logos* (Word) in the prologue is not quite matched by its this-worldly epilogue and differs sharply from the pairing of technical prologues and epilogues in Greco-Roman treatises.[28] Bauckham bolsters the point that the Johannine prologue and epilogue complement each other by counting 496 words in John 21:1–23 and 496 syllables in John 1:1–18. Utilizing the technique of *gematria*, the number 496 equals the value of the Greek word *monogenēs* or "only son" (cf. 1:14, 18).[29] Matching up words and syllables may be like comparing apples and oranges, but Bauckham has to have lots of confidence in the twenty-seventh edition of Nestle-Aland to reconstruct the original wording of the prologue and the epilogue from our extant manuscripts exactly, for an undetected copyist error would derail his calculations. He also has to exclude 21:24–25 from his word count by arguing that the epilogue is framed by two conclusions (20:30–31; 21:24–25) consisting of 43 words each.

There have been additional structural arguments for the unity of all twenty-one chapters. Peter F. Ellis and John Breck hang the authenticity of the epilogue on a chiastic structure that they adduce to be running through the entire text,[30] but their analysis

---

the closing summary of his *Histories* (39.8.4–6) with a few extra concluding comments (39.8.7–8), and Xenophon sprinkled concluding statements that summed up select events in different books of his *Hellenica* (3.5.25; 4.8.19).

26. Ellis, "Authenticity of John 21," 20; Breck, "Appendix," 28; Morris, *John*, 758; Blomberg, *Historical Reliability*, 272.

27. Thyen, *Entwicklungen*, 260; Ellis, "Authenticity of John 21," 21–22; Blomberg, *Historical Reliability*, 273; Köstenberger, *John*, 583–84; Bauckham, *Eyewitnesses*, 364; Bauckham, *Beloved Disciple*, 277–78.

28. See the review of the Greco-Roman convention in Baum, "Original Epilogue," 234–35.

29. Bauckham, *Eyewitnesses*, 364–65; Bauckham, *Beloved Disciple*, 275–77.

30. Ellis, "Authenticity of John 21," 24–25; Breck, "Appendix," 36–39,

has not commanded scholarly assent. Thomas L. Brodie discerns a threefold pattern in 19:35–37, 20:30–31, and 21:24–25 where the witness of an inanimate book is bracketed by flesh-and-blood witnesses before and after Easter,[31] but 21:24–25 juxtaposes the truthfulness of what the beloved disciple put into writing with a multiplicity of "books" (*biblia*). Bauckham builds on past studies about the amount of fish caught in the net in 21:11.[32] The total 153 is a triangular number, the sum of the first seventeen integers, and seventeen and 153 are equivalent to the Hebrew names Gedi and Eglaim through the application of *gematria*. Ezekiel 47:10 prophesied that a stream of water would pour out from the temple into the Dead Sea, purifying it into a fresh lake teeming with life, and fishers would wade into its shore from the spring of Gedi to the spring of Eglaim. In John 7:37–39, Jesus was the fountain of life. Bauckham's decoding of the symbolism of 153 fish is one of many vaunted solutions, from traditionalist scholars who take the number as a genuine reminiscence of a huge haul of fish[33] to researchers who have given up on cracking this code.[34] If Bauckham correctly deciphered the allusion to Ezekiel, it does not mean that the redactor could not have devised this puzzle on the basis of John 7:37–39. At this point, Bauckham tallies up how many times the key terms *sēmeion*, *pisteuein*, *Christos*, and *zōē* in John 20:30–31 occur in the Fourth Gospel. His totals are seventeen, ninety-eight, nineteen, and thirty-six respectively. Notice how there are seventeen occurrences of *sēmeion* and the sum of the last three numbers is 153.[35] Thus, Bauckham surmises that the evangelist smuggled the symbolic numbers seventeen and 153 into 20:30–31, but his list of key terms is selective and his choice of alternate ones (e.g.,

---

40–43.

31. Brodie, *John*, 572–74
32. Bauckham, *Beloved Disciple*, 278–80.
33. Carson, *John*, 671–73; Morris, *John*, 764–65; Blomberg, *Historical Reliability*, 276; Michaels, *John*, 1036–38.
34. See Brown, *John XIII—XXI*, 1075; Keener, *John*, 2.1231–33.
35. Bauckham, *Beloved Disciple*, 280–82.

THE BELOVED EVANGELIST?

Iēsous, graphein, huios, onoma) would throw off his math.[36] The arguments that John 21:1-25 is integral to the structure of the Fourth Gospel may be less than compelling.

If the plan was to close the curtain of the Fourth Gospel at John 20:30-31, it is conceivable that the same author returned to thoroughly revise the text at a subsequent date.[37] What makes this option doubtful, as Armin Baum stresses, is there is no explicit statement about resuming the narrative after a brief hiatus, nor was the concluding statement in 20:30-31 re-located to the end of the appended material.[38] Baum reckons that the redactor respected the literary integrity of the Fourth Gospel and kept its twenty chapters intact, supplementing it with auxiliary material after its original conclusion. There is precedent for this in the editorial attachment of two letters in front of the prologue for the book of 2 *Maccabees* (2 Macc 1:1-9; 1:10—2:18) and a prayer (*Sir.* 51:1-12), an autobiographical poem about the pursuit of wisdom (51:13-30), and a subscription following the conclusion (50:27-29) of the book of *Ben Sira*.[39]

Moreover, the narrative seems to be somewhat disjointed in the transition from chapter 20 to chapter 21.[40] When did the

36. Bauckham (ibid., 281) point out that *sēmeion, pisteuein, Christos*, and *zōē* occur for the last time in 20:30-31, but this is also the final occurrence of the noun *onoma* or "name" (John 1:6, 12; 2:23; 3:1, 18; 5:43; 10:3, 25; 12:13, 28; 14:13, 14, 26; 15:16, 21; 16:23, 24, 26; 17:6, 11, 12, 26; 18:10; 20:31).

37. Westcott, *St. John*, 359; Morris, *John*, 758; Carson, *John*, 668; Porter, "Ending," 73.

38. Baum, "Original Epilogue," 250-51, 254-55. Baum compares this with how Cornelius Nepo signaled his intent to add an appendix after his subject Atticus died (*De Vir. ill.* 25.19.1). M. J. Lagrange (*Saint Jean*, 520-21) argues for the originality of the epilogue by transposing 20:30-31 to the end of 21:1-25.

39. Baum, "Original Epilogue," 252-54; cf. Zumstein, *Kreative Erinnerung*, 303-305.

40. The following points are based on Bultmann, *John*, 701-702; Barrett, *John*, 577; Schnackenburg, *St. John*, 3.343-44; Brown, *John XIII—XXI*, 1078; Haenchen, *John*, 1.89; 2.222, 229; Beasley-Murray, *John*, 395-96; Braun, "Resisting John," 68-69; Witherington, *John's Wisdom*, 352; Schnelle, *Antidocetic Christology*, 14; Zumstein, *Kreative Erinnerung*, 8, 299-303, 305; Gaventa, "Archive of Excess," 245; Waetjen, *Two Editions*, 8; Von Wahlde, *Gospel and Letters*, 3.885; Thompson, *John*, 431.

disciples trek back to Galilee, why were they busy with a frivolous pastime like fishing after the Spirit empowered them to save lost people, why did they need a fresh vision of the risen one after Thomas was gently rebuked for demanding visible proof of the resurrection, and why was Jesus not recognizable to the disciples from their boat? Why had the weight of the emphasis shifted from Christology to ecclesiology, so that the stations of Peter and the beloved disciple in the church hierarchy were the most pressing matters (21:15–17), and from a largely realized to a futuristic eschatology (21:22–23)? Interestingly, if one skipped ahead from John 19:42 to 21:1, there would be more continuity in that the disciples reverted back to their former livelihoods before the risen Lord flipped their world upside down at the Sea of Galilee. This is what led Beverly Gaventa to posit dual endings in chapters 20 and 21, each proceeding with alternating accounts of what transpired after Jesus' burial in John 19:38–42.[41] The notification about the third time that Jesus "was manifested" (*ephanerōthē*) to the disciples in John 21:14, however, must be tied to his previous manifestations in 20:19-23 and 20:26-29 and undercuts her theory that the last two chapters were two independent endings.[42]

There may be points where critical scholars over-exaggerate the narrative incoherence in the progression from John 20:31 to 21:1. The transitional phrase "after these things" (*meta tauta*) is a temporal marker that some time elapsed since the initial reunions with the risen Jesus and the disciples could have travelled back to Galilee in the interim. To castigate the disciples' fishing venture as

---

41. Gaventa, "Archive of Excess," 247–49.

42. Witherington (*John's Wisdom*, 354) argues that John 21:24 alluded to two previous appearances to the seven disciples in 21:2 from an older source, but there is little reason why 21:14 cannot be recalling the two resurrection appearances to the collective group (20:1–23, 26–29) and excluding the individual appearance to Mary Magdalene (20:14–17). Gaventa ("Archive of Excess," 245) notes that the term *phaneroun* ("to manifest") is not used in chapter 20 and might be linked to the earlier revelations of Jesus' glory at 1:31 and 2:11, but it is more likely that the redactor is using his or her own preferred terminology for an Easter epiphany.

THE BELOVED EVANGELIST?

an act of "apostasy" may be a tad harsh;[43] the excitement fueled by the resurrection did not displace the basic necessity of toiling for food. There may be a profound theological lesson about the risen one's presence on both spiritual mountain tops and the mundane places of everyday labor.[44] Or gathering an abundance of fish may be a metaphor for the successful conversion rates resulting from the disciples' missionary preaching.[45] The misrecognition of the risen Jesus, evident when the disciples did not apprehend that it was Jesus hollering out to them from the shore, is a recurrent motif in the Easter accounts (cf. John 20:14–16; Matt 28:17; Luke 24:15–32).[46] Jesus' glorified body was both continuous and discontinuous with the body that had been buried in the ground (cf. 1 Cor 15:35–49), but Brodie reads too much into the lack of verbs of sight in his supposition that the risen Jesus was engaging with his disciples from a higher plane of existence besides the visible.[47]

On the other side, the sub-plot about Peter and the beloved disciple reaches a climatic resolution in chapter 21.[48] According to Bauckham, it is not until the epilogue that the reader has the full picture about how they embodied the ideals of active service and perceptive witness respectively.[49] At last Simon merited his cognomen *Petros* and became steadfast as a "rock" after his past failure to be loyal to Jesus to the point of death (cf. 13:36–38); he grew into a good shepherd who forfeited his life for the flock

---

43. Contra Hoskyns, *Fourth Gospel*, 552.

44. Brodie, *John*, 582–83; Keener, *John*, 2.1227–28.

45. Hoskyns, *Fourth Gospel*, 554–55; Barrett, *John*, 575; Quast, *Community in Crisis*, 135–139; Carson, *John*, 667; Ellis, "Authenticity of John 21," 20; Breck, "Appendix," 31; Blomberg, *Historical Reliability*, 273; Bauckham, *Beloved Disciple*, 77, 274; Von Wahlde, *Gospel and Letters*, 3.889.

46. Breck, "Appendix," 32; Blomberg, *Historical Reliability*, 274; Michaels *John*, 1031.

47. Brodie, *John*, 575.

48. Minear, "Original Function of John 21," 91–92; Ellis, "Authenticity of John 21," 18–19; Brodie, *John*, 581; Carson, *John*, 667; Blomberg, *Historical Reliability*, 273.

49. Bauckham, *Eyewitnesses*, 395–400; Bauckham, *Beloved Disciple*, 84–87.

(21:18–19; cf. 10:11). The beloved disciple's witness was enshrined in the form of the written testament (21:24–25). Be that as it may, the epilogue is not indispensable for bringing closure to these characters' storylines. The declaration that they each retired to their homes in John 20:10 may seem anti-climactic, but Peter's reinstatement to active duty was implicit when Jesus bequeathed the Spirit on the "Twelve" (20:24; cf. 6:70–71). Meanwhile, the beloved disciple's fundamental function was to be a reliable interpreter of the betrayal, death, and resurrection of Jesus in John 13–20. His trust in Jesus' post-mortem vindication did not have to be solidified by seeing the risen Lord for himself, exemplifying the ideal believer whose faith has no need for empirical proof (cf. 20:29), so he exited the stage in John 20:10 after his literary purpose was fulfilled.[50] The redactor may tie up the lingering loose ends about Peter and the beloved disciple in a more emotionally satisfying way for the reader, but an aesthetic preference is not a sound source-critical criterion.

Up until now, it may seem impossible to decide whether the evangelist or the redactor was the creative genius behind the Johannine epilogue. Perhaps as an afterthought, the evangelist re-edited a draft of the Fourth Gospel to archive the Christ movement's thriving missionary expansion, to firmly reinstate Peter to his pastoral office, and to plug the beloved disciple's enduring legacy in 21:1–25. What weighs against this is that the evangelist did not supply a clarificatory comment to that effect, did not reposition the concluding summary at John 20:30–31, and did not smooth over some of the resultant narrative discontinuities. It is the redactor who, opting to not interfere too much with the constituent parts of the Fourth Gospel, appended new material after John 20:30–31. I will now argue that two anachronisms—the authorial function of the beloved disciple and the mode of Peter's execution—reveal that this redactor was more at home in an early second-century *Sitz im Leben* ("situation in life").

---

50. For my reading that John 20:9 does not refer to the beloved disciple's ignorance after the discovery of the empty tomb, see chapter 1.

The Beloved Evangelist?

The Anachronism of Authorial Self-Representation

Unlike the historiographers and biographers in the Greco-Roman world who identified themselves, the New Testament Gospels were patterned on the history books of the Hebrew Bible and Ancient Near Eastern historians in giving maximum priority to their historical subjects.[51] The good news about Jesus Christ, not their personal reputations as evangelists, was front and center. Soon afterwards, there was a proliferation of gospel literature assigned to all sorts of first-century Christian personalities. The subscriptions pinned to the canonical Gospels, such as the "Gospel according to Matthew," had an impact on the subscriptions of non-canonical texts like the Gospels "according to Thomas" or "according to Mary."[52] Homage was paid to Didymus Judas Thomas in the incipit of the Gospel named after him for accumulating the secret sayings of Jesus. In the "Gospel According to Peter," Peter addressed the readers in the first person and mused about his emotional state in the aftershock of Jesus' crucifixion (26, 59–60). There was also the sporadic usage of the first-person plural in Acts 16:10–17, 20:5–15, 21:1–18, 27:1–37, and 28:1–16, but it is unlikely that the "we" in these chapters was a pseudonym (i.e., "false name").[53] John 21:24 may be the exception to the tendency of the canonical Gospels to not invoke a self-justifying authorial fiction and may fit the definition of an authorial fiction that Ismo Dunderberg borrows from John Kloppenborg as "the way in which the instruction represents its mode of production

---

51. Baum, "Anonymity," 120–42.

52. Koester, *Ancient Christian Gospels*, 20–22.

53. Ehrman (*Forgery*, 267–80) reviews the exegetical options that the 'we" in Acts reflects an eyewitness informant, an older source like a travel diary, a dramatic literary device, or a pseudonymous fiction. Ehrman mounts a defense for the last option, but the problem I have with this thesis is that the Lukan prologue would have been a more transparent way to push an authorial fiction on the reader and yet the author stayed anonymous (Luke 1:1–4; cf. Acts 1:1). My inclination is that the "we" was a literary device to put the reader right in the middle of the action.

or creation."⁵⁴ Mark Goodacre prefers the neutral description "authorial self-representation" and plots the Gospels on a timeline based on the growing demand for authorial self-representation as a mechanism for authenticating Gospel writings.⁵⁵

Contrastingly, the prior twenty chapters of the Fourth Gospel are consistent with the Synoptic Gospels in their deliberate anonymity. Chapters 13 to 20 did appeal to a Judean eyewitness who popped up at the upper room of a Jerusalem residence, the high priest's courtyard, the "place of the skull," and the sepulchre in the garden. According to Bauckham, the prevalence of authentic Palestinian Jewish names in the oldest strata of the Synoptic Gospels may likewise evince that some oral units integrated into them derived from local eyewitnesses of Jesus.⁵⁶ Granted, the extensive verbatim agreement across the Synoptic Gospels proves that the evangelists did not wholly rely on oral tradents. The prevalent scholarly solution to the Synoptic Problem, Markan priority, means that two of the Synoptic evangelists heavily borrowed from the Markan biographical outline of Jesus' life, while there is not yet a consensus about what hypothetical literary sources were utilized by the fourth evangelist (e.g., a Signs Source, a Passion Narrative, or a Synoptic Gospel). A mediating perspective may be that the anonymous evangelists had access to a rich assortment of oral and written sources and that some eyewitnesses played a limited role in the traditioning process. It was a far bolder assertion in John 21:24 that "the one who was writing these things" (*ho grapsas tauta*)—with "these things" naturally encompassing the whole book rather than a single private breakfast that Jesus ate with the seven disciples—was directly an eyewitness.

Many commentators translate the aorist participle *grapsas* in John 21:24 in a causative sense, cross-referencing it with the declaration in 19:19 that Pilate "wrote" (*egrapsen*) the inscription on the board nailed on the cross above Jesus' head when, obviously, he had

---

54. Dunderberg, *Beloved Disciple in Conflict*, 167.
55. Goodacre, *Thomas and the Gospels*, 174–79.
56. Bauckham, *Eyewitnesses*, 42, 46.

his subordinates do that job for him.⁵⁷ C. K. Barrett paraphrases John 21:24 as follows: "We, who are actually publishing the Gospel, recognize the authority and responsibility for it are both to be found in the beloved disciple, who gave us the necessary information, and thus virtually wrote the Gospel."⁵⁸ Bauckham refutes this translation as John 19:19 plainly meant that Pilate was accountable for the precise wording on the placard, even if he dictated it to an amanuensis. Taking John 21:24 at face value means that the beloved disciple was responsible for everything that was covered in the Fourth Gospel, regardless of whether or not a professional scribe was hired to transcribe it as his dictation.⁵⁹ Chris Keith references Esther 8:8–10 LXX as an example where the Persian ruler permitted Esther and Mordecai to freely draft up a letter in his name, but he sides with Bauckham that the context of John 21:24 rules out this wider usage of the verb *graphein* ("to write").⁶⁰

After the beloved disciple was commended in the third person as "the one who was writing these things" (*ho grapsas tauta*), the text switches to the first person with the exclamations that "we know" (*oidamen*) that the beloved disciple was truthful and that "I suppose" (*oimai*) that there were no books in all the world that could contain every last deed done by Jesus. Bauckham challenges the view that there were plural speakers in 21:24. He substitutes "I" in place of "we," for the first-person plural may be the "'we' of authoritative testimony" or the plural of majesty (cf. John 1:14;

---

57. Barrett, *John*, 587; Brown, *John XII—XXI*, 1123; Schnackenburg, *St. John*, 3.374; Beasley-Murray, *John*, lxxii, 415; Brodie, *John*, 595; Moloney, *John*, 561; Charlesworth, *Beloved Disciple*, 25–27, 46; Culpepper, *Life of a Legend*, 71; Thompson, *John*, 446.

58. Barrett, *John*, 119.

59. Bauckham, *Eyewitnesses*, 359–63; Bauckham, *Beloved Disciple*, 79. See also Culmann, *Johannine Circle*, 84; Thyen, "Entwicklungen," 294–95; Trobisch, *First Edition*, 96; Hengel, *Frage*, 218; Carson, *John*, 78, 683, 685; Morris, *John*, 776–77; Jackson, "Ancient Self-referential Conventions," 6–7, 29–30; Schnelle, *Antidocetic Christology*, 15; Blomberg, *Historical Reliability*, 28n 28, 282; Zumstein, *Kreative Erinnerung*, 24, 313, 322, 326–27; Theobald, "Der Jünger," 514–16; Köstenberger, *John*, 602–3; Köstenberger and Snout, "Witness, Author, Apostle," 215; Bennema, *Encountering Jesus*, 305.

60. Keith, "Competitive Textualization," 325n15.

The Beloved Apostle?

3:2, 11; 20:2; 1 John 1:2, 4, 5, 6, 7; 3 John 12).[61] Baum's rejoinder is that the authoritative pronouncements made by the Johannine characters are generally formulated in the first-person singular and that the examples of the "we" in the passages enumerated above might be genuine plurals.[62] A closely related hypothesis is that the "we" in 21:24 is a "dissociative we" where the beloved disciple was writing alongside a company of fellow eyewitnesses or colleagues[63] or an "associative we" that united the beloved disciple with his Christian audience.[64]

The critical weakness in the inclusion of the beloved disciple in the "we" is the degree of awkwardness for an author to jump from a self-reference in the third person to a self-reference in the first person in the same sentence. There may be one analogous example when Josephus (cf. *War* 3.202) communicated something about himself in the third person, retelling how the citizens of Jotapata entreated him to stay in their city, and interrupted his recap of this incident with the interjection "I cannot but think." Baum points out that the third person is implemented when Josephus narrated how he was a participant in the historical events, and the first person when Josephus wore the mantle of the narrator. If Bauckham's reading was correct, 21:24 incomprehensibly used both the third and the first person to denote the beloved disciple in his role as the narrator.[65] H. M. Jackson excuses the clumsy shift from an alleged self-reference in the third person to one in the first person on the grounds that both a documentary "subscription" (*hypographē*) and an epistolary postscript served as the templates for John 21:24. A public notary adjoined a subscription to a legal document such as

---

61. Bauckham, *Eyewitnesses*, 370–81; cf. Jackson, "Ancient Self-referential Conventions," 1–34; Köstenberger, *John*, 684; Köstenberger and Snout, "Witness, Author, Apostle," 216; Resseguie, "Ideal Point of View," 549. Bauckham offers Dionysius of Halicarnassus *Demosthenes* 58 as a parallel in that the author slips back and forth between the use of "I" and "we."

62. Baum, "Original Epilogue," 258.

63. Hoskyns, *Fourth Gospel*, 88–95, 560; Carson, *John*, 683–84; Keener, *John*, 2.1240–41.

64. Jackson, "Ancient Self-referential Conventions," 22–24.

65. Baum, "Original Epilogue," 258–59.

The Beloved Evangelist?

a contract or a will that might identify the principle beneficiary in the third person, while there may be a more informal address formulated in the first person in the postscript of an epistle.[66] Baum responds that 21:24–25 was not modelled on the subscriptions or colophons imprinted on a document by the scribal copyists publishing it, but was part of the epilogue as a creative piece of writing in its own right.[67]

A better reading is that the redactor signalled his or her affiliation with a coterie of likeminded associates, the dissociative "we" of 21:24b, who were appreciative of the beloved disciple's enduring legacy. Hence, the truthfulness of beloved disciple's testimony was ratified by multiple witnesses (cf. Deut 19:15). Since Westcott assigned John 21:1–23 to the evangelist, he bracketed the last two verses as the editorial "imprimatur" that the presbyters of the churches in Ephesus stamped on to the tail end of the chapter.[68] Cutting off 21:24–25 from the preceding section, though, would leave 21:1–23 without any formal denouement.[69] John 21:1–25 is a unified textual unit and a single editorial hand was behind the whole. Therefore, since the "we" explicitly took the credit for the twenty-five verses of the epilogue, the beloved disciple's individual authorship was delimited to the original twenty chapters of the Fourth Gospel.

Further, the redactor could not have been the beloved disciple if the latter was dead. Some scholars imagine that the beloved disciple, in his old age, would have wanted to silence any rumblings that Jesus had pledged to him that he would never experience death (21:22–23).[70] The conditional clause "if I [Jesus] will him [the beloved disciple] to remain alive until I come" (*ean auton thelō*

---

66. Jackson, "Ancient Self-Referential Conventions," 3–6.

67. Baum, "Original Epilogue," 265.

68. Westcott, *St. John*, 374; Lagrange, *Saint Jean*, 534; Blomberg, *Historical Reliability*, 38, 40, 280.

69. Baum, "Original Epilogue," 259.

70. Westcott, *St. John*, 373; Hoskyns, *Fourth Gospel*, 559; Morris, *John*, 775; Carson, *John*, 72, 78, 681–82; Ramsay, *John*, 1056; Jackson, "Ancient Self-referential Conventions," 21–22; Keener, *John*, 2.1240; Bauckham, *Eyewitnesses*, 420; Bauckham, *Beloved Disciple*, 80.

menein heōs erchomai), after all, was bound to cause bewilderment (21:22). However, why would the beloved disciple not have an inkling that, like Paul, he might be among the living to welcome Jesus for his eschatological homecoming (cf. 1 Thess 4:17)? There would be a stronger motivation to correct such a misconception after the beloved disciple's demise, lest the fact that the *parousia* ("coming") of Jesus had been delayed beyond the beloved disciple's lifetime prompt believers to abandon this hope altogether. As many scholars reconstruct the situation, the beloved disciple was the founder of the Johannine school or community and the news about his untimely departure shook them to the core.[71] Yet neither the circumstances surrounding the beloved disciple's death nor his history with the Johannine community was expounded. Instead, John 21:23 aimed to rebuff the misguided supposition that the first generation of Christ followers would not be extinguished before the eschatological consummation of history (cf. 1 Thess 4:13–17; Mark 9:1).[72] The redactor's point was that not even Jesus' dearest disciple was entitled to the presumption that Jesus would institute his rule on the earth within his lifespan, for that date has been predetermined in accordance with Jesus' sovereign will alone.

Sometime after the beloved disciple passed away, he was promoted to the author of the entire Fourth Gospel by the redactor. Perhaps this deduction was made on the basis of reading about the beloved disciple's sterling reputation in the handful of passages in John 13:23—20:10. Analogously, the Matthean modification that exchanged the name of Levi with that of the Apostle Matthew as

71. Cullmann, *Johannine Circle*, 71; 75; Haenchen, *John*, 2.228, 233; Schnackenburg, *St. John*, 2.371, 3.376–77, 379; Brown, *John I—XII*, xcix; Brown, *John XIII—XXI*, 1119; Brown, *Community*, 31; Thyen, *Entwicklungen*, 269, 29, 297–99; Quast, *Community in Crisis*, 17, 151–53; Grassi, *Secret Identity*, 9–10; Beasley-Murray, *John*, lxxi, 395–96; 412; Hengel, *Johannine Question*; 77, 80, 84; Hengel, *Frage*, 213–14; Charlesworth, *Beloved Disciple*, 45, 141–42; Witherington, *John's Wisdom*, 357; Moloney, *John*, 8, 561; Schnelle, *Antidocetic Christology*, 15; Culpepper, *Life of a Legend*, 70, 72, 84; Ramsay, *John*, 1056; Blomberg, *Historical Reliability*, 279–80; Von Wahlde, *Gospel and Letters*, 1.375, 2.906, 3.421–22, 426, 434; Thompson, *John*, 445.

72. Lindars, *John*, 639–40; Casey, *Is John's Gospel True?*, 162; Dunderberg, *Beloved Disciple in Conflict*, 124–27.

the crooked tax collector absolved by Jesus (Matt 9:9–10; 10:3; cf. Mark 2:14–15; Luke 5:27–29) may not have gone unnoticed and may have partly motivated the Patristic thinkers to ascribe the first canonical Gospel to the evangelist Matthew. This was not a case of pseudonymity, but of misattribution.[73] However, the "we" group to whom the redactor belonged was probably the Johannine community and the epilogue was appended at too early a date for the real evangelist to have been unknown to the redactor.

Therefore, it may be extrapolated that John 21:24 was an intentional pseudonymous device.[74] Raymond Brown encapsulates the reservations of many scholars about this extrapolation: "It is true that such an attribution may have been added to the Gospel as an attempt to clothe an anonymous work with the mantle of apostolic authority, but an attribution without a personal name does not seem specific enough for that purpose."[75] However, while the redactor may have been unfamiliar with the beloved disciple's actual name, the beloved disciple was the most suitable choice for a fictive author based on his exemplary virtue and perceptiveness within the Fourth Gospel.[76] The real evangelist may not have possessed any clout for Christians outside the small Johannine clique, so the redactor replaced him or her as the author with one of the evangelist's principal informants whose stellar qualifications as the "disciple whom Jesus loved" were on display for any general reader who perused the Fourth Gospel. There was ample Jewish precedent for fictitiously ascribing law codes to Moses, psalms to David, and wisdom books to Solomon.[77] Like them, the beloved disciple was an archetypal figure—the archetype of discipleship—and

---

73. For the difference, see Ehrman, *Forgery*, 30.

74. See Thyen, "Entwicklungen," 294–95; Theobald, "Der Jünger," 214–16.

75. Brown, *John I—XII*, xciii; cf. Hoskyns, *Fourth Gospel*, 560; Jackson, *Ancient Self-referential Conventions*, 7; Blomberg, *Historical Reliability*, 29, 32; Keener, *John*, 1.89; Bauckham, *Eyewitnesses*, 409; Bauckham, *Beloved Disciple*, 82.

76. Theobald, "Der Jünger," 315n117.

77. Casey, *Is John's Gospel True?*, 140–42. There were no unethical motives behind this literary convention.

consequently came to be regarded as the fountainhead of the Johannine tradition.

The Anachronism of Peter's Crucifixion

The beloved disciple was not the only character to undergo a thorough makeover in the Johannine epilogue. In John 21:15-19, Peter was rehabilitated and promoted to a pastoral office so that he might, in turn, feed Jesus' sheep. Peter's articulation of his devotion for Jesus three times as they sat near a charcoal fire (21:15-17), remorseful for his threefold denials of Jesus while warming himself before another charcoal fire (18:17-18, 25-27),[78] stirs the reader's emotions. Granted, Kevin Quast is right that Peter was never outright denigrated anywhere in the Fourth Gospel and could be portrayed neutrally or positively as the spokesperson for the Twelve in the first twelve chapters (e.g., 1:42; 6:68-69).[79] Still, the epilogue was an ecumenical petition to the wider flock who adored Peter as their symbolic shepherd.[80]

Much ink has been spilled on the connection between John 21:1-11 and Luke 5:1-11. Since there is no bountiful provision of fish in the call narratives in Mark 1:16-20 and Matthew 4:18-22, has the redactor of John 21:1-11 co-opted a piece of Lukan redaction?[81] Or was this a primitive Easter account of an epiphany

---

78. Bultmann (*John*, 712) is one of the rare commentators to deny the echoes of John 18:17-18, 25-27 here.

79. Quast, *Community in Crisis*, 27-54.

80. Ibid., 138-40, 153-54; Brown, *Community*, 162; Braun, "Resisting John," 69n.39, 70; Koester, *Ancient Christian Gospels*, 247; Waetjen, *Two Editions*, 24.

81. This thesis is best defended by Neirynck, "John 21," 326-31. On pages 321-25, Neirynck contests the view of Rudolf Pesch (*Der reiche Fischfang*, 321-23) that a fishing story and a meal tradition were combined. Neiryck contends that 21:4b is the sole addition that turns the miracle source in 21:1-8 into a resurrection appearance and, even though a few verses suggest that Jesus was in the process of cooking breakfast before the disciples brought their fish to him (21:9, 12, 13), a full-fledged Easter source cannot be reconstructed from these few verses.

of the risen Lord at the Sea of Galilee, which Luke transplanted to an earlier phase of Jesus' ministry?[82] Perhaps Jesus beckoned his disciples to lower their fishing net into the water on two separate occasions: the Lukan disciples strained to lift the net and the volume of fish caused their net to break and their boats to sink, while the Johannine disciples hauled the untorn net onto the beach. Apart from the terms for "fish" (*ichthys*) and "net" (*diktyon*), the vocabulary and details differ.[83] It would help to date the Johannine epilogue if the direction of influence from John 21:1–11 to Luke 5:1–11, or vice-versa, could be proven. Regrettably, the jury is out on this question along with the relationship between the third and fourth canonical Gospels more generally. These two excerpts cannot be discussed in isolation from the other parallels between the two Gospels such as the woman who anointed Jesus' feet (Luke 7:36–50; John 12:1–8), the naming of Lazarus and the sisters Mary and Martha (Luke 10:38–42; 16:19–31; John 11:1–44), the visit of Peter to the sepulcher (Luke 24:12; John 20:2–9), and the resurrection appearances localized in Jerusalem (Luke 24:1–11, 33–53; John 20:1–29). Whether these parallels are explicable on the grounds of literary dependence or common oral sources takes us beyond the scope of this study.[84]

Fortunately, there is an underappreciated clue to the general dating of the Johannine epilogue in the literary foreshadowing of Peter's death (21:18–19). Jesus contrasted a youthful Peter who was able to dress himself and had free mobility with an elderly

82. Bultmann, *John*, 701, 705; Brown, *John XII—XXI*, 1085–92; Culpepper, *Life of a Legend*. 22. According to James McGrath ("Mark's Missing Ending," np), Mark's Gospel closed the curtain at the women's fearful silence at 16 8, yet presupposed oral traditions about the Galilean appearances in 14:28 and 16:7. The oral traditions integrated into the Johannine epilogue would be a perfect continuation of Mark's story: the disciples, unaware that the women found an empty tomb, had resumed their former livelihoods in Galilee where the risen Jesus met up with them.

83. See Carson, *John*, 671; Witherington, *John's Wisdom*, 354, 405n8; Keener, *John*, 2.1222, 1226; Blomberg, *Historical Reliability*, 274–75, 275n405.

84. In a recent review of this debate, Gregory (*Reception of Luke*, 56–69) takes up Luke 24:12 and John 20:3–10 as a test case about the direction of influence and determines that the evidence for literary contact is inconclusive.

51

The Beloved Apostle?

Peter who stretched out his hands to be dressed and was guided by another to a place where he did not wish to go in John 21:18. According to Bultmann, this was once a proverb juxtaposing the freedom of youth with the dependency of old age.[85] The footnote that Peter's death glorified God in 21:19a, though, harkened back to Jesus' own glorification via his sacrificial death (cf. 12:23; 17:1).[86] Is John 21:19a a *Vaticinium ex eventu* or a "prophecy from the event" about Peter's martyrdom? Some scholars do not find the wording specific enough to be understood as such.[87] An allusion to Peter being "lifted up" on the cross might be more transparent (cf. 3:14; 12:32).[88] On the other hand, C. K. Barrett shines a spotlight on the Christian typological interpretations of subjects with outstretched arms as scriptural precursors for the crucified Christ (cf. *Barn.* 12:2, 4; Justin, *1 Apol.* 35; *Dial.* 90.4-5; Irenaeus, *Epid.* 79; Cyprian, *Test.* 2.20).[89] Ernst Haechen assembles the comparable allusions in Greco-Roman literature to the binding of a criminal's outstretched arms to a cross-beam (Epictetus, *Diatr.* 3.26.22; Artemidorus, *Onir.* 1.76; Plautus, *Mil. glor.* 2.4.7).[90] The redactor, then, may have deciphered a mystifying aphorism about Peter stretching out his arms as a representation of crucifixion.

According to Timothy D. Barnes, Peter was not tortured with the excruciating, prolonged agony of crucifixion. The Roman historian Tacitus rehearsed the torments that the Christ believers in Rome suffered under the emperor Nero, from being lit on fire while bound on crosses out of mockery to getting clothed in animal hides to be torn apart by wild beasts (*Ann.* 15.44.4). Correlating

---

85. Bultmann, *John*, 713-14.

86. Hoskyns, *Fourth Gospel*, 557; Barrett, *John*, 585; Brown, *John XII—XXI*, 1118; Hengel, *Johannine Question*, 76; Hengel, *Frage*, 210, 210n19; Beasley-Murray, *John*, 408; Carson, *John*, 679; Moloney, *John*, 556, 560; Witherington, *John's Wisdom*, 356; Waetjen, *Two Editions*, 14; Keener, *John*, 2.1237-38; Thompson, *John*, 443, 443n82.

87. Morris, *John*, 773; Blomberg, *Historical Reliability*, 278; Köstenberger, *John*, 773.

88. See Von Wahlde, *Gopel and Letters*, 2.896.

89. Barrett, *John*, 585.

90. Haenchen, *John*, 2.226-27.

Tacitus's account with John 21:18–19, Barnes argues that Peter was positioned in a cruciform posture and draped in a flammable tunic (*tunica molesta*) to be burned alive.[91] His hypothesis relies heavily on the meaning of the verb *zōnnymi* as girding oneself, as opposed to the crucifixion of males in the nude as an extra dose of humiliation.[92] However, John Granger Cook's recent monograph on crucifixions in antiquity digs up a little evidence that some crucified victims were not completely naked, from the crucifixion of youths celebrating the cult of Pan who were girded with the skins of their sacrificial victims around their loins (cf. Dionysius of Halicarnassus, *Rom. Ant.* 1.80.1) to a marble relief from Smyrna in the Ashmolean museum depicting some condemned slaves donning loin clothes and the Palatine graffito where the crucified ass had on some kind of an undergarment.[93] The term for "naked" (*gymncs*) was not incompatible with wearing an undergarment; Peter was not fishing in the nude (*gymnos*), for example, before he put on his outer garment in John 21:7.[94]

John 21:18–19 may be a preliminary stage in the burgeoning myth about Peter refusing to be crucified in the same manner as his Lord and the Romans happily obliging by hanging him upside-down (*Acts Pet.* 36–39; Tertullian, *Scorp.* 15.3). When did the image of the crucified Peter take root in the popular Christian imagination? On the one hand, there is the near total silence of the New Testament. Peter's mission to Rome seems to conflict with the division of labor over the proselytization of the "circumcised" and the "uncircumcised" ratified by Paul and the Jerusalem "Pillars" (cf. Gal 2:7–10), with Paul's letter to the Roman Christ associations that did not send greetings to Peter (Rom 16:1–23), and with the imprecise notice that Peter moved on to "another place" in Acts 12:17. Based on this data, Michael Goulder offers the groundless hunch that Peter probably died in his bed in Jerusalem around 55

---

91. Barnes, "'Another Shall Gird Thee,'" 81–83.
92. Ibid., 78–80.
93. Cook, *Crucifixion in the Mediterranean World*, 192–93.
94. For other examples, see ibid., 192–93n149.

CE.⁹⁵ Goulder grants that an epistle was fictitiously sent in Peter's name from "Babylon" (1 Pet 5:13), almost universally deciphered as a codename for Rome (cf. Rev 17), to Christians throughout the provinces of Asia Minor (1 Pet 1:1).⁹⁶ Otto Zwierlein clears even this evidence off from the table by rendering "Babylon" as part of the metaphorical apparatus envisaging Christians in the state of exile from their homeland in heaven (cf. 1 Pet 2:11).⁹⁷ There was also a veiled warning that the demonic ruler Beliar would be manifested as a lawless despot, by all appearances Nero since he committed the horrible offense of matricide, and that one of the Twelve would be delivered into his hands in the *Ascension of Isaiah* (4.1-4).⁹⁸ This may not be a "prophecy from the event" based on the sentence that the historical Nero handed down to Peter, but an unfulfilled prediction about the future revivification of Nero as an antichrist figure who would hunt down the last surviving member of the Twelve in this apocalyptic section.⁹⁹

On the other hand, there is fairly uniform textual evidence from the late first century onwards that situated Peter in Rome (*1 Clem* 5.4; Ignatius, *Rom.* 4.3; *Apoc. Pet.* 14.4–6; Dionysius of Corinth, in *Hist. Eccl.* 2.25.8; Irenaeus, *Adv. Haer.* 3.1.1; 3.3.2). Zwierlein moves the date for 1 Clement to around 125 CE¹⁰⁰ and what he disregards as the pseudo-Ignatian epistles to around 170 CE,¹⁰¹ which is much later than the conventional dates assigned to these epistles. In Zwierlein's estimation, Justin Martyr's mistranslation of the inscription *Semoni Sanco Deo Fidio* found on an altar at an island in the Tiber as a dedication "to Simon the holy god"

---

95. Goulder, "Did Peter Ever Go to Rome?," 380–383.

96. Ibid., 393. Since none of the Gospels put Peter at the scene of the crucifixion, Goulder avers that Peter's witness to Christ's sufferings in 1 Peter 5:1 attests to the belief that Peter had undergone the same sufferings as Christ in Rome by the date that the epistle was written.

97. Zwierlein, *Petrus in Rom*, 7–12.

98. Barnes, "'Another Shall Gird Thee,'" 93–94.

99. Goulder, "Did Peter Ever Go to Rome?," 396.

100. Zwierlein, *Petrus in Rom*, 316–30.

101. Ibid., 183–237.

THE BELOVED EVANGELIST?

(*Simoni Deo Sancto*) was the impetus for the myth of origins about Peter in Rome (cf. *1 Apol.* 26; 56).[102] Since Peter had reprimanded the magician Simon in Samaria (Acts 8:38–39), which did not deter him from spreading his cult in Rome (Irenaeus, *Adv. Haer.* 1.23.1–4), an imaginary battle was concocted between Peter and his old nemesis in the imperial capital during the second year of the emperor Claudius (Hippolytus, *Haer.* 6.15; Eusebius, *Hist. Eccl.* 2.14.1–6, 17.1; Jerome, *Vir. ill.* 1).

Even if Zwierlein's dating of 1 Clement wins the day, rather than the conventional view that it was mailed from the bishop Clement of Rome to the churches in Corinth between 94 to 98 CE, it still predated Justin's writings. 1 Clement 4–6 admonished against the deleterious effects of envy, parading seven examples from the Hebrew Bible and seven examples based on the near contemporaries of Clement. Peter suffered more than two trials (*1 Clem.* 5.4), Paul endured a litany of persecutions over the course of his missionary journeys before he departed from the world (5.6–7), and a myriad of Roman Christians were tortured at the behest of Nero (6.1–2). The mention of "Danaides and Dircae" (6.2) may be an allusion to the great fire in Rome that destroyed the temple of Apollo on the Palatine and the amphitheater of Taurus or the amphitheater of the Bull.[103] However, if 1 Clement's examples were rehashed in chronological order, 1 Clement 5:4 may touch on the three instances when Peter was arrested in Acts 4:1–21, 5:17–40, and 12:3–6 before Paul set sail for his first missionary journey.[104] Against this, Andrew F. Gregory's methodologically rigorous survey of the references to the Gospel of Luke and the book of Acts in the second century is adamant that an intertextual connection between Acts and 1 Clement cannot be substantiated.[105] Moreover,

---

102. Ibid., 129–33.

103. Barnes, "'Another Shall Gird Thee,'" 92. The temple to Apollo housed statues representing the daughters of the mythical King Danaus. Dirce, the mythical wife of the king of Thebes, was trampled and gored by a bull.

104. Goulder, "Did Peter Ever Go to Rome?," 389–91; Zwierlein, *Petrus in Rom*, 13–30, 255–62.

105. Gregory, *Reception of Luke*, 312–13.

while the aorist participle *martyrēsas* ("having borne witness") may have Peter's campaign of evangelism without the later connotations of martyrdom in mind, the euphemism for going "to one's own place" (*1 Clem.* 5.4, cf. 5.7; Acts 1:25; Ignatius, *Magn.* 5.1) seems to have denoted Peter's death and the paucity of details about the circumstances of Peter's execution by the state may have been politically shrewd.[106]

1 Peter and 1 Clement are the crucial linchpins for corroborating Peter's presence in Rome. If "Babylon" was a cipher for Rome in 1 Peter 5:13 and both writings dated to the last quarter of the first century, they may conserve a memory that Peter had been in Rome and was feasibly one of the casualties of Nero's pogroms against the Christ believers. This memory has been clouded over with legendary flourishes. Peter was probably not crucified upside down, nor did he wage a contest against Simon Magus over who could accomplish a greater supernatural feat. John 21:18–19 may be the first step in conforming Peter's martyrdom to the Passion of Jesus, which evolved into the *Quo Vadis* fable. In a poignant retelling of this myth in the *Acts of Peter* 35, Peter escaped from Rome when his life was endangered, but he bumped into Jesus heading into the city and asked him, "Lord, where are you going" (*Quo vadis, Domine*). Jesus responded that he was going to Rome to be crucified again, a signal that Peter ought to pick up his own cross and share in his master's fate.

Conclusion: The Contribution of the Johannine Epilogue

In addition to the telltale signs that the Johannine epilogue was adjoined to the text of the Fourth Gospel after John 20:30–31, I have underlined two additional reasons to contextualize the chapter in an early second-century milieu. John 21:18–19 coincides with the evolving social memories of Peter as the pre-eminent founder and martyr of the Christ associations in Rome, while John

---

106. Bockmuehl, *The Remembered Peter*, 124–30.

The Beloved Evangelist?

21:24 was engrossed in the deliberations over the legitimate authorship of the Gospels. The beloved disciple was upgraded from an eyewitness informant for what happened on Jesus' final day in Jerusalem to the one responsible for all the "things" written in the book from Jesus' anointing in Bethany beyond the Jordan to his Easter appearance to Thomas. As a fitting reward for his sagacity and virtue, the beloved disciple was eulogized as the fount of the whole Johannine stream of tradition. Nevertheless, the Johannine epilogue was published at an early enough date that the beloved disciple was not yet merged with the apostolic son of Zebedee in John 21:2. The next chapter will retrace the steps that spurred on this development.

3

Would the Real John Please Stand Up?

TO CAPTURE A FULLER picture of the beloved disciple, the dots were connected across the four New Testament Gospels and the *Acts of the Apostles*. Hence, some Christian readers could not fathom that the beloved disciple was not among the twelve apostles and the core three disciples within that collective who were the beneficiaries of private revelations at crucial junctures in the Synoptic outline. Since James perished in the onslaught of persecution under Herod Agrippa I, Peter's ministerial colleague John became the sole contender. The Twelve and the two sons of Zebedee, however, barely registered on the Fourth Gospel's radar screen. In spite of this, once the second-century Christians zeroed in on the Apostle John as the best match for the beloved disciple under the conditions set by the Synoptic Gospels and Acts, the Fourth Gospel was cross-referenced with the other writings in the putative Johannine corpus and with the *Exposition of the Oracles of the Lord* authored by Papias of Hierapolis to expand upon John's resume.

The Johannine Epistles afford readers a telling glimpse into the doctrinal and factional controversies that wreaked havoc on the harmony of the Johannine community or network of churches. In 2 John 1:1 and 3 John 1:1, greetings are sent from the "elder" or "presbyter" (*presbyteros*). This unusual signature enabled some Patristic and modern scholars to fuse the sender of the epistles with a charismatic pastor in Asia Minor whom Papias deferentially hailed as the Elder John (*Hist. Eccl.* 3.39.4, 15). There was also the

Would the Real John Please Stand Up?

Apocalypse or Revelation of John, one of the atypical exemplars of the apocalyptic genre in not masking its author behind a pseudonym (Rev 1:1, 4, 9; 22:8). Yet the "John" who was banished to the island of Patmos was not introduced as an *apostolos* or *presbyteros* and he paid tribute to the twelve apostles of the Lamb as the luminaries of a bygone era (21:14). Arguably the overlapping themes, imagery, and Christological titles such as Word (*logos*) and Lamb (*amnos* or *arnion*) might signify that the seer inhabited the same theological orbit as the Johannine Gospel and Epistles. He may have even been a product of the Johannine School, but common authorship of the Fourth Gospel and Revelation is definitively ruled out by their transparently dissimilar Greek writing styles down to the spelling of "Jerusalem" (*Hierosolyma* or *Ierousalēm*) and their eschatological outlooks that seem to be poles apart.[1] Later the Apostle John, the Elder John, and the seer John were amalgamated into one apostolic figurehead. This process was well underway when Justin Martyr maintained that the prophecies enclosed in the twentieth chapter of Revelation went back to the Apostle John (*Dial.* 81.4) and the fusion was completed by the time of Irenaeus. This chapter digs beneath these layers of accidental misidentifications.

Papias and the Elder John

Papias, the bishop of Hierapolis, was a collector of the Christian folklore floating around the area. Unluckily, there are no extant manuscripts of his *Exposition of the Oracles of the Lord* and it survives in the sparse, fragmentary quotations or summaries from its Christian readers in the succeeding centuries. Some of the fragments explicated eschatological pronouncements, from the bountiful vineyards in a future utopia on earth during the millennium (Irenaeus, *Adv. Haer.* 5.33.3; cf. Rev 20:1–6; *2 Bar* 29:5) to the downfall of the angelic government over the cosmos (Andrew

---

1. There is extensive coverage of the similarities and differences between the Fourth Gospel and Revelation in Jörg Frey's appendix in Hengel, *Frage,* 326–429.

of Caesarea, *Comm. Rev.* 34.12). Other fragments recited the ordinary or extraordinary actions done by Jesus or his motley crew of supporters: a corpse was resuscitated (Eusebius, *Hist. Eccl.* 3.39.9), Justus Barsabbas suffered no ill-effects after consuming poison (3.39.9), Mark aided Peter as his *hermēneutēs* or "interpreter" (3.39.15), Matthew transcribed the "oracles" (*logia*) in the Hebrew *dialektos* or "language" (3.39.16), a woman was indicted for many sins before the Lord (3.39.17), Judas's body swelled up to grotesque proportions before his life ended at his own place (Apollinarius of Laodicea fragment on Matthew 27.5), and the sons of Zebedee were slain (Philip of Side, *Codex Baroccianus* 142).[2]

Along with the comparable rhetorical tropes in the Lukan and Papian prologues about the proper investigatory and compositional methods that must be implemented by a biographer of Jesus (Luke 1:1-4; *Hist. Eccl.* 3.39.3-4, 15), Luke-Acts paralleled Papias in its inclusion of the sinful woman who was acquitted by Jesus (Luke 7:36-50; cf. John 7:53-8:11), the gruesome disembowelment of Judas on his own plot of land (Acts 1:18), the election of Justus Barsabbas to the rank of the twelfth apostle (1:23), the slaying of James with the sword (12:2), the affiliation of Mark and Peter (Acts 12:12; cf. 1 Pet 5:13), and the prophetic daughters of Philip (21:8-9). If the pastoral counsel in Acts 20:17-38 to the presbyters (*presbyteroi*) and bishops (*episkopoi*) of Ephesus to guard the flock under their care from the wolves eager to pounce when the Apostle Paul was no longer around to protect them was a mirror

---

2. For translations and commentary on the fragments, see Holmes, *Apostolic Fathers*, 722-67; Körtner, *Papias*, 50-71; Norelli, *Papia*, 174-499; Shanks, *Papias*, 105-260. Fölker Siegert published three Armenian fragments: one is found in the Armenian translation of the comments of Papias on Revelation 12:9 reproduced in the fifth-century commentary of Andrew of Caesarea and the other two are in Vardan Vardapet's thirteenth-century publication *Explanations of Holy Scripture* (cf. "Unbeachtete Papiaszitate," 605-14). Ulrich Körtner (*Papias*, 34-36), William Schoedel ("Papias," 260), and Enrico Norelli (*Papia*, 124, 394-411, 492-98) have cast critical suspicion on the authenticity of the Armenian fragments. For instance, it is unclear if the extended discussion on Revelation 12:9 and Luke 10:18 in the commentary of Andrew of Caesarea should be attributed to Papias and Vardan may have confused Papias with the fourth-century Alexandrian geographer Pappos.

into the historical situation of the writer of Luke-Acts, then Papias and the "evangelist Luke" had access to the oral lore that Christian elders and itinerant prophetesses spread around Asia Minor.³

An impressive consensus has arisen among specialists that Papias published the five volumes of his magnum opus around 110 CE.⁴ The first-generation disciples of the Lord had departed from this life, but their successors could communicate their instructions to Papias by word of mouth, and Papias conversed with the daughters of the first-generation evangelist Philip (*Hist. Eccl.* 3.39.3-4, 9). Papias's rebuke of dodgy innovators who cooked up newfangled sayings and unfamiliar commands (3.39.4) does not correspond to the complex systematic theologies of Marcion, Basilides, or Valentinus about the inferior creator deity or "demiurge" and the inner workings of the divine realm or *plērōma*, nor were Papias's five books a reaction against Basilides's twenty-four volume commentary *Exegetica*.⁵ Dating Papias before these controversial theologians rose to notoriety accords with Eusebius's placement of Papias as contemporaneous with the bishops Ignatius of Antioch and Polycarp of Smyrna, shortly after the bishop Clement of Rome died in the third year of the Roman emperor Trajan's reign in 100 CE (3.34.1; 3.36.1-2).⁶ Given Papias's acquaintance with two

---

3. See Norelli, *Papia*, 105-12, 124; Kok, *Margins*, 151-53. This seems to me to be a more probable scenario that either Papias's literary dependence of Luke (cf. Hill, "'Papian' Fragment," 625-28) or vice-versa (cf. Annand, "Four Gospels," 50; MacDonald, *Shipwrecked Gospels*, 43-66, 76-78).

4. The following arguments are based on Bartlet, "Papias's 'Exposition,'" 15-44; Körtner, *Papias*, 236, 261; Yarbrough, "Date of Papias," 186-91; Gundry, "Pre-Papian Tradition," 50-52; Schoedel, "Papias," 261; Norelli, *Papia di Hierapolis*, 48-54; MacDonald, *Shipwrecked Gospels*, 47; Shanks, *Papias*, 91-92; Kok, *Margins*, 110-11.

5. Contra Lightfoot, *Supernatural Religion*, 160-61; Barrett, *John*, 106; Koester, *Ancient Christian Gospels*, 34; Hill, "Papias of Hierapolis," 312-13.

6. David Sim ("R. H. Gundry," 286) objects that Eusebius may have been motivated to date Papias as early as possible to secure the general reliability of his traditions about the Gospels, especially after he denigrated Papias's own competence in *Ecclesiastical History* 3.39.13, but an earlier date works against Eusebius's own biases to sever Papias from having had any contact with the apostolic generation.

THE BELOVED APOSTLE?

Gospels, the Revelation of John, and the epistles of Peter and John (cf. *Adv. Haer.* 5.33.3; *Hist. Eccl.* 3.39.15-17; Andrew of Caesarea, *Comm. Rev.* 34.12), his literary productivity cannot be pushed into the first century.[7]

One piece of counter-evidence against this dating scheme is the purported fragment in the *Christian History* (ca. 430 CE) by Philip from Side in Pamphylia.[8] He summarized, but did not quote, Papias's alleged contention that those whom Jesus raised from the dead were still around in the time of Hadrian, Trajan's heir to the throne. Writing over a century after the fourth-century historian Eusebius's *Ecclesiastical History*, Philip of Side may have muddled up the hearsay that Papias disseminated about the supernatural revivification of a corpse (*Hist. Eccl.* 3.39.9) with the apologist Quadratus's certitude that some of those whom the Savior raised from the dead were living in his own day in his apology to Hadrian (4.3.2).[9] Monte Shanks is open to an underlying tradition from Philip of Side or Quadratus that stemmed from Papias and may have had the risen saints dwell on earth until Hadrian's lifetime rather than his reign (ca. 117-38 CE) per se. If so, it may not disprove the emerging consensus date of Papias's exposition.[10]

Among the accolades that Irenaeus lavished on Papias was that he was an "ancient man" (*archaios anēr*) and a "hearer of John" (*Adv. Haer.* 5.33.4). This is sharply at variance with Eusebius's resolute insistence that Papias's informant was the Elder John, not the Apostle John, and that Papias never had personal contact with either one of them (*Hist. Eccl.* 3.39.2, 5-7). Eusebius may have slipped up when admitting that Papias was, in fact, a first-hand

---

7. Contra Annand, "Four Gospels," 87-89; Yarbrough, "Date of Papias," 188; Perumalil, "Papias and Irenaeus," 33.

8. Bacon, "Syriac Translator," 17-18; Deeks, "Papias Revisited," 324; Hengel, *Johannine Question*, 16, 154-55n97; Hengel, *Frage*, 77. Norelli (*Papia di Hierapolis*, 52) grants that, if this Papian fragment is authentic, it could push the date of Papias's activity closer to 120 than to 110 CE.

9. Bartlet, "Date and Contents," 22; Körtner, *Papias*, 91; Schoedel, "Papias," 236; Gundry; "Pre-Papian Tradition," 51-52; MacDonald, *Shipwrecked Gospels*, 46, 46n5.

10. Shanks, *Papias*, 53-54.

hearer of the Elder John and Aristion (3.39.3, 7), so Papias may have briefly stayed with them in person as well as interviewed their cohorts who journeyed to Hierapolis.[11] A. C. Perumalil strains to fully align Irenaeus with Eusebius, since Irenaeus did not tag Papias's John as "the disciple of the Lord" nor brought up an accompanying citation from a writing in the Johannine corpus in *Against Heresies* 5.33.4.[12] Perumalil's argument is falsified by the wider literary context, for Irenaeus learned from Papias's fourth volume that John, "the disciple of the Lord," forecasted the abundant fertility of the earth when Christ ushers in his millennial rule (5.33.3-4). Influence from Revelation 20:1-6 was at the bottom of the popularity of millenarian theology in Asia Minor and Irenaeus was sure that Jesus' disciple John was the visionary behind it (4.14.2; 4.17.5; 4.18.6; 5.28.2; 5.30.1; 5.34.2). Justin's stance on the apostolicity of Revelation in *Dialogue* 81.4 may have also impressed itself on Irenaeus.[13]

As an exemplification of "apostolic succession," Irenaeus got a lot of apologetic mileage from allying Papias with the Apostle John. Eusebius's motivations for distancing Papias from this apostle were no less tendentious. Eusebius was not uninformed about the classification of Revelation among the "recognized" books, though his proclivity was to shelve it among the "spurious" ones (3.25.2, 4; cf. 3.28.2-5; 7.25.1-27), and did not hide his aversion to Papias's literal or "mythical" elucidation of the millennium (3.39.11-13).[14] Eusebius insulted Papias's intelligence (3.39.13)

---

11. Gundry, "Pre-Papian Tradition," 54, 57. Sim ("R.H. Gundry," 295) counters that Eusebius does not provide much support for the inference that Papias was a direct hearer of these two apart from the fact that Papias often names them and reproduces their teachings.

12. Perumalil, "Papias and Irenaeus," 333-34. Perumalil recognizes that "John" is named in *Against Heresies* 2.22.5 without a title or an accompanying textual citation, but he argues that the nearby reference to the "other apostles" clarifies that the apostle John was in mind in this passage.

13. Grant, *Irenaeus*, 40.

14. Perumalil, "Papias and Irenaeus," 335; Yarbrough, "Date of Papias," 187; Grant, *Irenaeus*, 36; Carson, *John*, 70; Gundry, "Pre-Papian Tradition," 54, 57-58; Michaels, *John*, 11-12; Shanks, *Papias*, 167, 173-74.

but Papias was sufficiently clever to dupe a theologian of the stature of Irenaeus into embracing pre-millennialism. To demote the Revelation of John, Eusebius deferred to the scholarly acumen of Dionysius, a bishop from Alexandria around 248 to 265 CE. Dionysius gauged the fourth evangelist's facility in the Greek language to far exceed that of the seer of Revelation (7.25.22–26) and submitted that there were two burial sites (*mnēmata*) dedicated to two different Johns in Ephesus (7.25.16). Modern historical critics may applaud Dionysius's astute attention to the diction and style of the Fourth Gospel and Revelation in refuting their unified authorship. His deduction about the two tombs is not as conclusive. Rival claimants may have quarrelled about where the Apostle John was laid to rest in Ephesus, two "memorial sites" may have been erected at the apostle's purported gravesite and house, or many persons named John may have been buried in Ephesus.[15] Shanks is positive that, if Eusebius had more to go on than a contentious reading of Papias's prologue and Dionysius's assumptions to substantiate the existence of his hypothetical Elder John, he would have put it on the table.[16]

Unlike his modern critics who are reliant on meager fragments, Eusebius's line of reasoning could have been tested against a full copy of the *Exposition of the Oracles of the Lord* readily available in his day. Eusebius may have correctly detected that Papias's Elder John was not the apostle of the same name, but his prejudices came into play when he forced the identification of the Elder John with John of Patmos in order to downgrade Revelation as a sub-standard, unapostolic artifact.[17] Papias's John was a chiliast who looked forward to the thousand year reign of Christ, but that does not necessitate that he was the visionary behind Revelation 20:1–6. Dionysius's proofs that Revelation was by some non-apostolic John were not drawn out of Papias's books; he disconnected the seer John from the fourth evangelist on the basis of the lin-

---

15. Gundry, "Pre-Papian Tradition," 57; cf. Morris, *John*, 21; Michaels, *John*, 11; Shanks, *Papias*, 134, 167.

16. Shanks, *Papias*, 167–68.

17. Schoedel, "Papias," 252.

guistic and stylistic traits of the Fourth Gospel and Revelation and the existence of the two tombs or memorials for John in Ephesus. To choose between the readings of Irenaeus or Eusebius, we must closely attend to the grammatical structure of Papias's prologue.

Papias outlined his usual *modus operandi* in this fashion (*Hist. Eccl.* 3.39.4): whenever someone "who had followed" (*parēkolouthēkōs*) the elders came along, Papias "was inquiring" (*anekrinon*) about the "words of the elders" (*tous tōn presbyterōn . . . logous*), about "what" (*ti*) the Lord's "disciples" (*mathētai*) such as Andrew, Peter, Philip, Thomas, James, John, or Matthew "said" (*eipen*) or what Aristion and "the elder John" were "saying" (*legousin*).[18] Papias complicated matters by marking Aristion and the Elder John as "disciples of the Lord" (*tou kuriou mathētai*) as well. It is tempting to delete this duplication of "disciples of the Lord" as a scribal gloss since it is omitted in the Syriac version of this Papian fragment,[19] or to opt for a hypothetical textual emendation where *hoi toutōn mathētai* ("the disciples of these ones") was corrupted to *hoi tou kuriou mathētai* ("the disciples of the Lord").[20] Based on the text-critical criterion that there is a greater probability that the *lectio difficilior* ("harder reading") may be more original, the repetition of "disciples of the Lord" should not be excised from the text.[21] Papias may have thought that Aristion and the Elder John were "disciples" of Jesus, but were not handpicked to be among Jesus' twelve *apostoloi* or "messengers," regardless of

18. The full Greek sentence reads *ei de pou kai parēkolouthēkōs tis tois presbyterois elthoi, tous tōn presbyterōn anekrinon logous, ti Andreas ē ti Petros eipen ē ti Philippos ē ti Thōmas ē Iakōbos ē ti Iōannēs ē Matthaios ē tis heteros tōn tou kuriou mathētōn ha te Aristiōn kai ho presbyteros Iōannēs, tou kuriou mathētai, legousin*. For the Greek text of *Ecclesiastical History* 3.39.4, see Holmes, *Apostolic Fathers*, 733.

19. See Mommsen, "Papianisches," 156-59; Abramowski, "Memoirs of the Apostles," 329-30n.28. However, Bacon ("Syriac Translator," 11-12) responds that there must have been some designation for the newly introduced Aristion and the Elder John and that the Syriac translator might have omitted the phrase because he did not find these two names in the lists of the twelve apostles (cf. Matt 10:2-4; Mark 3:16-19; Luke 6:14-16).

20. Bacon, "Syriac Translator," 11, 19.

21. Munck, "Presbyters," 230.

the historical accuracy of his belief.²² Alternatively, Papias may have levelled the playing field by affirming that all true Christians who guarded the communal storehouse of tradition were the "disciples of the Lord" against pseudo-believers with their manifold innovations.²³

There is disagreement about whether the "elders" and the "disciples of the Lord" were one group or two. Were the "elders" a class of ecclesiastical presbyters who ranked beneath the Lord's disciples and their singular episcopal successors (cf. Acts 11:30; 14:23; 15:2, 4, 6, 23; 16:4; 20:17, 21:18; 1 Tim 4:14; 5:17; Tit 1:5; Jas 5:14; Ignatius, *Magn.* 6.1; *Tral.* 3.1; *Smyrn.* 8.1; Irenaeus, *Adv. Haer.* 2.22.5; 3.2.2; 4:28.1; 5.5.1; 5.30.1; 5.36.1-2; 6.33.3)?²⁴ Reading these passages as suggesting that a monepiscopacy was in place in Papias's time, so that he defined *presbyteroi* as subordinate church officers under a presiding bishop, has been contested by Alistair C. Stewart. His thesis is that the economic affairs of a congregation meeting in a household were always managed by one *episkopos* (bishop) and, when the domestic bishops gathered together in a city-wide federation, they were collectively labelled as "presbyters" (*presbyteroi*).²⁵ When it appears that there were plural *presbyteroi* within one domestic Christian assembly (e.g., 1 Tim 4:14; 5:17), Stewart translates the term as senior benefactors or "elders" donating their finances or exercising teaching duties in an unofficial capacity.²⁶ It is in the late second century that a monarchial episcopate grew out of the collective presbyterate; a *monepiskopos* came to have oversight of multiple Christian

---

22. The scholars who accept this interpretation and yet take Papias to be in error include Barrett (*John*, 108) and Schnackenburg (*St. John*, 1.80–81n19, 89).

23. See Munck, "Presbyters," 232. Munck cites Acts 9:1 as an example of a more general referent for the "disciples of the Lord" that was not confined to the Twelve.

24. Bacon, "Syriac Translator," 11n21; Schnackenburg, *St. John*, 1.80; Körtner, *Papias*, 116–21; Schoedel, "Papias," 251; Bauckham, *Eyewitnesses*, 17; Bauckham, *Beloved Disciple*, 64; Sim, "R. H. Gundry," 293–94.

25. Stewart, *Original Bishops*, 15–53.

26. Ibid., 149–65.

assemblies in a geographic area and the presbyters became his subordinate ministers.[27] If Stewart's thesis is right, it would be anachronistic to impute monepiscopacy back to Papias's situation.[28] But if Stewart has misjudged the evolution of the monepiscopacy in the Ignatian epistles, then it is theoretically possible that Ignatius's near contemporary Papias similarly held the *presbyteroi* to have been church officers subservient to the apostolic overseers in various locales.

The question is whether the Greek syntax permits the differentiation of the "disciples of the Lord" from the "elders" in this extract from Papias. Some translators render the interrogative pronoun *ti* ("what") as an "accusative of general reference," meaning that the elders' "words" did not deviate from "what" the previous "disciples of the Lord" had spoken to them. If there were two groups, the first consisted of seven disciples and the second of two elders. Otherwise, Papias should have chosen an all-encompassing label, either disciples or elders, for a single group.[29] On the other hand, a more natural reading of the Greek is that the interrogative pronoun *ti* is an "appositive," meaning that Papias alternated between denoting the same group as "disciples of the Lord" and as "elders" and was restating his objective of ascertaining the elders' (i.e., the disciples') words or what they had said.[30] Appositional accusatives were a typical grammatical construction, while an "accusative of general reference" was rare in Koine Greek and in the process of being replaced by instrumental datives.[31] Shanks stresses that "accusatives of general reference" should be the translator's

27. The causes of this centralization are discussed in ibid., 299–352.

28. See also Shanks, *Papias*, 142.

29. Barrett, *John*, 107; Brown, *John I—XII*, xci; Haenchen, *John*, 1.10; Schnackenburg, *St. John*, 1.80; Culpepper, *Life of a Legend*, 110; Hill, "Papias," 310n4; Bauckham, *Eyewitnesses*, 16–18; Sim, "R.H. Gundry," 292; Kok, *Margins*, 59, 62.

30. Lightfoot, *Supernatural Religion*, 145; Bartlet, "Date and Contents," 16–18; Munck, "Presbyters," 236; Annand, "Four Gospels," 47–48; Deeks, "Papias Revisited," 296–97; Carson, *John*, 70; Gundry, "Pre-Papian Tradition," 53–54; Köstenberger, *John*, 7n17; Shanks, *Papias*, 140–43.

31. Shanks, *Papias*, 142.

The Beloved Apostle?

last resort and that the conditions for translating an accusative in this way are not present in this passage.[32]

Additionally, the adjective *presbyteros* does not have to be defined as an official post in the ecclesiastical social structure, but can be an accolade applying to any elderly figure of repute, apostolic or otherwise.[33] For instance, Peter petitioned the elders (*presbyteroi*) as a "fellow elder" (*sympresbyteros*) in 1 Peter 5:1 and the same basic sentiment may have been behind Paul's paternal metaphor in Philemon 1:10.[34] While the advice in 1 Peter 5:1–5 may have been aimed at the official Christian presbyterate in the provinces of Asia Minor, it may be more likely that the *presbyteroi* of 1 Peter were senior patrons who informally advised and cared for the *neōteroi* ("younger men") based on the wisdom and humility that comes with age.[35] Papias may have used the term *presbyteros* for a venerable, senior Christian role-model, irrespective of whether or not this person was also an ecclesiastical officeholder.[36]

Papias's sloppy phrasing can be blamed for the lack of interpretive clarity. On purely grammatical grounds, there may be a stronger likelihood that the "disciples of the Lord" stand in an appositional relationship to the "elders" so that they were one and the same group.[37] There may have been nine elders (i.e., Andrew,

---

32. Ibid., 140–42. Shanks defines "an accusative of general reference" as qualifying a statement that might otherwise be false by limiting the reference for the verbal action. It applies when a verb denoting a state or an adjective is limited by an accusative, when discussing a part of the greater whole, when examining the qualities or attributes of an object, or when referring to a sphere in general or indefinite relations between clauses.

33. See Lightfoot, *Supernatural Religion*, 146; Munck, "Presbyters," 234–36; Deeks, "Papias Revisited," 296–97; Schoedel, "Papias," 251; Hill, "Papias of Hierapolis," 110; Stewart, *The Original Bishops*, 142–43; Von Wahlde, *Gospel and Letters*, 3.416.

34. Carson, *John*, 70; Gundry, "Pre-Papian Tradition," 53, 54; Köstenberger and Snout, "Witness, Author, Apostle," 220; Shanks, *Papias*, 36–37.

35. Stewart, *Original Bishops*, 202–6.

36. Contra ibid., 297. If the seven apostles were also *presbyteroi*, they were not part of the presbyterial college in Asia Minor but were respected "elders" of a previous generation for Papias.

37. Shanks's book has persuaded me that I was mistaken to translate this

Peter, Philip, Thomas, James, John, Matthew, Aristion, and the Elder John), with the last two surviving until Papias's day.[38] This is why Eusebius's quotation of Papias switched from the aorist tense *eipen* ("they said") to the present tense *legousin* ("they are saying") when the subject changed from the seven disciples to Aristion and the Elder John (*Hist. Eccl.* 3.39.14). The number of elders could be cut down to eight if the same John surfaced twice, once in each list. In this view, John was one of the apostolic disciples—a group that had mostly passed away—and was, together with Aristion, one of the last living eyewitnesses of Jesus.[39] If Papias used an anaphoric article to refer back to the first mention of a substantive that was anarthrous when it was introduced, *ho presbyteros Iōannēs* could be translated as "the aforementioned Elder John."[40] However, the article does not have to be anaphoric.[41] Although they were all "elders" given their seniority over Papias, the article accentuated the titular nature of "Elder" that Papias affectionately bestowed on the second John, perhaps due to his exceptionally old age and Papias's admiration for him. There are solid reasons to discriminate between the Apostle John among the seven apostles and the Elder John who was paired with Aristion. It would be redundant to repeat the same John twice in one sentence without explanation, the title prefacing the second John's name distinguishes him from the first John, and the Apostle John may have died before the *Exposition of the Oracles of the Lord* was published.

The seven apostolic elders were dead when Papias was a bishop in Hierapolis. We do not know the ages of the apostles

---

as an "accusative of general reference" in Kok, *Margins*, 62.

38. I am not convinced by Rupert Annand ("Four Gospels," 47–48) and Urban C. Von Wahlde (*Gospel and Letters*, 3.418) that Aristion and the Elder John were the subject of *parēkolouthēkōs* and, hence, were followers of the elders.

39. Carson, *John*, 70; Gundry, "Pre-Papian tradition," 55; Köstenberger and Snout, "Witness, Author, Apostle," 219; Michaels, *John*, 11; Shanks, *Papias*, 133.

40. Carson, *John*, 70; Blomberg, *Historical Reliability*, 26; Köstenberger and Snout, "Witness, Author, Apostle," 219; Shanks, *Papias*, 19–21, 154–55.

41. Deeks, "Papias Revisited," 297.

when they were summoned by Jesus to his mission, but someone between the ages of ten and twenty years old in 30 CE would have been in their nineties in 110 CE.[42] Few in the ancient world could boast of lengthy lifespans. Markus Bockmuehl estimates that the average life expectancy in the ancient world was around thirty-five years old, while 20 to 25 percent reached middle age and 5 percent of the population celebrated their sixtieth birthdays.[43] Of course, high infant mortality rates have to be factored into these low statistics and every year that one did not succumb to death by natural or violent causes increased the chances of making it to old age. Christian examples such as the sixty-five-year-old Polycrates (*Hist. Eccl.* 5.24.7) or the ninety-year-old Pothinus (*Hist. Eccl.* 5.5.8) were not unheard of, but the apostles John and Philip may have been memorialized as old men because they were mixed up with the Elder John and the evangelist Philip (Irenaeus, *Adv. Haer.* 2.22.5; 3.3.4; Eusebius, *Hist. Eccl.* 3.31.3; 5.24.2-3; Epiphanius, *Pan.* 30.24.6; Jerome, *Vir. ill.* 9) and Quadratus's apologetic about the extended lifespans of the re-embodied saints was in the realm of the fantastic (Eusebius, *Hist. Eccl.* 4.3.2).[44] Since the imperfect tense of *anakrinō* means that Papias "was cross-examining" his informants over a continuous period in the past, it might be possible to translate *legousin* as a historic present so as to confine the speaking days of Aristion and the Elder John to the past too.[45] While Bauckham dates Papias's inquiries back to the 80s CE,[46] there is no indication that decades elapsed between Papias's interviews and his setting down his interviewees' responses in writing. There is no signal that Aristion and the Elder John had stopped "speaking" at the time when Papias was writing.

42. See Barrett, *John*, 108; Schnackenburg, *St. John*, 1.89-90; Körtner, *Papias*, 125-26; Sim, "Response to R. H. Gundry," 292; Kok, *Margins*, 63, 168-69.

43. Bockmuehl, *Seeing the Word*, 179.

44. Bockmuehl (ibid., 178-79) accumulated several texts to prove his contentions about the "living memory" that lasted until the second century, but does not always seem to critically sift through these texts.

45. Hill, *Johannine Corpus*, 384.

46. Bauckham, *Eyewitnesses*, 18.

Would the Real John Please Stand Up?

Granted, the sobriquet "Elder" could fit an aged apostle still alive in Trajan's reign. The odds that *two* personal disciples of Jesus lived into their nineties are exceedingly low. Robert Gundry, Andreas J. Köstenberger, and Monte Shanks aver that, while Aristion was among Jesus' larger following among the crowds, he was denied the epithet "elder" because Jesus had not authorized him as one of the apostolic custodians of the tradition.[47] We have seen that *presbyteros* could be an adjective honoring any senior benefactor commanding respect or a title for an ecclesiastical official, but there are no ancient Christian texts where the term had such a restrictive definition that it could not be applied to anyone besides the apostles. Instead, the Elder John's nickname emphatically underscored his old age, but Aristion's age did not stand out as noteworthy. Aristion was probably not a first-generation disciple of Jesus, but a second-generation disciple of the risen Lord. This is confirmed by the lack of any record of Aristion among the named disciples of the historical Jesus.[48] It is pure speculation to include Aristion among the seventy-two disciples in Luke 10:1[49] or the two anonymous disciples in John 21:2.[50] Both Aristion and the Elder John were bracketed together and apart from the seven apostles, the likely reason being that they were influential "disciples" of the second Christian generation.

Finally, the Apostle John's life may have been cut short as a martyr. The fifth-century historian Philip of Side (*Codex Baroccianus* 142) and the ninth-century monk George the "Sinner" or *Harmartōlos* (*Chronicle* 3.134.1, in MS *Codex Coislinianus* 305) reproduced a fragment where Papias unjustly scapegoated the Jews for the deaths of James and John. Their martyrdoms are eulogized in a Syrian martyrology from Edessa (ca. 411 CE) and the

---

47. Gundry, "Pre-Papian Tradition," 55; Köstenberger, "Witness, Author Apostle," 219; Shanks, *Papias*, 153–54, 156–57.

48. Körtner, *Papias*, 125–26; Sim, "Response to R. H. Gundry," 292, 294; Kok, *Margins*, 63.

49. Contra Brown, *John I—XII*, xci; Perumalil, "Papias and Irenaeus," 334.

50. Hengel, *Question*, 19; Bauckham, *Eyewitnesses*, 415; Bauckham, *Beloved Disciple*, 79n.16; Von Wahlde, *Gospel and Letters*, 419n13.

The Beloved Apostle?

Calendar of Carthage (ca. 505 CE). Yet there may be a reasonable cause for skepticism about this purported Papian fragment.[51] The evidence is late, Philip's reliability is questionable, and the reference to the deaths of James and John may have been interpolated into a single manuscript of George's *Chronicle*. There may be other explanations: Papias's report that James was killed could have been corrupted under the influence of the prophecy in Mark 10:39 that both brothers would be baptized into Jesus' suffering. Alternatively, the "witness" (*martyria*) that the seer John bore in his patient endurance under exile (Rev 1:2; cf. George the Sinner on Origen, *Comm. Matt.* 16.6) or the tribute to John of Ephesus as a "witness" (*martys*, cf. Eusebius, *Hist. Eccl.* 3.31.3; 5.24.3) may have been augmented with the additional connotations of martyrdom. Names could have gotten mixed up; the confusion is evident when the Calendar of Carthage marked the passing of "John the Baptist" and James on the same day.

On the other hand, Eusebius may have suppressed a genuine Papian fragment since it stood against the prevailing Patristic standpoint that the Apostle John died peacefully in Ephesus during Trajan's reign from 98 to 117 CE (Irenaeus, *Adv. Haer.* 2.22.5; 3.3.4; Eusebius, *Hist. Eccl.* 3.23.4; Epiphanius, *Pan.* 30.24.6; Jerome, *Vir. ill.* 9).[52] Shanks disbelieves that Eusebius would have suppressed something that backed up his valorization of martyrdom and his anti-Jewish prejudices,[53] but the social memory that John, the son of Zebedee, lived to a ripe old age may have become too ingrained and Eusebius could have chalked up Papias's error as one more example of the naïve credence that he placed in local myths. If Papias attested to the martyrdoms of James and John, they may not have died at the exact same point of time (cf. Acts

---

51. The following reasons in this paragraph are compiled from Barrett, *John*, 103-4; Brown, *John I—XII*, LXXXIX; Schnackenburg, *St. John*, 1.87-88; Lindars, *John*, 30; Schoedel, "Papias," 240-41; Blomberg, *Historical Reliability*, 37; Culpepper, *Life of a Legend*, 171-74; Shanks, *Papias*, 219-25, 239-40.

52. Bultmann, *John*, 11; Haenchen, *John*, 1.10; Hengel, *Question*, 21; Hengel, *Frage*, 88-91, 317, 319 Charlesworth, *Beloved Disciple*, 240-41; Waetjen, *Two Editions*, 57; Norelli, *Papia*, 369-71.

53. Shanks, *Papias*, 221-22.

12:2).⁵⁴ However, the authenticity of this Papian fragment would shut the case for equating the Apostle John with the Elder John, for the Elder John was preaching around the same time as when Papias was publishing his exposition.

Papias and the Evangelist John

The Elder John may have not been an apostle, but that has not diminished his importance within certain scholarly reconstructions. For some modern scholars, the Elder John was the one whom the Johannine Christ-followers fondly nicknamed as the "disciple whom Jesus loved" (John 13:23; 19:26; 20:2, 7; 21:20) and as their "elder" (2 John 1:1; 3 John 1:1).⁵⁵ In contrast, while some Christian scholars in antiquity linked the Elder John with the book of Revelation (Eusebius, *Hist. Eccl.* 3.39.6) or with the second and third Johannine Epistles (Jerome, *De vir. ill.* 9), the undisputed Papian fragments from Irenaeus (*Adv. Haer.* 5.33.4) and Eusebius (*Hist. Eccl.* 3.39.3-4, 15-17) did not broach the subject of the Fourth Gospel at all.

One piece of ancient evidence that did explicitly tie Papias to the Fourth Gospel, the "Anti-Marcionite Prologue" to the Fourth Gospel, contended that Papias transcribed the Fourth Gospel at the dictation of the Apostle John. Donatien de Bruyne isolated the Latin prologues to the Gospels of Mark, Luke, and John in thirty-one manuscripts from the fifth to the fourteenth centuries and theorized that they were all formulated during the Marcionite crisis in the latter half of the second century.⁵⁶ Subsequent scholarship has overturned de Bruyne's theses on the early dating, common authorship, and unitary anti-Marcionite agenda of these

---

54. See MacDonald, *Shipwrecked Gospels*, 59; Shanks, *Papias*, 220. Note that both Philip of Side and George the Sinner harmonized this fragment with the tradition of John's long life extending into the reign of Trajan.

55. Hengel, *Johannine Question*, 124-32; Hengel, *Frage*, 204-74; Bauckham, *Eyewitnesses*, 384-471; Bauckham, *Beloved Disciple*, 73-75; Von Wahlde, *Gospel and Letters*, 3.419, 421-22; Thompson, *John*, 1.

56. Bruyne, "prologues Latines," 193-214.

Latin prologues.⁵⁷ While the Latin prologues are late witnesses, and "Anti-Marcionite" may be a misnomer, J. B. Lightfoot wanted to figure out how the premise that Papias was John's scribe came about. Since the imperfect tense in the indicative mood has identical endings in the first-person singular and the third-person plural, Lightfoot guessed that Papias commented somewhere to the effect that the churches "were recording" (*apegraphon*) the Fourth Gospel at John's dictation and a Latin scribe misread it as "I [i.e., Papias] was recording."⁵⁸ A simpler explanation is that the so-called "Anti-Marcionite" Prologue has twisted things beyond repair and is useless for the historian: Papias was misremembered as the Apostle John's amanuensis rather than the Elder John's fan, Papias's book was misspelled as *Exoteric*, and the Apostle John was pictured as Marcion's adversary in spite of the chronological difficulties that this creates.⁵⁹

Since the Eusebian citations of Papias strictly concerned the Elder John's postulations about the evangelist Mark (*Hist. Eccl.* 3.39.15), and maybe the evangelist Matthew if the following line was also from the Elder John (3.39.16), Eusebius may have ignored what Papias had to say about the evangelist John because it was uninteresting.⁶⁰ More controversially, Eusebius may have censored Papias's claim that the Fourth Gospel was authored by the Elder John.⁶¹ To fortify this argument, some scholars look for indirect signs of Johannine influence on Papias.⁶² Papias's seven disciples

---

57. Jürgen Regul's *Die antimarcionitischen Evangelienprologe* is a full-scale refutation of de Bruyne's article. See also Gutwenger, "Anti-Marcionite Prologues," 393–409; Heard, "Old Gospel Prologues," 1–16; Haenchen, *John*, 1.17; Culpepper, *Life of a Legend*, 130.

58. Lightfoot, *Supernatural Religion*, 214; Carson, *John*, 27. For another option, Gutwenger ("Anti-Marcionite Prologues," 405–6) supposes that Papias wrote down a description of the Fourth Gospel based on the information given to him about it by the elder John.

59. See Heard, "Old Gospel Prologues," 12–13; Haenchen, *John*, 1.18; Schnackenburg, *St. John*, 1.83, 90.

60. See Lightfoot, *Supernatural Religion*, 46, 51, 178–85.

61. Bauckham, *Eyewitnesses*, 424; Bauckham, *Beloved Disciple*, 57–58.

62. The following evidence for Papias's use of the Johannine literature is

may have been enumerated in the chronological order in which they are narrated in the Fourth Gospel (John 1:40-44; 11:16; 21:2), his partiality towards the commandments given by faith and in accordance with the truth has a conspicuously Johannine ring to it, and his deprecation of the *taxis* or "order" of the evangelist Mark's Gospel may have assumed a contrast with the fourth evangelist's neat biographical outline structured around the Jewish festival calendar (*Hist. Eccl.* 3.39.3-4, 15). Papias's use of *First John* may increase the odds that he had knowledge of the Fourth Gospel (3.39.17). Irenaeus assigned traditions to a collective body of elders (cf. *Adv. Haer.* 2.22.5; 5.5.1; 5.30.1; 5.33.3; 5.36.1-2)—it is feasible that Papias was among them—and some of them were exegetical observations about verses such as John 14:2 on the heavenly mansions that Jesus prepared for his elect (5.36.2) and John 8:57 on the age of maturity for a religious sage (2.22.5-6).

None of these arguments are unassailable.[63] Any of the elders in Asia Minor could have trained Irenaeus to be a skilled exegete. Johannine traditions and literature were floating around the general geographical area where Papias resided, but it is not evident that Irenaeus's exegesis of the Fourth Gospel was derived from Papias's exposition. In Papias's estimation, it was Matthew who carefully "arranged" (*sunetaxato*) the oracles about Jesus (*Hist. Eccl.* 3.39.16). Matthew's coverage extended from Jesus' birth to his ascension and he organized the didactic material into five great discourses, so Matthew's Gospel was the gold standard of rhetorical arrangement for Papias. Papias considered Matthew's Gospel to have been a translation of a Semitic original and advocated on

---

compiled from Lightfoot, *Supernatural Religion*, 186-216; Deeks, "Papias Revisited," 325-26; Grant, *Irenaeus*, 35; Hengel, *Johannine Question*, 20-22; Hengel, *Frage*, 80-87; Hill, "New 'Papian' Fragment," 582; Hill, *Johannine Corpus*, 385-86; 407-9; Bauckham, *Eyewitnesses*, 226-33, 423-25; Bauckham, *Beloved Disciple*, 51-58, 62-63; Nagel, *Rezeption*, 474; Hill, "'Orthodox Gospel,'" 286; Shanks, *Papias*, 149, 260n534, 260n540; Von Wahlde, *Gospel and Letters*, 3.419.

63. For the following arguments against Papias's usage of the Fourth Gospel, see Lindars, *John*, 30; Körtner, *Papias*, 173-76, 198-99; Koester, *Ancient Christian Gospels*, 246; Norelli, *Papia*, 114-23; MacDonald, *Shipwrecked Gospels*, 17n.26; Watson, *Gospel Writing*, 463; Kok, *Margin*, 198-99.

behalf of the translators as they had worked to the best of their abilities "as each was able" (*hōs hēn dynatos hekastos*).⁶⁴ To align Papias's list of disciples with the Fourth Gospel, one must skip over a bunch of names to move from the first three names in John 1:40–44 (i.e., Andrew, Peter, Philip) to Thomas in John 11:16 and to "those of Zebedee" in John 21:2. Rather, Papias's seven disciples almost match up with Matthew 10:2 (cf. Mark 3:16–19), except that the names are in a slightly different order and Bartholomew dropped out due to his insignificance. Papias's Johannine-sounding language may be a residue from *First John*, but nothing necessitates that the Johannine epistle circulated with the Fourth Gospel among all Christian interpretive communities.⁶⁵

Mention should be made of Richard Bauckham's and Charles Hill's quest to isolate undetected Papian fragments. Bauckham postulates that a few lines in the Muratorian Canon derived from a missing portion of Papias's writings. In lines 9 to 16, John, one of the disciples, was urged by his fellow disciples and bishops to write and Andrew, one of the apostles, had a vision that John ought to comply with their request. Line 33 certified that John arranged Jesus' wondrous deeds in "order." For Bauckham, the source of the Muratorian Canon was referring to the Elder John since it detached him from the "apostles" and was making the statement about John's excellent order with Mark's Gospel as the point of comparison.⁶⁶ However, Bauckham may over-interpret the trivial variation between "disciples" and "apostles," for John and Andrew were not directly juxtaposed and were separated by a larger body of "disciples and bishops."⁶⁷ The "disciples and bishops" were

---

64. There is no deprecration of the translator's work in *Ecclesiastical History* 3.39.16 (cf. Watson, *Gospel Writing*, 126n25; contra Bauckham, *Eyewitnesses*, 225).

65. This is the case even if 1 John was intended as an orthodox commentary on the Fourth Gospel. A parallel with Luke-Acts is instructive: while Acts was the sequel to the Gospel of Luke, the Gospel and the book of Acts had separate transmission histories as documented by Gregory, *Reception of Luke and Acts*.

66. Bauckham, *Eyewitnesses*, 431; Bauckham, *Beloved Disciple*, 61–62.

67. Köstenberger, "Witness, Author, Apostle," 222.

Would the Real John Please Stand Up?

likely the communal "we" who attested to the truthfulness of the Fourth Gospel in John 21:24, except that the Muratorian Canon did not hold that the beloved disciple had died before this verse was penned since it included John among their number.[68] There is no need to seek out a negative foil for John's order. The standpoint of the Muratorian Canon was that all of the canonical Gospels cohere together in matters of general substance from the nativity to the second coming of the Lord (lines 19–26), so it would not have condoned Papias's castigation of Mark's inadequate order (*Eccl. Hist.* 3.39.15).

Hill's hypothesis is that Eusebius preserved Papias's commentary on the origins of the Fourth Gospel, but without proper acknowledgement, in *Ecclesiastical History* 3.24.5–7 and 11–13. If this is true, Papias attributed two of the Gospels to the historical disciples of Jesus, Matthew and John (3.24.5). Hill's case is strengthened by how Eusebius prefaced 3.24.5, 8a with the words "the record holds" (*katechei ho logos*) and 3.24.7, 11 with "they say" (*phasin*), which may be technical terms for when Eusebius had recourse to a written source.[69] By identifying Papias as that source, Hill maps out how the Patristic theologians advanced Papias's points (*Hist. Eccl.* 2.15.1–2; 3.24.5–7, 11–13, 3.39.15–16) about how the hearers of the evangelists begged them to compose their Gospels, how the Gospels were sanctioned by the apostles as accurate transcripts of their recollections about Jesus, and how the fourth evangelist supplemented the order or arrangement of the Synoptic Gospels.[70]

What is indicative of a written source in *Ecclesiastical History* 3.24.5–8 is the inclusio beginning and ending with "the record holds" (*katechei ho logos*), but the informal *phasi* ("they say") in 3.24.11 may show that Eusebius's discussion shifted to the rationalizations given to the Christian laity in his own day

---

68. Barrett, *John*, 124; Schnackenburg, *St. John*, 1.84.

69. Hill, "New 'Papian' Fragment," 589–92.

70. Ibid., 592–606; cf. Bartlet, "Date and Contents," 26–27; Hill, *Johannine Corpus*, 387–92; Hill, "Papias," 312; Blomberg, *Historical Reliability*, 25; Hill, "'Orthodox Gospel,'" 287–94.

for the chronological differences between the four Gospels.⁷¹ Eusebius gravitated towards a particular resolution to this dilemma in 3.24.8b–13, namely that the Fourth Gospel logged the miracles that Jesus performed before John the baptizer was thrown into prison (cf. John 3:24), but this excuse for why the Gospels diverge from one another was out of step with Papias's blanket declaration that the "order" (*taxis*) of Mark's Gospel was defective.⁷² Moreover, the precise solution in *Ecclesiastical History* 3.24.8b–13 that the Fourth Gospel chronicled what happened before the incarceration of the baptizer is not traceable to any Patristic thinkers prior to Eusebius and may have been devised as a counterpoint to Origen's admission that the Gospels were not harmonizable at the literal level (*Comm. Jo.* 10.2).⁷³

As for the written source behind *Ecclesiastical History* 3.24.5–8a, the sixth chapter of Clement's *Hypotyposeis* accentuated the authorial humility of the evangelist Mark, the endorsement of Mark's Gospel by Peter when he discovered that Mark had transcribed notes from the apostle's sermons for his Roman hearers at their request, and the supplementation of the Synoptics with the fourth evangelist's spiritual Gospel (*Eccl. Hist.* 2.15.1–2; 6.14.5–7). These were Clement's points and, in Eusebius's eyes, Papias may have agreed with Clement to the extent that Mark was Peter's interpreter (2.15.2).⁷⁴ Clement may have gone on to talk

---

71. Bauckham, *Eyewitnesses*, 534–34; Manor, "Epiphanius' *Alogi*," 137; Manor, "Papias, Origen, and Eusebius," 11. Hill ("New 'Papian' Fragment, "591n.21) locates only two places where Eusebius sourced a written text with "they say" (*Hist. Eccl.* 7.12; 2.15.2), but the informal language in 2.15.2 may communicate that Eusebius had very loosely paraphrased the sixth chapter of Clement's lost *Hypotyposeis* (cf. 6.14.5–7).

72. Bauckham, *Eyewitnesses*, 435–36; Kok, *Margins*, 197. Hill ("'Orthodox Gospel,'" 291) objects that the incompleteness of Mark's account may be behind Papias's criticisms of Mark's *taxis* if he thought that Mark omitted Jesus' miracles before the imprisonment of John. The problem is that there is no veiled criticism of Mark's order in *Ecclesiastical History* 3.24.5–13, since Eusebius presumed that the chronologies of the Gospels were harmonizable.

73. Manor, "Epiphanius' *Alogi*," 133–36, 139–41; Manor, "Papias, Origen, and Eusebius," 7–10, 13–15.

74. Kok, *Margins*, 206–13.

about the circumstances that prompted the evangelists Matthew and John to write, so his lost *Hypotyposeis* may have been the source for *Ecclesiastical History* 3.24.5–8a.⁷⁵ Against the objections that the canonical ordering of the Gospels in *Ecclesiastical History* 3.24.6–7a contradicts Clement's take that the Gospels with the genealogies (i.e., the Gospels of Matthew and Luke) were "written first" (*progegraphthai*) in 6.14.5,⁷⁶ the verb *prographein* can mean "to write before the public" and Clement may have surmised that Mark's Gospel was compiled for a private audience in Rome rather than for wider public dissemination like the more refined Gospels of Matthew and Luke.⁷⁷ Margaret Mitchell labels this as an "audience request tradition" in which the intended audience compelled a reluctant author to write down his or her wisdom and this trope that surfaced in the Muratorian Canon as well may have been commonplace.⁷⁸

To wrap up the threads so far, the Elder John was not among the seven apostles of Jesus enumerated by Papias and the Fourth Gospel has not turned up in the undisputed Papian fragments. A single word, *presbyteros*, is a flimsy basis to liken the Elder John to the elder or presbyter of 2 John 1:1 and 3 John 1:1. Thus, I find Ulrich H. J. Körtner's suspicions that the Johannine epistles were pseudonymously ascribed to the Elder John to give Johannine theology a foothold in Asia Minor to be unnecessary.⁷⁹ Rather, when John, the son of Zebedee, came to be identified as the beloved disciple and the author of the Johannine corpus, 2 John 1:1 and 3 John 1:1 may have been the pegs that enabled him to be merged with Papias's Elder John.⁸⁰ Our information about the

75. Gregory, *Reception*, 37. suspects that Clement might be Eusebius's source; contra Hill, "New 'Papian' Fragment," 586n11,

76. Hill, "New 'Papian' Fragment," 586n11; Manor, "Epiphanius *Alogi*," 130n.341.

77. For this translation, see Stephen Carlson, "'Order' of the Gospels, 118–225. I build on this translation in Kok, *Margins*, 210–11.

78. See Mitchell, "Patristic Counter-Evidence," 50n42, 51.

79. Körtner, *Papias*, 198–202.

80. Grant, *Irenaeus*, 37; Casey, *Is John's Gospel True?*, 164–69; Culpepper, *Life of a Legend*, 307; Watson, *Gospel Writing*, 464–67, Kok, *Margins*, 62, 80.

Elder John is meager. This is disappointing in light of the enormous influence that his hunches that the evangelist Mark was a second-hand reporter of the deeds of the Lord that had been spoken about by Peter and that the evangelist Matthew directed his Gospel towards the Jewish people in their own language had on the reception history of these two Gospels for nearly two millennia (*Hist. Eccl.* 3.39.15–16). There may be a few more facts about the shadowy Elder John that can be gleaned from Irenaeus's *Adversus Haereses* below.

Justin Martyr and the Seer John

Justin divulged his upbringing in Flavia Neapolis in Syria Palestina at the outset of his *First Apology* (*1 Apol.* 1.1). His next publication, the *Dialogue with Trypho the Jew*, was based on his chats with a Jewish refugee named Trypho and his friends in the aftermath of the Romans' brutal suppression of a Jewish revolt in 135 CE. Trypho had initiated a dialogue with Justin when he spotted him donning the stereotypical garb of a philosopher (*Dial.* 1.2) and Justin relayed the steps in his own intellectual journey. After sampling the philosophical schools of a Stoic, a Paripatetic, a Pythagorean, and a Platonist, an older gentleman introduced Justin to the antique Hebrew prophets who foretold the advent of the Christ (2.3–8.1). Henceforth, Justin prided himself as a Christian philosopher and launched his own school in Rome. Running afoul of the Cynic philosopher Crescens, he was denounced to the Roman governing authorities. Justin's surname "martyr" was bequeathed to him after he was sentenced to death by the Urban Prefect Q. Junius Rusticus (cf. Tatian, *Oratio* 19; Eusebius, *Hist. Eccl.* 4.16.7–9). While Justin's philosophical training may have been shallow, he paved the way for translating Christian tenets into a philosophical medium and making philosophy accessible for ordinary Christians.[81]

Justin approved of what John, one of Christ's apostles, forecasted about the occupation of Jerusalem by the servants of Christ

---

81. Parvis, "Justin Martyr," 59–60.

for a thousand years before the everlasting judgment and resurrection from the dead (*Dial.* 81.4; cf. Rev 20:1-6). Justin's beliefs and ethics were also formed by the "memoirs of the apostles" (*apomnēmoneumata tōn apostolōn*), or what his Christian contemporaries were styling as the *euangelia* or the "Gospels" (*1 Apol.* 66.3; *Dial.* 10.2; 100.1).[82] There is scholarly disagreement over whether Justin pigeonholed the Gospels as fitting into a known genre of literature, the memorabilia of a renowned philosopher, or whether the noun *apomnēmoneumata* ("memoirs") was related to the verb *apomnēmoneuein* ("to remember") inasmuch as the Gospels were comprised of the memories of the apostles (cf. *1 Apol.* 33.5; 66.3; cf. Papias, in *Hist. Eccl.* 3.39.3-4, 15).[83] Most of Justin's citations of the memoirs are clustered in a section of the *Dialogue* (98—107) that centered on an extended exegetical analysis of Psalm 22 in the context of debunking "docetist" disavowals of the corporeal existence of Jesus as a flesh-and-blood human being.[84]

One could scan through the apostolic memoirs or archives to research what Jesus accomplished in history; whatever Justin conceived the "Acts of Pilate" to be, they also sufficed to document the historicity of Jesus (*1 Apol.* 35.9; 48.3).[85] We should not underestimate the liturgical reading of the apostolic memoirs alongside the Hebrew prophets during Christian worship services (*1 Apol.* 67.3).[86] A diary entry from the high priest Caiaphas or the Roman

82. Abramowski ("Memoirs," 323, 326) argues for the originality of Justin's references to the *euangelia*.

83. See Heard, APOMNÊMONEUMATA, 125-26; Abramowski, "Memoirs," 328; Koester, *Ancient Christian Gospels*, 38-39; Stanton, *Jesus and Gospel*, 104; Kok, *Margins*, 112-13.

84. See Abramowski, "Memoirs," 329-31.

85. Gamble, *New Testament Canon*, 28-29; Campenhausen, *Christian Bible*, 168; Koester, *Ancient Christian Gospels*, 41-42. However, Hill (*Johannine Corpus*, 332-35; "'Orthodox Gospel,'" 261-63) argues that Justin's "Acts of Pilate" should not be identified with the apocryphal *Acts of Pilate* nor with Pontius Pilate's personal journals, but was an alternate shorthand title for the canonical "memoirs of the apostles." I contest Hill's view that the "Acts of Pilate" contains details that could only derive from the Fourth Gospel in *1 Apology* 35 below.

86. Farmer and Farkasfalvy, *Ecumenical Approach*, 142; Metzger, *Canon*,

prefect Pontius Pilate, were they recoverable, would not have been on par with the "memoirs of the apostles." Some scholars find that the wording of *Dialogue* 103.8 on the memoirs of the "apostles and their followers" stipulates that there had to be at least four memoirs that were accorded scriptural status (*Dial.* 103.8).[87] Graham Stanton was mindful that the assumption that Justin vouched for *our* fourfold gospel canon may be wrongheaded: we might correlate Matthew and John with the two apostles and Mark and Luke with the two helpers of the apostles, but Justin acclaimed the second canonical Gospel as the memoirs of Peter (*Dial.* 106.3).[88] The conjunction *kai* ("and") denoted that all of the memoirs were joint-ventures of the apostles and their assistants; just as Mark was Peter's *hermēneutēs* or "translator" who drafted up the Gospel at Peter's dictation (cf. Papias, in *Eccl. Hist.* 3.39.15), Justin may have reasonably deduced that it was the normal practice for the apostles to be assisted by secretaries.[89]

The inclusion of the Fourth Gospel among Justin's indefinite number of apostolic memoirs cannot be taken as a given. There is debate about if, and to what degree, Justin cited the Fourth Gospel. To give two well-known scholarly surveys that lean towards maximalist results, F. M. Braun counted eleven points where Justin's writings had contact with the Fourth Gospel.[90] Edouard Massaux

---

6; Stanton, *Jesus and Gospel*, 100; Hill, *Johannine Corpus*, 337; Hill, "'Orthodox Gospel,'" 252–53.

87. Westcott, *St. John*, lxv; Blomberg, *Historical Reliability*, 24; Hengel, *Johannine Question*, 13; Hengel, *Frage*, 67; Stanton, *Jesus and Gospel*, 100–101; Hill, *Johannine Corpus*, 338–40; Hill, "'Orthodox Gospel,'" 263.

88. Stanton, *Jesus and Gospel*, 101–2. For other scholars who read the "memoirs of him" (*apomnēmoneumasin autou*) as a possessive genitive with Peter as the nearest antecedent (i.e., Peter's memoirs), see Heard, APOMNĒMONEUMATA, 127; Ehrman, *Forgery*, 325; Kok, *Margins*, 113–14. This contrasts with the translation given by Paul Foster ("Gospel of Peter," 108) where *apomnēmoneumasin autou* is an objective genitive meaning the "memoirs about him" (i.e., Jesus).

89. Pryor, "Justin Martyr," 155; Watson, *Gospel Writing*, 476n106.

90. Braun, *Jean le théologien*, 136–38. From the *First Apology*, he lists chapters 32 (John 1:1, 14); 35 (John 19:13); 61 (John 3:3); and 66 (John 6:53, 55). From the *Dialogue*, he lists chapters 17 (cf. John 1:9; 4:34; 5:23; 6:38); 63

WOULD THE REAL JOHN PLEASE STAND UP?

jotted down a compilation of potential references or allusions to the Fourth Gospel in Justin's *First Apology*, *Second Apology*, and *Dialogue*, measuring the level of certainty that can be granted to each individual parallel.[91] On the opposite side of the spectrum, some scholars extrapolate that Justin was either ignorant of the Fourth Gospel or purposely avoided it.[92] A few scholars inclined towards more minimalistic results concede that Justin may have marked the beginning of the tentative use of the Fourth Gospel by a non-gnostic Christian authority.[93] These divergent results are the outcome of implementing dissimilar methodologies for determining an intertextual reference.[94]

The "maximalists" are flexible in granting literary dependence on a source text when there are extensive verbal or thematic correspondences with it and lesser affinities with other potential literary parallels. In light of the proliferation of oral and written traditions about Jesus (cf. Luke 1:1-2; John 20:30; 21:25; 2 Pet 1:16; Papias, in *Hist. Eccl.* 3.39.4), the primary requirement of the

---

(John 1:13); 88 (John 1:20, 23); 91 (John 3:14-17); 106 (John 13:3; cf. 5:22-26; 10:29; 17:2, 6, 24). 111 (John 14:34; cf. 1:29, 36); and 121 (John 3:17; 1:17; 11:9; 15:15). He deems the parallels in *1 Apology* 61 and *Dialogue* 63, 66, and 91 to contain the most striking parallels.

91. Massaux, *St. Matthew*, 3.46-47, 94-95. From the *First* and *Second Apology*, he lists *1 Apol.* 6.2 (John 4:24); 32.10 (John 1:14); 32.11 (John 1:13); 33.2 (John 14:29); 35.8 (John 19:13); 52.12 (John 19:37); 61.4-5 (John 3:3-5); 63.15 (John 1:1); and *2 Apol.* 6.3 (John 1:3). From the *Dialogue*, he lists 14.1 (John 4:10; 7:38; cf. *Dial.* 69.6); 32.2 (Zech 12:10-14, John 19:37; cf. *Dial.* 118.1); 62.3 (John 1:13; cf. *Dial.* 54.2; 61.1; 76.1; 84.2); 94.5 (John 3:14-15); 100.1 (John 10:18); 105.1 (John 1:18); 117.4 (John 1:18); and 136.3 (John 5:23, 46). Like Braun, Massaux is most impressed by the parallel in *1 Apology* 61.4-5.

92. Hillmer, "Second Century," 72-73, 79-80; Bellinzoni, *Sayings of Jesus*, 140; Haenchen, *John*, 2.13; Gamble, *New Testament Canon*, 28; Koester, *Ancient Christian Gospels*, 360.

93. See Sanders, *Early Church*, 31; Barrett, *John*, 111; Watson, *Gospel Writing*, 474, 477n113.

94. See Batovici, "Survey of Methodologies," 398-402. Batovici summarizes the methods of Massaux (*St. Matthew*, 1.xxi-xxii, xviii), Hillmer ("Second Century," 6), Koester (*Ancient Christian Gospels*, 297), Nagel (*Rezeption*, 34-45), Hill (*Johannine Corpus*, 67-70; "'Orthodox Gospel,'" 235-42), and Gregory and Tuckett ("Method," 61-82).

"minimalists" is that a writer has to replicate an evangelist's editorial modifications to a source to prove that there was contact with that evangelist's own writing rather than with his or her sources. Since the vast majority of specialists on the Synoptic Problem favor Markan Priority, Matthean or Lukan redaction may be perceptible from their additions, omissions, or alterations to the text of Mark.[95] Since there is no unanimity among scholars about the sources of the Fourth Gospel (e.g., a Christological Hymn, a Sign's Source, a Passion Narrative, or a Synoptic Gospel), this criterion becomes harder to implement without coming to far-reaching decisions about the extent of the fourth evangelist's literary creativity or fidelity to prior hypothetical sources.[96] Since this is not an exact science, Dan Batovici is willing to mull over the literary echoes and allusions detected by the maximalists with their less stringent criteria, but cautions that "one should be very wary about claiming dependence of knowledge, in the absence of the positive results at the scrutiny of the 'minimalist' criterion."[97]

Many of the proposed parallels to the Fourth Gospel pertain to Justin's *logos* and incarnational Christology (cf. *1 Apol.* 5.4; 10.6; 21.1; 22.2; 23.2; 32.9–10; 60.7; 63.2, 15; 66.2; *2 Apol.* 6.3; *Dial.* 61.1; 84.2; 100.2).[98] Stoic and Neoplatonic philosophy had the concept that there was a cosmic rational principle undergirding the physical universe, but the affirmation that the *logos* (reason, word) was the supreme divinity's begotten son who became a human (*1 Apol.* 5.4; *2 Apol.* 6.3) seems to imprecisely imitate the language of the Johannine Prologue (cf. John 1:14, 18). The incarnation of Jesus

---

95. Even here it is possible that the differences of Matthew and Luke from Mark may be based on alternating between sources on the same incident rather than a Matthean or Lukan redactional change. See Gregory, *Reception of Luke*, 13–14; Gregory and Tuckett, "Method," 76–77.

96. See Gregory and Tuckett, "Method," 79; Batovici, "Survey of Methodologies," 405.

97. Batovici, "Survey of Methodologies," 405.

98. See Westcott, *St. John*, lxvi; Massaux, *St. Matthew*, 3.4647, 94–95; Braun, *Jean le théologien*, 136–38; Hengel, *Johannine Question*, 13; Hengel, *Frage*, 65; Pryor, "Justin Martyr," 162–63; Stanton, *Jesus and Gospel*, 102; Hill, *Johannine Corpus*, 317–28; Hill, "'Orthodox Gospel,'" 257–60; Thompson, *John*, 20.

through an act of divine will rather than through the intermingling of human blood or seed seems akin to the Western reading of John 1:13 (*1 Apol.* 23.2; 32.11; Dial. 54.2; 61.1; 63.2; 76.1).[99] Again, this involves far-reaching decisions: did the Johannine Prologue redact an older Christological hymn, and, if so, is it feasible that this hymn was still being disseminated in the mid-second century? Were there any other traditional streams aside from the Johannine Prologue that may have flowed into Justin's *logos* Christology?

For another example, Justin imagined that the multitude who gathered at Jesus' trial were "mocking" (*diasyrontes*) him by forcefully seating him on the judgment seat, which inadvertently fulfilled the prophecy in Isaiah 58:2 where the people implored their deity to render a judgment (*1 Apol.* 35.4). The *Gospel of Peter* literally pictured a mob shouting "let us drag away [*syrōmen*] the Son of God" and seating Jesus on the judgment seat out of mockery (3.6–7), but Justin's term for "judgment seat" (*bēma*) corresponds to John 19:13 and Justin might have mistaken Jesus rather than Pilate as the subject who "sat down" (*ekathisen*) on it. The nail marks in Jesus' hands, in fulfillment of the piercing of the righteous sufferer's hands and feet in Psalm 22:16 (*1 Apol.* 35.7), could be drawn from either Gospel (John 20:25, 27; cf. *Gos. Pet.* 6:21). Justin could be dependent on the Fourth Gospel, on the *Gospel of Peter*, or on a common source underlying the Fourth Gospel and the *Gospel of Peter*.[100]

The "born again" saying in *1 Apology* 61.4–5 is the clearest test case. Justin's form of the saying differs at points from John 3:3: Justin left out the double amen formula, used the compound verb for "reborn" (*anagennaō*) while John 3:3 used the verb "born"

---

99. Hill, *Johannine Corpus*, 318–19, 323–24; Hill, "'Orthodox Gospel,'" 258. The Western reading changes the plural subject and verb to a singular so that this is a reference to Jesus' own birth rather than to the spiritual rebirth or adoption of believers.

100. On the complicated question of the relationship between these three sources, see Braun, *Jean le théologien*, 141–43; Koester, *Ancient Christian Gospels*, 396–97; Pilhofer, "das Petrusevangelium," 69–75; Hill, *Johannine Corpus*, 306–9, 330–32; Foster, "Gospel of Peter," 108–11; Ehrman, *Forgery*, 326; Watson, *Gospel Writing*, 379–80; Hill, "'Orthodox Gospel,'" 261–62.

The Beloved Apostle?

(*gennaō*) along with the adverb "again" or "above" (*anōthen*), had the phrase "kingdom of heaven" (*basileia tōn ouranōn*) instead of "kingdom of God" (*basileia tou theou*), and warned that one might not "enter" (*eiserchomai*) rather than "see" (*oraō*) the kingdom (but cf. John 3:5). It is on these grounds that Helmut Koester and Arthur J. Bellinzoni held that Justin's form of the saying was independent of and more primitive than John 3:3 and 5.[101] Justin's phraseology about entering the kingdom was more in line with the Synoptics (cf. Matt 5:20; 7:21; 18:3; 19:23-24; Mark 9:47; 10:15, 23-25; Luke 18:17, 25), whereas seeing the kingdom in John 3:3 was equivalent to experiencing the eschatological reality (cf. John 1:50-51), and lacked the ambiguity over whether *anōthen* meant "again" or "above" which set up Nicodemus's query about the impossibility of literally being reborn a second time in John 3:4. Koester and Bellinzoni hypothesize that Justin took the saying from a baptismal liturgy (cf. 1 Pet 1:3, 23; Hippolytus, *Haer.* 8.10.8; Ps.-Clem. *Hom.* 11.26.2; *Apos. Const.* 6.15.5). Both Justin's interpretation of Christ's words in reference to the regeneration that comes about through baptism and the Fourth Gospel's clarification that one must be born of water and the spirit (John 3:5) evinced the logion's original baptismal function or "situation in life" (*Sitz im Leben*).[102]

James Barker catches some of the circularity in Koester and Bellinzoni's argumentation for an originary baptismal setting for Jesus' saying, for one might flip their argument around so that a free-floating saying about spiritual rebirth acquired the connotations of baptism from the Fourth Gospel's redactional framework and, consequently, informed Justin's construal of it.[103] It is just as defensible that Justin loosely paraphrased John 3:3, 5 and conflated its wording with Matthew 18:3 and 1 Peter 1:3, 23. What is more conclusive is that Justin goes on to state the obvious that

---

101. Bellinzoni, *Justin Martyr*, 135-38; Koester, *Ancient Christian Gospels*, 257-58, 360-61.

102. Koester, *Ancient Christian Gospels*, 257-58; Bellinzoni, *Justin Martyr*, 136-37. However, see Barker's case that all of these parallels are dependent on John 3:3, 5 ("Patristic Parallels," 548-58).

103. Barker, "Patristic Parallels," 547-48.

no one can re-enter their mother's womb (*1 Apol.* 61.5), picking up on Nicodemus's follow-up question in John 3:4. Thus, Justin was not in the dark about the dialogue between Jesus and Nicodemus that framed the saying in John 3:1-21.[104] Finally, while Justin's elucidation of Moses' bronze serpent (Num 21:8-9) as a type foreshadowing the crucified Christ in *1 Apology* 60.2-3 may not require an intertextual link with John 3:14, for the same typological interpretation showed up the *Epistle of Barnabas* 12:5-7 independently of the Fourth Gospel, the fact that there were two allusions to John 3:1-21 in near proximity to each other in the *Dialogue* increases the likelihood that Justin had read this section of the Fourth Gospel.[105]

Since *1 Apology* 61.4-5 passes the minimalist's redaction criterion,[106] the rest of the parallels unearthed with the maximalist's toolkit may be worthy of further consideration.[107] These parallels are not extensive and Justin had a transparent penchant for the Synoptic tradition because it furnished his prophetic prooftexts and his system of ethics.[108] Moreover, his selections from the "memoirs of the apostles" (cf. *1 Apol.* 66.1-3; 67.3; *Dial.* 100.4; 101.3; 102.5; 103.6, 8; 104.1; 105.1, 5, 6; 106.1, 4; 101.7) were often different combinations of the texts of Matthew and Luke except for one instance when he alluded to Mark 3:17 (*Dial.* 106.3).[109]

104. Braun, *Jean le théologien*, 1.138-139; Hengel, *Frage*, 64; Nagel, *Rezeption*, 99-100; Hill, *Johannine Corpus*, 327-28; Hill, "'Orthodox Gospel,'" 255-56; Kok, *Margins*, 180; Barker, "Patristic Parallels," 549-50.

105. Hengel, *Frage*, 64. Others who argue that *1 Apology* 61.5 (or *Dialogue* 91.4; 94.5 and 112.1-2) references John 3:14 include Braun, *Jean le théologien*, 139; Massaux, *St. Matthew*, 95; Hengel, *Johannine Question*, 151n72.

106. Barker ("Patristic Parallels," 549) judges Batovici's maximalist-minimalist dichotomy to mischaracterize the debate surrounding *1 Apology* 61.5, for this saying passes the minimalist criterion with flying colors.

107. See Braun, *Jean le théologien*, 136-44; Massaux, *St. Matthew*, 3.46-47, 94-96; Hengel, *Johannine Question*, 12-14; Hengel, *Frage*, 63-67; Nagel, *Rezeption*, 94-116; Hill, *Johannine Corpus*, 314-51; Hill, "'Orthodox Gospel,'" 252-65.

108. Hengel, *Johannine Question*, 13; Hengel, *Frage*, 65, 66; Hill, *Johannine Corpus*, 328.

109. See Stanton, *Jesus and Gospel*, 100-101; Kok, *Margins*, 113-15; contra

There may be a few exceptions where the Fourth Gospel was included in the "memoirs of the apostles." In *Dialogue* 100.4, Justin filled in the signifier "Son of God" with his own understanding of Jesus' pre-existence in the form of Wisdom and birth from a virgin mother. Five chapters later, Justin was satisfied with the proofs from the "memoirs of the apostles" that the "only" or "begotten" one (*monogenēs*), the Father's *logos* and power, condescended to be born as a human through a virgin (*Dial.* 105.1). What Justin found in the "memoirs" may have been confined to the virginal conception that he had previously gone over in *Dialogue* 78.3.[110] Hill insists that the incarnation of the only-begotten of the Father must have been taken from the "memoirs" as well, since the Matthean and Lukan infancy narratives do not have to be construed as the incarnation of a pre-existent being into the womb of the Virgin Mary without the input from the Fourth Gospel and Justin had "proven" the existence of the *logos* from the Jewish Scriptures in *Dialogue* 61.1–62.5.[111] However, while Justin was knowledgeable about personified attributes or divine hypostases (e.g., *logos*, wisdom, glory) and intermediary agents (e.g., the Angel of Yahweh) from the Jewish Scriptures and the Johannine Prologue, he may have brought this lens to bear on the infancy narratives in Matthew's and Luke's apostolic memoirs. Justin would have seen the story that Mary was impregnated without the agency of a human father as totally congruent with his theological viewpoint that the one who was begotten of the Father from eternity past descended into her womb.

There is one more example where Trypho put his finger on a conflict between Justin's belief in the pre-existence of the Messiah in the Godhead and the prophecy in Isaiah 11:1–3 that the Messiah was to be endowed with the Spirit at a specific point in time (*Dial.* 87.2). Justin's response was that Jesus was not in need of spiritual charisms as if he did not possess them beforehand, but that Jesus consented to be baptized and anointed by the Spirit so that he

Ehrman, *Forgery*, 326.
   110. Pryor, "Justin Martyr," 156–57.
   111. Hill, "'Orthodox Gospel,'" 259–60.

could fulfill the messianic prophecies in full public view and so that all the spiritual gifts apportioned to the prophets of old might find their fulfillment in him (87.3–5; 88.4, 6). His description of the baptism encompassed canonical details like the attire and diet of the baptizer (88.7; cf. Matt 3:4; Mark 1:6) and apocryphal details like the fire that lighted up the Jordan River (88.3). His language that the Spirit rested on Jesus may be reminiscent of John 1:32–33 (*Dial.* 87.3, 5) and the repetition of the baptizer's disclaimer that "I am not the Christ" (*ouk eimi ho Christos*) seems to be a verbal echo of John 1:20 (*Dial.* 88.7).[112]

Koester is unwavering in discounting any references to the Fourth Gospel from Justin, maintaining that Justin had the baptizer repudiate that he was the Messiah due to the prophecy about him as the messenger preparing the way in the wilderness in Isaiah 40:3 and the crowd's misguided assessment of John as a potential messianic candidate in Luke 3:15.[113] I do not see why Justin could not have taken over a unique detail from John 1:20, but that does not mean that Justin took it from an apostolic memoir. What the apostles of Christ explicitly testified to was that Jesus was baptized in the Jordan River and that the Spirit descended on him like a dove (*Dial.* 88.3; cf. Matt 3:16–17; Mark 1:9–10; Luke 3:21–22). Curiously, the Fourth Gospel had the baptizer retell his vision of the Holy Spirit's descent like a dove while bypassing the actual baptism of Jesus (John 1:32–34). Of course, Justin was conversant with extra details about this event drawn from a variety of oral and written sources, not all of which were categorized as the "memoirs of the apostles." Hill argues that the plural apostles of Christ in *Dialogue* 88.3 must be Matthew and John,[114] but Justin was speaking about the oral testimony of the collective apostles about the baptism of Jesus that was eventually written down in the memoirs.

---

112. Stanton, *Jesus and Gospel*, 76; Hengel, *Frage*, 64; Nagel, *Rezeption*, 100–102; Hill, *Johannine Corpus*, 329.

113. Koester, *Ancient Christian Gospels*, 391.

114. Hill, *Johannine Corpus*, 329.

The Beloved Apostle?

The Gospels of Matthew, Mark, and Luke were Justin's "memoirs of the apostles." Justin had familiarized himself with the contents of the Fourth Gospel, a text that was foundational for his *logos* Christology in all likelihood, but it was not yet on the same level as the Synoptic Gospels. The Fourth Gospel's fortunes would soon dramatically change. Justin's pupil Tatian squeezed Synoptic episodes into the structure of the Fourth Gospel in his *Diatessaron* ("through four"), his harmonized version of the four Gospels, and the emerging fourfold gospel canon placed the Synoptic and Johannine Gospels on equal footing. It was the devotional reading of the four Gospels in concert with one another within the canon that convinced Christians that the Apostle John was the beloved disciple and lead to the subscription "the Gospel according to John." For Justin, it was the book of Revelation that the Apostle John had left for posterity.

Irenaeus and the Apostle John

There is a great deal of uncertainty in reconstructing Irenaeus's birthplace and upbringing.[115] Eusebius copied a letter that Irenaeus sent to Florinus, a presbyterial colleague whom Irenaeus reprimanded for his attraction to dubious philosophical tenets, and it spelled out the extent of Irenaeus's tutelage under the bishop Polycarp in Smyrna (in Eusebius, *Hist. Eccl.* 5.20.4–8). Irenaeus had risen in the ranks of his own Christian congregation in the city of Lugdunum when a wave of persecution swept over the Christians in Gaul in 177 CE and he hand-delivered a letter from these Christian confessors to the bishop Eleutherus of Rome (5.1; 5.4.1–2). After his ordination as a bishop of Lugdunum, Irenaeus produced his most famous heresiological treatise aptly titled *On the Detection and Overthrow of Knowledge Falsely So-Called*, also known by the shorthand heading *Against Heresies* (*Adversus haereses*). A date for Irenaeus's birth between 130 to 140 CE satisfies his personal acquaintance with Polycarp, his succession to an episcopal chair in

---

115. For overviews on our meagre date for Irenaeus's life, see Grant, *Irenaeus of Lyons*, 1–10; Osborn, *Irenaeus of Lyons*, 1–7; Minns, *Irenaeus*, 1–3.

Lugdunum after the martyrdom of the 90-year old bishop Pothinus, and his literary activity in the late second century.[116]

Papias and Polycarp had a formative impact on Irenaeus's worldview. We saw above how Irenaeus thought that Papias had an audience with the Apostle John himself (*Adv. Haer.* 5.33.4). Many scholars defer to Irenaeus's reminiscences about Polycarp's appointment to his episcopal office by John and by the rest of the apostles (*Adv. Haer.* 3.3.4; Eusebius, *Hist. Eccl.* 5.20.5–6; 5.24.16).[117] Other scholars distrust the accuracy of Irenaeus's perceptive faculties as a "child" (*pais*),[118] but Perumalil is incredulous at the thought that a boy younger than fifteen years of age would have voyaged from Gaul or Rome to Smyrna to study with Polycarp.[119] It would not be farfetched for Irenaeus to have been a little child at the feet of Polycarp if he was reared in Asia Minor and later immigrated to Rome and then Gaul to pursue a career in rhetoric or to serve as a missionary.[120] Irenaeus accumulated vivid mental notes about Polycarp's physical appearance, discourses, mannerisms, and lifestyle over a lengthy span of time, all the way "from childhood" (*ek paidōn*) (in Eusebius, *Hist. Eccl.* 5.20.6) until his transition into adulthood (*ēlikia*) as an adolescent (*Adv. Haer.* 3.3.4).[121] Irenaeus had memories of Florinus as a childhood companion within Polycarp's circle of influence, so he

---

116. Grant (*Irenaeus of Lyons*, 2) settles for a date for Irenaeus's birth around 140 CE and his visitation of Polycarp around 155 CE, while Osborn (*Irenaeus of Lyons*, 2) prefers to date Irenaeus's birth shortly before 130 CE.

117. See Westcott, *St. John*, lxii; Morris, *John*, 16n.43; Perumalil, "Papias and Irenaeus," 336–37; Carson, *John*, 25, 68; Osborn, *Irenaeus*, 128–29, 172; Bauckham, *Eyewitnesses*, 455–57; Mutschler, "Mirror of Irenaeus of Lyons," 324–27; Shanks, *Papias*, 73–78.

118. See Barrett, *John*, 105; Schnackenburg, *St. John*, 1.79; Beasley-Murray, *John*, lxviii.

119. Perumalil, "Papias and Irenaeus," 336.

120. Minns, *Irenaeus*, 1.

121. Perumalil, "Papias and Irenaeus," 336; Mutschler, "Mirror of Irenaeus of Lyons," 325–26; Shanks, *Papias*, 74–78.

The Beloved Apostle?

was not at liberty to totally fabricate what they both had heard in the presence of Polycarp.[122]

Irenaeus christened John, the evangelist behind the Fourth Gospel (1.8.5; 2.2.5; 3.1.1; 3.11.1, 3; 5.18.2), as "the disciple of the Lord" (Greek: *ho tou kuriou mathētēs*; Latin: *discipulus Domini*). This appellation was reserved for him alone and John was mentioned about sixty times, more than the other three evangelists combined.[123] John had taken up residence in Ephesus and had lived until the rise of the Roman emperor Trajan to imperial power (2.22.5; 3.1.1). One of Polycarp's most memorable yarns about John was that he had quickly absconded from a public bathhouse when the heretic Cerinthus approached him, for he feared that the walls would collapse on everyone inside in an outpouring of divine wrath against this "enemy of the truth" (3.3.4). For the vast majority of scholars, the "disciple of the Lord" that Irenaeus had in mind was one of the twelve apostles.[124] Bauckham demurs from the consensus in supposing that the Christian residents of Asia Minor had lionized their own illustrious disciple, the Elder John, and that Irenaeus mused over Polycarp's affiliation with this individual rather than with the son of Zebedee mentioned in *Against Heresies* 2.24.4 and 3.12.3-5, 15.[125]

Lorne Zelyck has issued a cogent rebuttal against Bauckham's thesis. First, the passages where it is undeniable that "John" was a

---

122. Culpepper, *Life of a Legend*, 126; Bauckham, *Eyewitnesses*, 35; Mutschler, "Mirror," 326; Shanks, *Papias*, 76.

123. Mutschler, "Mirror of Irenaeus of Lyons," 320. See *Against Heresies* 1.8.5; 1.16.3; 2.2.5; 2.22.3; 2.22.5; 3.1.1; 3.3.4; 3.11.1; 3.11.3; 3.16.5; 3.16.8; 3.22.2; 4.20.11; 4.30.4; 5.18.2; 5.26.1; 5.33.3; 5.35.2. See also *Ecclesiastical History* 5.24.16.

124. Sanders, *Fourth Gospel*, 5; Brown, *John I-XII*, lxxxviii; Schnackenburg, *St. John*, 1.79; Barrett, *John*, 100-101; Haenchen, *John*, 1.15-16; Lindars, *John*, 29; Wiles, *Spiritual Gospel*, 9; Hengel, *Johannine Question*, 3; Murray, *John*, lxvi; Culpepper, *Life of a Legend*, 124; Osborn, *Irenaeus of Lyons*, 124; Köstenberger and Snout, "Witness, Author, Apostle," 223-25; Michaels, *John*, 7; Von Wahlde, *Gospel and Letters*, 410; Mutschler, "Mirror of Irenaeus of Lyons," 323; Zelyck, "Authorship of the Fourth Gospel," 239-58.

125. Bauckham, *Eyewitnesses*, 452-63; Bauckham, *Beloved Disciple*, 70-71; cf. Annand, "Four Gospels," 47.

member of the Twelve are due to the surrounding context where John was part of the triumvirate of Peter, James, and John in the Synoptic Gospels (2.24.4; 3.12.15) or was paired with Peter in Acts 3 and 4 (3.12.3–5). This John was never explicitly described by Irenaeus as Zebedee's son; "Zebedee" was named in a single instance when Irenaeus paraphrased the interaction that Jesus had with the mother of the "sons of Zebedee" in Matthew 20:20–22 (1.21.2) and "Zebedee" was surely the unnamed father who was deserted in his boat when the apostles were obliged to leave everything behind for Jesus (4.5.4; cf. Mark 1:20 par).[126] Second, the "disciple John" was marked as an "apostle" (1.9.2–3) and classed among the "apostles" (2.22.5; 3.3.4; 3.5.1; 3.11.9; 3.21.3). Third, Irenaeus sometimes used "disciples" interchangeably with "apostles" (1.25.2; 3.5.1).[127] Irenaeus's preference to pay homage to John as the "disciple" rather than the "apostle" of the Lord is noticeable. Yet it is the seventy-eight occurrences of *mathētēs* ("disciple") in the Fourth Gospel, in comparison to the total absence of the term *apostolos*, and the Fourth Gospel's tribute to the "disciple whom Jesus loved" that prompted Irenaeus to switch to his favorite moniker for John.[128]

When the "disciple John" seems to have been identified as an apostle, Bauckham is forced to maintain that Irenaeus coopted the title "apostle" from his Valentinian opponents who had imputed it to John (1.9.2–3) or that he realigned the title with a general conception of "apostolicity" that could be extended to John the baptizer (3.11.4), Barnabas (3.12.14), and the "Seventy" in Luke 10:1–20 (2.21.1).[129] "Barnabas" should be deleted from Bauckham's counter-examples since he was neither explicitly nor implicitly called an apostle in *Against Heresies* 3.12.14.[130] There is a notable reservation in applying the label "apostle" to John the baptizer or

---

126. Zelyck, "Authorship of the Fourth Gospel," 241–42.

127. Ibid., 252.

128. Mutschler, "Mirror of Irenaeus of Lyons," 321; Zelyck, "Authorship of the Fourth Gospel," 253.

129. See Bauckham, *Eyewitnesses*, 458–63; Bauckham, *Beloved Disciple*, 70–71.

130. Zelyck, "Authorship of the Fourth Gospel," 248.

The Beloved Apostle?

to the Seventy. Even when the logic of Irenaeus's argument seems to have been that the baptizer had been entrusted with an apostolic mission that made him superior to the prophets (3.11.4; cf. Matt 11:9; Luke 7:26; 1 Cor 12:28) or that the coded symbolism that the Valentinians culled out of the number twelve was foolish since Jesus had seventy other disciples (2.21.1), the title "apostle" seems to have been restricted to the Twelve or to Paul as "the apostle" (*ho apostolos*) par excellence.[131] The latter usage was in line with Paul's preferred self-designation (Rom 1:1; 11:3; 1 Cor 1:1; 4:9; 9:2; 15:9; 2 Cor 1:1; 12:11–12; Gal 1:1). John, the "disciple of the Lord," was the Apostle John in Irenaeus's eyes.

Irenaeus was not the first person to champion the Johannine authorship of the Fourth Gospel, but he may have been the first to defend the apostolic succession of Polycarp and Papias. Other hagiographic accounts of Polycarp's life were oblivious to the affiliation that Polycarp may have had with the Apostle John. Polycarp's reputation was built on his years of faithful service and his noble death, patterned after the Passion of Jesus in the New Testament Gospels, in the *Martyrdom of Polycarp*. He was eulogized as an "apostolic and prophet teacher" (*M. Poly.* 16.2) because he had been a guardian of the apostolic heritage of the church in Smyrna; the *Martyrdom of Polycarp* did not specify his relationship to any individual apostles.[132] In Pionius's adulatory *Life of Polycarp* (20-23), Bucolus preordained Polycarp to be his successor in the episcopal chair of Smyrna and the decision was ratified by the deacons and laity after Bucolus's demise.[133] Polycarp could have wielded much more religious capital if he was installed into his office by an apostle.

Regrettably, there was just one epistle that has not been lost out of Polycarp's extensive correspondence. Polycarp's *Letter to the Philippians* was immersed in the Pauline epistles and set up

---

131. For criticism of Bauckham along these lines, see Köstenberger and Snout, "Witness, Author, Apostle," 224-25; Watson, *Gospel Writing*, 464 n. 48; Zelyck, "Authorship of the Fourth Gospel," 248-51.

132. Contra Hill, *Johannine Corpus*, 359.

133. Barrett, *John*, 105; Casey, *Is John's Gospel True?*, 167-68.

WOULD THE REAL JOHN PLEASE STAND UP?

Paul as an exemplary figure (3.2; 9.1; 11.2-3) without uttering a word about the Apostle John or the Fourth Gospel. Now, Polycarp should not be expected to have recapped his whole autobiography in an occasional epistle and he may have been standing in solidarity with the Philippians by extolling Paul as their apostolic founder.[134] Polycarp loosely recited the Johannine Epistles when he railed against those who refused to confess the incarnation, the cross, or the final judgment and resurrection as belonging to the devil (*Phil.* 7.1; cf. 1 John 4:2-3; 5:6-8; 2 John 7), but what Hill puts forward as parallels to the Fourth Gospel are much weaker.[135] The tools at our disposal cannot verify Polycarp's knowledge of the Fourth Gospel.[136]

The quandary is that the line of apostolic succession that Irenaeus sketched from the Apostle John to Polycarp was not independently attested and could be an apologetically-motivated invention to chide Florinus for deviating from apostolic norms (*Adv. Haer.* 1.10.1; 2.9.1; 3.11.1),[137] but there are no intimations

---

134. Hengel, *Frage*, 72; Hill, *Johannine Corpus*, 416-17.

135. Hill, *Johannine Corpus*, 418-20; Hill, "'Orthodox Gospel,'" 268-69. Even if 1 John 5:6-8 was indebted to the "blood and water" in John 19:34-35 and 1 John 4:2-3 and 2 John 7 to the denunciation of the children of the devil in John 8:44, it cannot be extrapolated that Polycarp used 1 John's source text when he cited 1 and 2 John. The same applies to the admonition in *Phil.* 7.2 to return back to the word delivered from the beginning: if it is sufficient to chalk this up as a reference to 1 John (2:7, 24; 3:11) and 2 John (5), there is no need to turn to John 1:1 and 13:34 as well, even if the epistles were building on the language of the Fourth Gospel. The hope of a future resurrection (*Phil.* 5.2) was an elemental Christian doctrine and did not require John 6:40, 44, 54 to be in the background. Hill admits that the phrase "loving the brotherhood" had more in common with 1 Peter 2:17 than with John 13:34. Lastly, Hill speculates that Polycarp was the "elder" or "presbyter" who influenced Irenaeus's choice of Johannine proof-texts in *Adv. Haer.* 4.31.1 (cf. John 8:56) and 4.33.2 (cf. John 19:34-35), but there is no reason why Irenaeus would not have named him if that was the case and it may be likely that Irenaeus kept him anonymous because this person was not a bearer of the kind of ecumenical clout that Polycarp was known for (cf. Myllykoski, "Cerinthus," 230).

136. See Sanders, *Early Church*, 14; Barrett, *John*, 105; Haenchen, *John*, 1.8-9; Holmes, "Polycarp's Letter," 197-99.

137. Minns, *Irenaeus*, 135-37; Zelyck, "Authorship of the Fourth Gospel," 254-57.

The Beloved Apostle?

that Florinus accused Irenaeus of outright lying. The theory that seems to me to best satisfy all of the evidence is that Polycarp was a student of Papias's Elder John and divulged memorable incidents from the lifetime of his aged benefactor to Irenaeus when he was young, but Irenaeus mixed him up with the Apostle John who had come to be regarded as the author of the entire Johannine corpus.[138] In Ehrman's taxonomy, homonymity or the accidental confusion of individuals with the same name should be distinguished from the conscious adoption of a pseudonym.[139] There were no intentions to deceive on Irenaeus's part. The other accounts about Polycarp passed over his affiliation with the Elder John because the latter individual did not have the stature of an apostle for them to take any notice. Analogously, Eusebius (*Hist. Eccl.* 3.31.3; 5.24.2) failed to correct Polycrates error when he mixed up the evangelist Philip (cf. Acts 6:5; 8:5–6, 26–40; 21:8–9) with the Apostle Philip (cf. Mark 3:18 par; John 1:43–46; 6:5–7; 12:21–22; 14:8–9; Acts 1:13).[140] With the small pool of common Jewish names, accidental misidentifications were inevitable. Thus, we have a few more scraps of information about the Elder John: he was a resident of Ephesus, lived until the time of Trajan, and had a dramatic confrontation with Cerinthus.[141]

Although C. K. Barrett was dismissive of putting too much weight on the Elder John as an attractive yet fallacious conjecture,[142] I believe that my conjecture has more cogency than his. Barrett's hypothesis was that the Apostle John had migrated to Ephesus

---

138. Casey, *Is John's Gospel True?*, 164–69; Watson, *Gospel Writings*, 464–67; Kok, *Gospel on the Margins*, 62, 116.

139. Ehrman, *Forgery*, 47–49.

140. Shanks (*Papias*, 169) argues that the Apostle Philip could have also settled in Hierapolis and had daughters who became prophetesses, but Papias and the author of Acts seem to have shared traditions about the apostle Justus Barsabbas and the prophetic daughters of the evangelist Philip (cf. Acts 1.23; 21.8–9; *Hist. Eccl.* 3.39.9).

141. Contra Bacon, "Syriac Translator," 19. Bacon identified the Elder John as the seventh Jerusalem bishop who died in 117 CE (cf. Eusebius, *Hist. Eccl.* 4.5.3).

142. Barrett, *John*, 108.

where he trained the fourth evangelist, the "elder" of 2 John 1:1 and 3 John 1:1, and the seer of Revelation as his students.[143] In Barrett's view, the memory of Saint John of Ephesus as the evangelist sprung out of the Ephesian provenance of the Fourth Gospel.[144] Perhaps an Asia Minor provenance of the Fourth Gospel can be retained: it explains the overlapping parallels with the book of Revelation and the relatively early attestation of Johannine literature in Asia Minor. The Fourth Gospel had a huge impact on Christians in the region and was at the root of the Quartodeciman crisis over when Easter should be observed. However, the Fourth Gospel was not associated with the Apostle John until the mid-second century. Moreover, the New Testament writings and Patristic authorities preceding Irenaeus such as Ignatius of Antioch and Justin Martyr are silent about the Apostle John's ministry in Ephesus. The Ephesian tradition about the Apostle John was launched by Irenaeus, who confused the apostle with Papias's and Polycarp's Elder John who was active in Ephesus, and I will argue that Polycrates of Ephesus and the apocryphal *Acts of John* were not independent witnesses to the Irenaean tradition.[145]

To start with Polycrates, he disclosed one unusual detail that was unparalleled in Irenaeus: John, the one who reclined on the Lord's bosom and was laid to rest in Ephesus, wore the sacerdotal plate (*petalon*) of the high priest (*Hist. Eccl.* 3.31.3; 5.24.2). According to Bauckham, John 18:15 and Acts 4:6 were the textual underpinnings of Polycrates's image of John as a high priest.[146] It seems unthinkable that Polycrates would mistake the "John" who was part of the high priest's extended family with the "John" who was an apostle of Jesus when the two appear as antagonists in the trial scene in Acts 4:5-21, though J. Ramsay Michaels paid Polycrates the backhanded compliment that his "gift for muddying the

143. Ibid., 133.

144. Ibid., 28.

145. I am grateful to James Barker for reading over a preliminary draft of this chapter and encouraging me to factor the data of the *Acts of John* and its relationship to the Johannine corpus more into my proposal.

146. Bauckham, *Eyewitnesses*, 445-52; Bauckham, *Beloved Disciple*, 41-50.

The Beloved Apostle?

waters seems to know no bounds."[147] The conjoining of unrelated verses in a leap of exegetical ingenuity has ample precedent: medieval Christians spun a whole backstory about how the evangelist Mark's disfigurement disqualified him from the priesthood on the slim basis of his perplexing sobriquet *kolobodaktylos* or "stump-fingered" (Hippolytus, *Haer.* 7.18) and his kinship with the Levite Barnabas (Acts 4:36; 15:37; Col 4:10).[148]

Acts 4:6 may have not been the proof-text drawn on by Polycrates. John 18:15 may have been sufficient for him as it had the beloved disciple intermingling with those in priestly circles. Or Polycrates may have made the same moves as other exegetes who combined the names of the women at the cross, so that Zebedee's wife became Jesus' aunt (Matt 27:56; John 19:25). Further, noting that one of Mary's relatives was the priest Zechariah (Luke 1:5, 36), Polycrates may not have thought that it was a stretch that there was more than one priestly lineage within Jesus' extended family.[149] Frankly, the short excerpt from Polycrates quoted by Eusebius is far too brief to hazard a guess about what communal memories or scriptural proof-texts spurred on Polycrates to envisage John in this fashion. Bauckham may be too quick to discard the metaphoricity of the priesthood of Christian believers or of their leaders as an analogue (cf. 1 Pet 2:5, 9; Rev 1:6; 5:10; 20:6; *Did.* 13.3; Hippolytus, *Haer.* 1.proeum.6), judging the specification about the high priest's *petalon* to be an awfully obscure way of communicating that general point.[150] It is no more subtle than how the precious stones adorning the foundational walls of the New Jerusalem in Revelation 21:19-20 corresponded to the

---

147. Michaels, *John*, 9.

148. For an analysis of this various explanations for the evangelist Mark's nickname in the Anti-Marcionite and Monarchian Prologues to the second canonical Gospel, see Kok, *Margins*, 225-26.

149. See Blomberg, *Historical Reliability*, 35; Köstenberger and Stout, Witness, Author, Apostle," 223.

150. See the argument of Bauckham (*Eyewitnesses*, 447-48; *Beloved Disciple*, 47) against Braun (*Jean Le Théologien*, 339-40; cf. Schnackenburg, *St. John*, 1.81).

jewels on the high priest's breast plate.[151] Revelation 21:19-20 was a round-about way of announcing that the redeemed citizens of the heavenly city were a community of priests. Polycrates had no independent knowledge of the Elder John, but was building upon what Irenaeus had said about John resting on the Lord's chest and ending his days in Ephesus with the additional metaphor about John's priestly service.

The *Acts of John* was a composite work that was gradually enlarged over stages.[152] Chapters 18 to 86 and 106 to 115 contained tales of the Apostle John's thrilling adventures in Asia Minor and peaceful *metastasis* or "departure" in Ephesus. An older, gospel-like narrative with recognizable allusions to the calling of the disciples and the transfiguration was integrated into chapters 87—105. One of its most fascinating elements was its polymorphic Christology, in which Jesus manifested himself to different onlookers in diverse guises simultaneously (e.g., 88.5-9). It also had an idiosyncratic perspective about what the symbol of the "cross of light" evoked (98—101) and how it had nothing to do with a fleshly, vicarious sacrifice. When John fled to the Mount of Olives because he could no longer bear to look on Jesus' sufferings (97.3; cf. John 19:26-27), he saw an apparition of the Lord in a cave and the Lord reassured him that the torments that he bore on the cross were illusory (97.1—101.14). Jesus was not truly pierced with lances and reeds nor did blood flow out from him (97.3; 101.7-8, 11).

For Pieter J. Lalleman and Hill, these utterances were a polemical inversion of the plain sense of John 19:34-35.[153] Yet Richard Pervo and Harold Attridge stress that the *Acts of John* was on the radical trajectory of Johannine thought in stretching its dualistic cosmology to the limits and emphasizing the revelatory

---

151. Reader, "Twelve Jewels," 435-48.

152. For specifics about the redactional strata that were unified in the final form of the text, see Schäferdiek, "Acts of John," 157-59; Lalleman, *Acts of John*, 25-66; Hill, *Johannine Corpus*, 259; Attridge, "Acts of John," 257-58; Pervo, *Acts of John*, 3-4. I am consulting Pervo's recent translation of the *Acts of John* (pp. 28-78).

153. Lalleman, *Acts of John*, 116; Hill, *Johannine Corpus*, 260-61.

The Beloved Apostle?

nature of the cross on which Jesus was "lifted up."[154] Although Istvan Czachesz has made a valiant effort to demonstrate that this embedded Gospel was more primitive than the Fourth Gospel,[155] John's befuddlement about why Jesus felt either soft or hard as a rock when he leaned on his chest at the table (89.5–6) assumed John 13:23 and took the late identification of this character as the Apostle John for granted.[156] Czachesz stressed that the sensual overtones of this passage in the *Acts of John* were modelled on the intimacy between a teacher and a pupil in the Neo-Platonic tradition (e.g., Plato's *Symposium*), but his argument that this theme was erased from the Fourth Gospel because it offended its author's Jewish sensibilities is improbable.[157] It is more plausible that the *Acts of John* amplified the relationship between Jesus and the beloved disciple in accordance with Greek cultural mores than that the fourth evangelist left stray verses about the beloved disciple behind instead of removing the character altogether.

As for the final form of the text, its date and provenance have not been settled upon. Commentators have located it in Asia Minor,[158] Egypt,[159] or Syria.[160] The dates for it have ranged from the second quarter of the second century,[161] the mid-point of the second century,[162] the late second century,[163] and the first half of the third century.[164] Dating the text according to when polymorphic Christology might have been fashionable to the best of our knowl-

---

154. Attridge, *Acts of John*, 260–65; Pervo, *Acts of John*, 21.

155. Czachesz, "The Gospel in the Acts of John," 49–72.

156. Nagel, *Rezeption*, 270–71; Attridge, "Acts of John," 259.

157. Czachesz, "The Gospel in the Acts of John," 56–58, 65–66, 68.

158. Lalleman, *Acts of John*, 256–66.

159. Bauckham, *Eyewitnesses*, 464; Czachez, "Acts of John," 49. Czachesz argues that the final revision occurred in Alexandria, but early material may have stemmed from Asia Minor.

160. Schäferdiek, "Acts of John," 166.

161. Lalleman, *Acts of John*, 268–70; Attridge, "Acts of John," 256.

162. Braun, *Jean le Théologien*, 200–204; Hill, *Johannine Corpus*, 259.

163. Pervo, *Acts of John*, 16.

164. Schäferdiek, "Acts of John," 167.

edge seems too uncertain and teasing out the literary relationship between the five apocryphal *Acts* seems too disputed. There was no secure external reference to the *Acts of John* before Eusebius (*Eccl. Hist.* 3.25.6).¹⁶⁵ The *Acts of John* presupposed that the beloved disciple was the Apostle John, which was the result of harmonizing the four canonical Gospels, and John's travel itinerary as he journeyed from Ephesus to Smyrna may have been oriented around the letters to seven churches in Asia Minor in Revelation 2–3 (*Acts John* 56.1).¹⁶⁶ I agree with Pervo's argument that the earliest edition of the *Acts of John* cannot be dated before 190 CE on the following grounds:

> The decisive factor for dating the work is the circulation of the understanding that John the son of Zebedee wrote the fourth gospel and died a peaceful death in Ephesus, as the author seeks to capitalize on this tradition rather than propound it. The various elements of this legend emerge in the course of the second half of the second century but do not appear together before Irenaeus (approximately 180).¹⁶⁷

Conclusion: The Construction of the Ephesian John

The portrait of Saint John of Ephesus was constructed, piece by piece, from the Fourth Gospel, the Johannine Epistles, the book of Revelation, and the *Exposition of the Oracles of the Lord*. We can outline how the process unfolded step by step:

1. The Apostle John was a pillar of the messianic sect in Jerusalem, the seer John visualized the impending apocalypse on

---

165. Ibid., 152–53; contra Lalleman, *Acts of John*, 137, 151.

166. Schäferdick, "Acts of John," 164; Hengel, *Frage*, 53; Hill, *Johannine Corpus*, 259n.214 contra Lalleman, *Acts of John*, 18–19. James Barker first pointed out this detail to me.

167. Pervo, *Acts of John*, 16.

the island of Patmos, and the Elder John was a senior Christian benefactor in Ephesus who was held in high esteem.

2. Justin Martyr determined that the Apostle John was the prophet who forecasted Jesus' millennial kingdom in Revelation 20:1–6.

3. As the fourfold Gospel canon was taking shape, verses in the Synoptic and Johannine Gospels were correlated with each other and the Apostle John emerged as the beloved disciple and the fourth evangelist.

4. Both the Valentinian Ptolemy and the bishop Irenaeus were familiar with the attribution of the Fourth Gospel to the Apostle John, while Irenaeus's confusion of the Apostle John with the Elder John sparked the Ephesian tradition about the fourth evangelist.

4

Why Does The Authorship of the Fourth Gospel Matter?

THE DECISION OVER WHETHER the Fourth Gospel was compiled by an apostle appointed by Jesus himself or by a team of undistinguished editors may have larger theological ramifications. Aside from some notable ancient dissenters to the majority ruling, the Fourth Gospel, the three Johannine Epistles, and the Apocalypse all passed the criterion of apostolicity in order to be canonized. Andreas J. Köstenberger has plotted when the doubts about the apostolic origins of the Fourth Gospel began to surface among modern biblical critics in France, England, and Germany in the eighteenth and nineteenth centuries.[1] Their justifications for doubting were manifold: the detection of discrepancies between the Johannine and Synoptic chronologies or the stylistic variations within the Johannine Corpus, the deduction that there was little early external attestation for the Fourth Gospel, the supposition that the Fourth Gospel was immersed in Greek Platonic philosophy, or the adoption of Enlightenment incredulity towards age-old dogmas. As a defensive reaction against the more radical theses that the Fourth Gospel dated to the late second century and was devoid of historical substance, the Pontifical Biblical Commission

---

1. See Köstenberger, "Early Doubts of the Apostolic Authorship," 17–47; cf. Charlesworth, *Beloved Disciple*, 197–201. Köstenberger's survey goes back as far as the suggestion by the French Roman Catholic scholar Richard Simon in 1695 that the titles of the Gospels reflect their apostolic contents rather than their apostolic authorship.

103

re-affirmed that the Johannine authorship of the Fourth Gospel was non-negotiable on May 29, 1907.[2]

The stakes over the authorship of the Fourth Gospel do not have to be so dramatic. Neither the historical reliability of its sources nor the theological inspiration of its message has to be compromised for communities of faith by querying the ecclesiastical traditions that did not begin to be imputed to the Fourth Gospel until the latter half of the second century.[3] Nonetheless, this chapter will delve into the question of why there has been so much personal investment in the authorship of this text among both ancient and modern readers. If the author is a known entity, readers may bring their own expectations about what the said author would or would not have intended to communicate through the text to their reading process.

What Does an Author Do?

For some readers, the authenticity and meaning of this text is bound to the qualifications of its author. This is corroborated by the etymology of the term "author" in the word "authority," for it is entrenched in an individual's claim to possess the rights over an original literary creation.[4] To prevent misleading impressions, it must be clarified that the evangelist, whether John or someone else, was not quite an "author" in this modern sense of the term. Roland Barthes defines the "author" as the product of English empiricism, French rationalism, Reformation fideism, and capitalist ideology which is manifested in the fascination with biographies, diaries,

---

2. For discussion, see Hoskyns, *Fourth Gospel*, 24; Schnackenburg, *St. John*, 1.76; Charlesworth, *Beloved Disciple*, 203. The documents from the Pontifical Biblical Commission can be accessed in Italian and Latin at http://www.vatican.va/roman_curia/congregations/cfaith/pcb_doc_index.htm.

3. Keener (*John*, 82) rightly points out that a secondhand reporter can have access to historically verifiable information while a firsthand participant can be an inaccurate and biased reporter.

4. Vanhoozer, *Is There a Meaning*, 45.

and interviews about the "individual genius."⁵ Kevin J. Vanhoozer assents to Barthes's definition inasmuch as the conceptualization of the author as an autonomous, sovereign subject and creator of meaning is an Enlightenment invention.⁶ Patristic theologians would have recoiled at the thought that the evangelists were creative inventors of their material. It is better to speak of them as authorized performers and guarantors of the Jesus tradition.

All the same, for literary theorists who deem the author to be the locus of meaning, the text acts as a surrogate presence or extension of the author and the interpreter's goal is to recover the authorial intention.⁷ E. D. Hirsch defines verbal meaning as "whatever someone has *willed* to convey by a particular sequence of linguistic signs and which can be conveyed (shared) by means of those linguistic signs."⁸ Hirsch declares that a sequence of signs is meaningless apart from human consciousness that wills it to mean something.⁹ Aware of the pitfalls in reifying internal mental processes,¹⁰ Vanhoozer borrows the definition of a text as a concrete act of communication from a communicative agent that is embodied in writing from an approach known as "speech act theory."¹¹ He expands on how "[a] text is a complex communicative act with *matter* (propositional content), *energy* (illocutionary force), and *purpose* (perlocutionary effect)."¹² Much of biblical scholarship is driven by author-centered approaches as it enquires about what "John" intended to communicate in his socio-historical

---

5. Barthes, "Death of the Author," 142–43.

6. Vanhoozer, *Is There a Meaning*, 45. Vanhoozer summarizes the "secularization thesis" that the attributes previously granted to the divine became transferred to the human individual in modernity.

7. Vanhoozer, *Is There a Meaning*, 43–44.

8. Hirsch, *Validity in Interpretation*, 31, emphasis mine. Hirsch expands on this definition when he discusses how communication cannot occur unless the meaning is shareable and the interpreter can render the author's categories intelligible based on his or her prior experience on pp. 66–67.

9. Ibid., 3.

10. Vanhoozer, *Is There a Meaning*, 83, 220, 231.

11. Ibid., 225, 231, 253.

12. Ibid., 228.

context. Kyle Keefer reckons that post-eighteenth century exegetes generally steered clear of the Patristic interpretations of biblical writings because they did not erect an unambiguous wall between exegesis and eisegesis, between drawing out meaning from a text or imputing meaning into it.[13]

Some literary theorists have serious reservations about the accessibility and feasibility of capturing the authorial intention, especially for ancient persons who are no longer around to be interrogated. Besides, there may be a surplus of meaning encoded into the text that had escaped the author's conscious perception.[14] Hirsch's rebuttal to these arguments has a few nuances. The author's intended "meaning" is fixed in the text, but an author may not have total command of the subject matter and may be unaware of all the implications of his or her argument in relation to the terminology or concepts he or she has utilized.[15] The "significance" of a literary work will also be constantly revised as it enters into dialogue with ever-changing historical, social, and political circumstances.[16] Vanhoozer carves out a comparable distinction between the past communicative action and its resultant effects, whether foreseen or unintended.[17]

There may be another fallacy in locating meaning in the biography of the author. In their well-known explication of the "intentionalist fallacy," W. K. Wimsatt and Monroe C. Beardsley examine how literary critics appraise a poem by studying its internal linguistic features, inquiring about the biography of the poet, or checking the denotative and connotative meanings of words in their cultural milieu. It is illegitimate, they aver, to conjure up the textual meaning by consulting private oracles about the psychological makeup of the poet rather than the publicly available semantic and syntactic structures of the poem itself.[18] This has encouraged

13. Keefer, *Branches*, 5
14. Bockmuehl, *Seeing the Word*, 41.
15. Hirsch, *Validity*, 20–21, 57–61.
16. Ibid., 8–10, 63.
17. Vanhoozer, *Meaning*, 261.
18. Wimsatt and Beardsley, "Intentional Fallacy," 10, 11, 18; cf. Barthes,

narrative critics to bracket the tentative historical reconstructions of the world behind the text in favor of closely attending to the linguistic and structure elements of the text itself. Markus Bockmuehl also affirms that a text envisions a model or ideal reader who, in the case of the Fourth Gospel, is an ecclesiastically-situated convert invested in the truth claims therein (John 20:30–31).[19]

Roland Barthes destabilized the text along with the author. For him, a text is "a tissue of quotations drawn from the innumerable centres of culture," a web of intertextual references to prior writings re-arranged in a fresh pattern and expressed in an antecedent system of signs beyond the author's control, so textual meanings are endlessly deferred.[20] He advocates for the "reader" as the final arbiter of meaning: the reader has a bird's-eye perspective of the multiplicity of textual meanings whose unity is to be found in its destination rather than its origin.[21] Some literary critics might cringe at the prospect that meaning is governed by the subjective whims of an idiosyncratic reader, but Stanley Fish rebuts the charge of subjectivism by denying that an individual subject ever stands outside any one interpretive community at a time with its shared assumptions, norms, and values that enable his or her understanding.[22] It is the collective and normative interpretive strategies of the community, according to Fish, that constitute the properties of the text and assign them intentions.[23] A finite number of interpretive strategies are certified by a literary institution, so eccentric readings are not permitted if there is no elaborated interpretive procedure for constituting the text in such a fashion.[24]

Anthony Thiselton faults Fish's approach for undermining the hermeneutical ideal of a fusion of the horizons of the text and

---

"Death," 143.

19. Bockmuehl, *Seeing the Word*, 68–72.
20. Barthes, "Death of the Author," 146–47.
21. Ibid., 148.
22. Fish, *Interpretive Communities*, 319–20.
23. Ibid., 171.
24. Ibid., 342, 345–49.

the interpreter, so that texts have the power to transform readers and confront dominant ideologies as much as readers bring their interpretive questions to bear on texts.[25] Hans Robert Jauss developed the "fusion of the horizons" model by focusing on the objectifiable horizon of expectations that a reader builds up from his or her past reading experience and that is endlessly malleable as a new text confirms, surpasses, frustrates, or refutes the reader's expectations.[26] A text is not a timeless repository of aesthetic properties, for it has ongoing effects so long as readers continue to bring its latent capabilities to fruition and successively build on the readings preceding them over the course of history.[27]

The hermeneutical debate over where meaning resides—the author, the text, or the reader—has not abated. Chastened by these critiques, the defenders of authorial intention concede that certainty is elusive in the efforts to approximate the author's intended meanings and that the lens that readers bring to the act of interpretation are contextually-bound.[28] Still, Hirsch worries that banishing the author cedes the lone sound principle for adjudicating the validity of conflicting readings.[29] Barthes, who chiselled the epitaph on the author, welcomes this brave new world when he opines that "[t]o give a text an Author is to impose a limit on that text, to furnish it with a final signified, to close the writing."[30] Or, as Michel Foucault puts it, "[t]he author therefore is the ideological figure by which one marks the manner in which we fear the proliferation of meaning."[31] If the author is subtracted from the equation, readers will search for other devices to delineate the

---

25. Thiselton, *New Horizons*, 539–46. Thiselton is borrowing an image from Gadamer, *Truth and Method*, 305.

26. See the second and third theses in Jauss, *Aesthetic of Reception*, 22–27. The "horizon of expectations" could include the reader's pre-understanding of genre, textual forms and themes, and aesthetic tastes.

27. Jauss, *Aesthetic of Reception*, 19–20; cf. Keefer, *Branches*, 10–12.

28. Hirsch, *Validity of Interpretation*, 16–17; Vanhoozer, *Is There a Meaning*, 184.

29. Ibid., 3.

30. Barthes, "Death," 147

31. Foucault, "What is an Author," 222.

limits of the text and other controls for interpretation.³² Hence, theorists can come to an agreement on what the "authorial function" is supposed to accomplish. Foucault expounds on how the classification of a text under a reputable name bestows a seal of authenticity and a definite status on it in a given society based on the social and cultural capital of the author.³³ Additionally, it presumes a degree of internal homogeneity within a text as well as its conformity with related works in the authorial corpus.³⁴ Foucault parallels these modern ideas about authorship to Saint Jerome's criteria for discriminating between authentic and pseudonymous writings: consistent literary quality, conceptual or theoretical coherence, and stylistic uniformity, along with the absence of historical anachronisms.³⁵ Ultimately, for Foucault, the "author function" is a discourse about the ownership of a text.³⁶

The Criterion of Apostolicity

This theoretical foundation is germane to the deliberations over the apostolic credentials of the Gospels in the Patristic period. As the memoirs about Jesus by his apostolic successors, Justin Martyr mined the Gospels for historical information.³⁷ Irenaeus turned his readers' attention from the "apostles" as a collective body to the biographies of the individual evangelists. Denis M. Farkasfalvy and

---

32. I am grateful to Hannah M. Strømmen for pointing out to me that Foucault, unlike Barthes, did not simply seek to do away with the "authorial function" as much as to engage how it works as a controlling and limiting device (see ibid., 209, 211).

33. Ibid., 211. See also the discussion of economic, social, and cultural capital in Bourdieu, "Forms of Capital," 46–58.

34. Foucault, "What is an Author," 211.

35. Ibid., 214.

36. Ibid., 212.

37. Although I agree that Justin employed the memoirs as historical sources (cf. Gamble, *New Testament Canon*, 28–29; Campenhausen, *Christian Bible*, 168; Koester, *Ancient Christian Gospels*, 41–42), the liturgical reading of the memoirs alongside the "prophets" during Sunday worship services should not be underestimated (cf. *1 Apol.* 67.3).

The Beloved Apostle?

Tomas Bokedal elevate apostolicity to Irenaeus's primary benchmark for regulating which books and doctrines should be backed as normative.[38] The criteria espoused for delimiting the contents of the Christian canon in the fourth century were apostolicity, orthodoxy, antiquity, and catholicity.[39] Eusebius branded Christian writings as "accepted" (*homologoumena*), "disputed" (*antilegomena*), or "spurious" (*notha*) partly on the basis of their authorship and discredited non-canonical Gospels and Acts under the names of various apostles as forgeries (cf. *Hist. Eccl.* 3.25.1–7). Bruce Metzger explains that "apostolic origin, real or putative, of a book provided a presumption of authority."[40]

Undoubtedly, apostolic authorship was not an absolute requirement for canonization, nor was this criterion applied in isolation from the rest of the tests put to the documents.[41] The evangelists Mark and Luke were not remembered as apostles themselves, but as associates of the apostles Peter and Paul who mediated their kerygmatic proclamations in their Gospels. Although the epistle to the Hebrews was accepted as a Pauline writing by numerous Christians, especially among the eastern churches, it did not commend itself as Pauline to some of the Christians in Rome (cf. Eusebius, *Hist. Eccl.* 3.3.5; 6.25.14). Christian intellectuals such as Origen (in *Hist. Eccl.* 6.25.11–14) or Jerome (*Epist.* 129) were hesitant about its unsubstantiated Pauline authorship, but they valued the epistle for its concord with apostolic doctrine and its long history of usage.[42] Even so, Tertullian depreciated Marcion's

---

38. Farmer and Farkasfalvy, *Ecumenical Approach*, 144; Bokedal, *Christian Biblical Canon*, 68, 249–50.

39. For overviews of the four criteria, see Grant, *New Testament*, 181–87; Bruce, *Canon of Scripture*, 256–63; Gamble, *New Testament Canon*, 67–72; Metzger, *Canon*, 251–54; MacDonald, *Biblical Canon*, 405–20.

40. Metzger, *Canon*, 103. Macdonald (*Biblical Canon*, 407) adds, "In this sense, apostolicity insured acceptance."

41. Campenhausen, *Christian Bible*, 204–5, 330; Farmer and Farkasfalvy, *Ecumenical Approach*, 148; Gamble, *New Testament Canon*, 68; Macdonald, *Biblical Canon*, 411.

42. Campenhausen, *Christian Bible*, 232–33; Bruce, *Canon of Scripture*, 258; Gamble, *New Testament Canon*, 50; Metzger, *Canon*, 253; MacDonald,

Why Does the Authorship of the Fourth Gospel Matter?

Gospel by belittling the evangelist Luke as a subordinate "apostolic man" (*Marc.* 4.2.4).[43]

The category "apostles," therefore, functioned as a theologoumenon, much like the heading "prophets" did for the Jewish Scriptures.[44] The crucial matter was that the Christian canon was designed to mediate the effects that the Christ event had on the original founders of the Christ movement in a stable textual form, to prevent their pronouncements from getting distorted beyond recognition in an era beyond their lifetimes.[45] Taking apostolicity in the broadest sense, Tomas Bokedal elucidates the *raison d'être* of the canon as "an act of continuous preservation and actualization of the church's foundational literary tradition, for the sake of mediating continuity with apostolic Christianity, historic and contemporary."[46]

One obstacle that the canon-makers faced was how to weed out the writings that were pseudonymously ascribed to one of the apostolic founders. In the case of Serapion of Antioch, he tolerated devotional meditations on the *Gospel of Peter* within a Christian assembly in Rhossus in Syria. Upon further study of its alleged "Docetic" Christology that negated the humanity of Jesus, Serapion censured this Gospel (cf. *Hist. Eccl.* 6.12.2).[47] Lee Martin Macdonald judges that "[i]n this example, apostolicity and antiquity

---

Biblical Canon, 408, 414.

43. Macdonald, *Biblical Canon,* 407.

44. Farmer and Farkasfalvy, *Ecumenical Approach,* 123.

45. Grant, *New Testament,* 184–85; Farmer and Farkasfalvy, *Ecumenical Approach,* 146–48; Gamble, *New Testament Canon,* 58; Macdonald, *Biblical Canon,* 411; Bokedal, *Christian Biblical Canon,* 166.

46. Bokedal, *Christian Biblical Canon,* 9.

47. For discussion about this incident, see Grant, *New Testament,* 149; Campenhausen, *Christian Bible,* 169, 174; Farmer and Farkasfalvy, *Ecumenical Approach,* 29–30. Bruce, *Canon of Scripture,* 201, 260–61; Gamble, *New Testament Canon,* 50; Metzger, *Canon,* 119–20, 172; MacDonald, *Biblical Canon,* 410. For the inadequacy of "Docetism" as a label summarizing the Christology of the *Akhmîm* fragment, which is generally identified with the *Gospel of Peter,* see Head, "Gospel of Peter," 209–24.

The Beloved Apostle?

evidently took a back seat to the criterion of truth."[48] However, my perspective on this incident is that the criteria of truth and apostolicity were inseparable; Serapion repudiated that the Apostle Peter would have had anything to do with a text that had a supposedly aberrant Christology that deviated from the apostolic norms. The causal link between apostolicity and orthodoxy was self-evident to Serapion because of his theological conviction that the *monepiskopos* was the apostles' duly appointed successor, the custodian of the "rule of faith" passed down over successive generations.

The ideology of "apostolic succession" furnished the basic controls for interpretation. The *kanōn* or the "rule" of faith was the appropriate lens for deciphering the apostolic archives. This public rule of faith had to be handed down approved channels; the *episkopoi* or superintending bishops of the Christian assemblies in a local jurisdiction had to be part of an official line of succession stretching back to an apostle. Irenaeus displayed the official succession list of the Roman See (3.3.2-3); he did not do so because the church in Rome was pre-eminent over every other locale, but because it was tedious to run through multiple ecclesial lists and the Roman Christian congregations had a stellar pedigree from two leading apostles.[49] If Peter and Paul inaugurated the line of "apostolic succession" in Rome, the episcopal succession in Asia Minor passed through the apostle John to Polycarp and Papias in Smyrna and Hierapolis respectively (cf. *Adv. Haer.* 3.3.4; 5.33.4; Eusebius, *Hist. Eccl.* 5.20.5-6; 5.24.16). The successors of the apostles were in the best position to pontificate on the apostolic texts.

What kind of cultural capital did the Fourth Gospel acquire by getting associated with the Apostle John? As the written testimony of an outstanding representative of the "Twelve" and of the "Pillars" headquartered in the Jerusalem mother church (cf. Mark 3:13-19 par; John 6:67-71; Acts 1:13-26; 1 Cor 15:5; Gal 2:6-10), the Fourth Gospel set the bar for what Christian beliefs and practices had to measure up to. The Fourth Gospel was stamped with an apostolic seal of approval and sanctioned for use among the

48. Macdonald, *Biblical Canon*, 410.
49. See Osborn, *Irenaeus*, 147; Minns, *Irenaeus*, 138-39.

Christian laity. Moreover, the inclusion of other writings in a "Johannine corpus" enabled the reciprocal explication of all the writings contained within it. No matter how high the Christological rhetoric of the Fourth Gospel soars, it cannot be detached from the full reality of Jesus' incarnation in the "flesh" (*sarx*) and of his blood that he spilled in his vicarious sacrifice (1 John 2:2; 4:2; 5:6; 2 John 7; cf. John 1:14; 19:3). The mostly realized eschatology of the Fourth Gospel was to be held in tension with Revelation's futurist apocalyptic scenario. On the other hand, some Patristic scholars who unreservedly endorsed the apostolicity of the Fourth Gospel were reluctant to attribute the shorter epistles (cf. Jerome, *Vir. il.* 18) or the Apocalypse (cf. Dionysius of Alexandria, in *Hist. Eccl.* 7.25) to the Apostle John.

Possession of the apostolic archives could not overcome the fundamental challenge of interpretive pluralism. The differing purposes and goals of interpretive communities routinely dictate their reading strategies.[50] Take, for instance, the "New Prophecy" heralded by Montanus, Prisca, and Maximilla that swept through the province of Phrygia in the latter half of the second century. For the partisans supporting this prophetic trio, their charisms were gifts from the "Paraclete" (*paraklētos*) or "Advocate" who leads believers into all truth (John 14:16–17, 26; cf. Tertullian, *Prax.* 1. 30; *Jejun* 1, 12; *Mon.* 14). Nor did the Valentinian Ptolemy's agreement that the fourth evangelist was the "disciple John" stop him from turning the Johannine Prologue into fodder for his cosmogonic myth about a series of divine emanations that, in effect, divorced the highest transcendent deity in the spiritual realm known as the *plērōma* or "fullness" from the ignorant "demiurge" or "craftsman" of the physical world (*Adv. Haer.* 1.8.5). Irenaeus ruthlessly lampooned the Valentinians' fanciful etymologies and context-less scriptural proof-texts (1.4.4; 1.9.4; 1.11.4).[51] Worse, he grumbled that they strayed from the publicly accessible rule of faith. Unlike the Valentinians' eccentric, atomistic exegesis, hermeneutics for

---

50. Fish, *Interpretive Communities*, 15.

51. For an analysis of Irenaeus's parodies of his Valentinian opponents, see Osborn, *Irenaeus*, 157–59.

Irenaeus was a corporate, ecclesiastical affair (cf. 4.26.2; 4.21.3).[52] What made Irenaeus a more trustworthy exegete of the Fourth Gospel was his indirect connection with the Apostle John through his previous relationship to Polycarp.

The Gospel according to Cerinthus?

There was a recurring accusation that one or more of the Johannine writings were forged by the arch-heretic Cerinthus (cf. Eusebius, *Hist. Eccl.* 3.28.2, 4–5; 7.25.3; Epiphanius, *Pan.* 51.3.6, 4.1–2; Dionysius bar Salibi, *Comm. Apoc.* 1–2).[53] This minority authorial tradition deserves a fresh hearing. Our predicament is that Cerinthus did not leave any writings behind and his actual theology must be filtered through the polemical distortions of his adversaries. In the first strand of polemic, Cerinthus taught that the material cosmos was designed by an inferior power and that Jesus was an ordinary human born through the intercourse of Mary and Joseph who was selected to be the vessel for an impassible pneumatic entity called "Christ" (cf. Irenaeus, *Adv. Haer.* 1.26.1; Hippolytus, *Haer.* 7.33.1–2; 10.21.1–3).[54] The second strand of polemic from Gaius of Rome and Dionysius of Alexandria was that Cerinthus dreamt up a millennial paradise brimming with sensual delights (cf. Eusebius, *Hist. Eccl.* 3.28.2, 4–5; 7.25.3). Because Irenaeus likened Cerinthus's Christology to that of the Jewish Christian sect known as the Ebionites or the "poor ones" (*Adv. Haer.* 1.26.2), the fourth-century heresiologist Epiphanius of Salamis contrived a whole biography for Cerinthus as a full-fledged

---

52. Minns, *Irenaeus*, 135–37; Osborn, *Irenaeus*, 146; Thiselton, *New Horizons*, 146–56, 166. However, Kyle Keefer (*Branches*, 51) notes that Irenaeus did not explicitly reflect upon his own hermeneutical methodology and describes Irenaeus's hermeneutics as pragmatic.

53. For a historical survey of critical scholarship on Cerinthus, see Hill, "Gnostic or Chiliast," 140–43; Myllykoski, "Cerinthus," 221–24.

54. Schnelle, *Antidocetic Christology*, 69–70; Hengel, *Johannine Question*, 59–61; Hengel, *Frage*, 176–77, 177n76; Hill, "Gnostic or Chiliast," 149–59; Myllykoski, "Cerinthus," 225–36.

WHY DOES THE AUTHORSHIP OF THE FOURTH GOSPEL MATTER?

Judaist Christian who thwarted the *Torah*-free Gentile mission at every turn (cf. *Pan.* 28.2, 4, 5).[55] Ostensibly, a deprecation of the physical creation and a thisworldly millennialism are contradictory. The tension between these two positions could be alleviated if Cerinthus, like Marcion (cf. Tertullian, *Marc.* 3.4, 21, 24; 4.6), expected that the inferior creator deity or demiurge would fulfill the Hebrew prophecies about the restoration of the Jewish nation and the resumption of the temple cult during the millennium, whereas the spiritual salvation unveiled by Jesus for his elect had the ethereal goal of liberation from materiality altogether.[56] Another possibility is that Irenaeus wrongly allied Cerinthus with the demiurgical theology of the Valentinians, albeit in an embryonic form, because they both had a "possessionist" and diphysite Christology where a celestial entity indwelled in the human Jesus from the moment of his baptism.[57] If that is the case, Cerinthus may have been a proponent of a more primitive Christology and a more literalist eschatology that some of his Christian peers decried as unacceptable. In either scenario, Cerinthus's outlook was caricatured.

Why would anyone have given credence to the Cerinthian authorship of the Johannine literature? An effective method to debunk Cerinthus's chiliastic excesses may have been to attack it at its root in Revelation 20:1–6. As for the Fourth Gospel, perhaps there was anxiety over the verses that might be exploited by someone who was swayed by Cerinthus's views.[58] Did Jesus' disclosure of a heavenly Father whom no one had ascended to nor seen (John 1:18; 3:13; 5:37; 6:46) and his denunciations of his interlocutors as children of a diabolical father (8:44) lend itself to a demiurgical theology? Was the soteriological dualism where the light invaded

---

55. Hill, "Gnostic or Chiliast," 143–49; Manor, "Epiphanius' *Alogi*," 99–100; Myllykoski, "Cerinthus," 218–20, 244.

56. See Hill, "Gnostic or Chiliast," 159–70.

57. See Myllykoski, "Cerinthus," 232–36, 240–45.

58. For exegesis along these following lines, see Pagels, *Gnostic Exegesis*; Lattke, "Gnostic Jesus of John," 151–52; Sloyan, "Gnostic Adoption," 129; Rasimus, "Ptolemaeus," 158–69; DeConick, "Catholic-Gnostic Debate."

a world plunged in darkness (1:4–5; 3:19–21; 8:12; 9:15; 11:9–10; 12:35–36) transmuted into a cosmological dualism between spirit and matter? Did the omission of Jesus' miraculous conception, along with John the baptizer's vision of the divine Spirit descending on the adult Jesus (1:32–34), open the door for taking the enfleshment of the heavenly *logos* in John 1:14 in a "possessionist" rather than in an "incarnational" sense?

Then again, the actual complaints that were levelled in the ancient sources were against the chiliasm and obscure symbols of Revelation and the chronological difficulties in the Fourth Gospel, with nary a word breathed about the Fourth Gospel's theological difficulties.[59] If the objective was to impugn the integrity of the Johannine literature by any means necessary, would any loathed sectarian have done the trick, or were the original intentions behind tying this corpus specifically with Cerinthus forgotten? It would help to discover who was the first to demean the Johannine writings in this fashion. A full exploration of the Patristic and medieval Syriac texts on this subject would take us beyond the scope of this monograph, so a brief overview will have to suffice.[60] The comprehensive doctoral dissertation by Joseph Daniel Smith Jr. is illustrative of the older synthesis that the irreproachably orthodox presbyter, Gaius of Rome, ran a concerted campaign against Montanism and assailed the Johannine corpus because it was the Montanist's textual underpinnings.[61] Allen Brent, Charles C. Hill, and T. Scott Manor have deconstructed this synthesis piece by piece.[62] Nonetheless, they are all remarkably in agreement that Gaius did not go as far as to vilify the author of Revelation or the Fourth Gospel as a forger.[63]

59. Hill, *Johannine Corpus*, 176–77; 191–92; Hill, "'Orthodox Gospel,'" 264, 264–65n90; cf. Culpepper, *Life of a Legend*, 121.

60. For a history of scholarship on this subject, see Smith, *Gaius*, 13–115, Hill, *Johannine Corpus*, 172–90; Manor, "Epiphanius' *Alogi*," 19–44, 197–211.

61. Smith, "Gaius."

62. Brent, *Hippolytus*, 133–84; Hill, *Johannine Corpus*, 172–204; Manor, "Epiphanius' *Alogi*;" Manor, "Papias, Origen, and Eusebius," 15–21.

63. See Smith, "Gaius," 170, 324–27; Brent, *Hippolytus*, 133–37, 140–41, 144, 146; Hill, *Johannine Corpus*, 174–75, 177, 182, 191–92; Manor,

Why Does The Authorship of the Fourth Gospel Matter?

To begin with the chronologically oldest data, Irenaeus railed against "others" (*alii*) who discounted the blessing of the Paraclete in John 14:16 (cf. *Adv. Haer.* 3.11.9). For Smith, Irenaeus's indictment of anonymous "others" conceals that Gaius was his true target and was not named out of respect for his ecclesiastical rank.[64] This does not line up with Eusebius's dating of Gaius and his dialogue partner, the Montanist Proclus, during the pontificate of Zephyrinus between 199 to 217 CE (*Hist. Eccl.* 2.25.6–7; 3.31.4 6.20.3).[65] In fact, Gaius was not ranked as a "bishop" (*episkopos*) until the ninth century when Photios I, the Ecumenical Patriarch of Constantinople, gathered that Gaius was a "bishop of the nations" from a dubious note in the margins of a book entitled *On the Essence of the Universe* (cf. *Bibl.* 48).[66] Nor was this a polite squabble among friendly colleagues; Irenaeus's *alii* committed the unforgivable sin against the Holy Spirit.[67] They may not have unequivocally rebuffed the Fourth Gospel, but their contempt for the Paraclete had practically the same effect.[68] I am not persuaded by Hill's conflation of the *alii* in 3.11.9 with the schismatics who were partial to a possessionist Christology in 3.11.7 on the slim basis that Irenaeus sandwiches an anonymous group between Marcion and the Valentinians in both 3.11.7 and 3.11.9.[69] It is not their Christology, but their pneumatology, that merited Irenaeus's disdain. Maybe the *alii* confined the gift of the Paraclete to the

---

"Epiphanius *Alogi*," 167, 221–37.

64. Smith, 'Gaius," 141–68; Cf. Culpepper, *Life of a Legend*, 121.

65. For a defense of this dating, see Manor, "Epiphanius *Alogi*," 180–84.

66. Brent, *Hippolytus*, 131–33; Hill, *Johannine Corpus*, 195–98; Manor, "Epiphanius *Alogi*," 179–80. They explain that Gaius was either confused with the presbyter Hippolytus of Rome or that the work entitled *The Labyrinth* which is now a part of the tenth book of Hippolytus's *Refutation of All Heresies* was misattributed to Gaius to make Gaius a "counselor" to a variety of ethnic groups (cf. *Haer.* 10.34.1).

67. Hill, *Johannine Corpus*, 112.

68. Brent, *Hippolytus*, 139; Manor, "Epiphanius' *Alogi*," 97.

69. Hill, *Johannine Corpus*, 111–17, 173–74, 191.

apostolic age, but the drive to tame charismatic enthusiasm need not be motivated by anti-Montanist animus.[70]

Next, Eusebius quotes Gaius of Rome and Dionysius of Alexandria. Gaius reviled Cerinthus for pretending that he acquired the revelations of a "great apostle" about a thousand years of lavish marriage festivities in Jerusalem (3.28.2). Since the apostle is not named and the wording and ideas in this excerpt are not a perfect match to the lamb's wedding feast and the millennium in Revelation 19:9 and 20:1-6, Cerinthus may have peddled his own forged apocalyptic work.[71] This is what Theodoret of Cyus (393-458 CE) maintained in his *Compendium of Heretical Fables* (*Haer. Fab.* 3.3). However, Revelation's apostolicity was presupposed since Justin Martyr (*Dial.* 81.4) and Gaius presented a caricature rather than an impartial description of either Cerinthus's viewpoint or his source text. It is probable that Gaius was a vocal detractor of Revelation. A link between Revelation and the "Gaian heresy," if that is the text-critically correct reading, may be as old as Tertullian (*de praes. haer.* 33. 10).[72]

Dionysius of Alexandria (190-248 CE) was a critic of chiliasm too, but he could tolerate an otherwise orthodox Egyptian bishop, Nepos, who had been perturbed by his fellow Alexandrians for allegorizing away the literal prophecies of Revelation (3.24.1-9). When Dionysius had Cerinthus in his sights, he exaggerated the carnal pleasures and cultic imagery of Cerinthus's millennium (3.28.4-5; 7.25.3). Although mindful of the grave suspicions out there that Revelation was pseudonymous (7.25.2), Dionysius did not distrust that some holy person named John was the recipient of the visions as long as they were decrypted through his allegorical hermeneutic (7.25.4-7). Smith posits that Gaius's *Dialogue with Proclus* was Dionysius's written source for the chatter from

---

70. Brent, *Hippolytus*, 139; Hill, *Johannine Corpus*, 111-12; Manor, "Epiphanius' *Alogi*," 96, 98, 190-91.

71. Smith, "Gaius," 181-82; Hill, *Johannine Corpus*, 174; Brent, *Hippolytus*, 134; Manor, "Epiphanius' *Alogi*," 153-56.

72. See Hill, *Johannine Corpus*, 200-203.

Why Does The Authorship of the Fourth Gospel Matter?

"certain people" (*tina*) about Revelation's authorship.[73] It may be the effect of Eusebius's juxtaposition of Gaius's and Dionysius's critiques against millennialism that gives the misleading impression that one was dependent on the other.[74] Dionysius can be taken at face value: the sneaking suspicions of some Alexandrian Christians that Cerinthus penned Revelation 20:1–6 was an overreaction against bishop Nepos.[75]

The slander about Revelation's Cerinthian origins was independently attested by Gaius in Rome and Dionysius in Alexandria. Neither quotation extends the allegation to the Fourth Gospel. Eusebius may have suppressed a hostile view about the Fourth Gospel, but his censors were less sensitive to a smear against Revelation since he was ambivalent about whether it should be categorized as acceptable or spurious (*Hist. Eccl.* 3.25.2, 4).[76] Eusebius admitted that Gaius excluded the epistle to the Hebrews from the canon of Pauline epistles (6.20.3)—a stance that was not beyond the pale in Eusebius's day (3.3.5)—but he may not have complimented Gaius as a "learned churchman" (*ekklēsiastikos anēr*) if Gaius had maligned a canonical Gospel in his *Dialogue Against Proclus*.[77] It is unclear whether Eusebius was aware that the Fourth Gospel had been lumped together with Revelation as fakes by Cerinthus, but Epiphanius of Salamis was crystal clear that the *Alogi* touted this inflammatory charge (cf. *Pan.* 51.3.6).

Epiphanius's tome *Panarion* was a "treasure chest" of medicinal cures for the poisonous stings of heresy and he devoted his fifty-first section to the *Alogi*, a sect dated shortly after all the fuss over the dating of Easter (i.e., the Quartodeciman crisis) in the late second century. The corroboration for a group resembling the

73. Smith, "Gaius," 184–90.

74. Brent, *Hippolytus*, 134–37; Hill, *Johannine Corpus*, 175; Manor, "Epiphanius' *Alogi*, 152.

75. Manor, "Epiphanius' *Alogi*," 157–58.

76. Smith, "Gaius," 191–92; Hengel, *Johannine Question*, 6; Hengel, *Frage*, 87; Bauckham, *Beloved Disciple*, 35, 56–58; Watson, *Gospel Writing*, 486; Kok, *Margins*, 180–81.

77. Brent, *Hippolytus*, 148; Hill, *Johannine Corpus*, 193; Manor, "Epiphanius's *Alogi*," 185–89; Manor, "Papias, Origen, and Eusebius," 17.

Alogi at this date is non-existent.[78] Epiphanius coined this label for them, for those who willingly deprived themselves of the discourses of the Johannine *logos* were, frankly, illogical (51.3.1–3). Their protestations were that the wedding hosted in Cana soon after Jesus' baptism in John 2:1 was not easy to mesh with the Synoptics on Jesus' wilderness temptations over forty days (*Pan.* 51.4.9–10; 51.21.15–16; cf. Matt 4:1–11; Mark 1:12–13; Luke 4:1–13), that the Fourth Gospel doubled the Passover festivals that Jesus attended (51.22.1), and that Revelation has nonsensical symbolism of angels and trumpets (51.32.2; 51.34.2–3). Notably missing are the Montanist themes on spiritual charisms or church offices and hierarchies.[79] There may be one allusion to Montanism, though, in the denial of the *Alogi* that there was a church in Thyatira (contra Rev 2:18) ever since the Phrygians infiltrated it and caused a mass apostasy (51.33.1–3).[80]

Smith again reduced the membership of the *Alogi* to a solitary enthusiast, Gaius of Rome.[81] As we will see below, "Gaius" acts as a spokesperson for a comparable laundry list of grievances about Revelation and the Fourth Gospel in the Syriac evidence dating to the twelfth century. Instead of letting data removed from Epiphanius by approximately eight centuries set the agenda, an alternate hypothesis is that Epiphanius invented a composite

---

78. Manor, "Epiphanius' *Alogi*," 13; Manor, "Papias, Origen, and Eusebius," 18–19.

79. Brent, *Hippolytus*, 138, 143.

80. Brent (ibid., 142–43) argues that it was the Montanists themselves who spurned Revelation because Revelation 2:18 was used as a Catholic proof-text against them. Yet the logic of the section is that the Phrygians converted the whole town to the Montanist heresy, precipitating the *Alogi's* objection that the apostasy of the church in Thyatira falsifies Revelation 2:18, so it is more likely that Epiphanius has shifted the subject from the Phrygians back to the *Alogi* when speaking about "the ones" (*hoi*) who repudiated the Apocalypse. Manor ("Epiphanius' *Alogi*," 164) argues that the point about Thyatira echoes the kind of geographical corrections that an informed textual critic like Origen might make to a biblical text, but the point cannot be evaded that the observation that there was no church in Thyatira is premised on the denial that the Montanists constituted a true church.

81. Smith, *Gaius*, 137, 168, 265–66, 427, 249.

"heresy" out of the preceding apologies for the Johannine corpus from Irenaeus of Lyon, Dionysius of Alexandria, Origen of Alexandria, and Eusebius of Caesarea, along with the criticisms of it from the non-Christian Greek philosophers Celsus, Porphyry, and Philosabbatius (cf. *Pan.* 51.8.1).[82] If this is correct, it does not mean that Epiphanius extrapolated the Cerinthian authorship of the whole Johannine corpus from the more limited authorship of Revelation or amalgamated Irenaeus's Johannophobes with Dionysius's anti-Revelation allegorists.[83] He may have genuinely heard a rumor that Cerinthus was behind the Fourth Gospel from his sources, a rumor that struck him as absurd given what the Fourth Gospel promulgated about the eternality of the *logos* (51.4.1–2), so he concentrated his energy on the controversies over the Johannine chronology.

Starting in 1888, a flood of new data about "Gaius" burst onto the scene that altered the perception of Gaius from a "learned churchman" to a "heretic." The Syriacist John Gwynn published five fragments from a *Commentary on the Apocalypse* by Dionysius bar Salibi, the twelfth century Jacobite bishop of Amid.[84] All five fragments exhibited a condensed objection from the "heretic Gaius" (*Caius haereticus*) and a rebuttal from "Hippolytus of Rome" over Revelation's compatibility with other scriptural eschatologies. Like the *Alogi*, bar Salibi's "Gaius" groused about the avenging angels released to slaughter a third of humankind in Revelation 9:15; like Epiphanius, bar Salibi's "Hippolytus" reached for Deuteronomy 32:8 to demonstrate the indissoluble connection between angels and nations (cf. Epiphanius, *Pan.* 51.34.2–8; Bar Salibi, *Comm. Apoc.* 10).[85] Firm evidence that the attacks of

---

82. This is most extensively argued in Manor, "Epiphanius' *Alogi*," 88–167; cf. Brent, *Hippolytus*, 141, 143; Hill, *Johannine Corpus*, 185–90.

83. Westcott, *St. John*, lx; Brent, *Hippolytus*, 140; Manor, "Epiphanius' *Alogi*," 167; Hill, "'Orthodox Gospel,'" 264–65n90; Brent, *Hippolytus*, 176; Hill, *Johannine Corpus* 186.

84. Gwynn, "Heads Against Caius," 397–418.

85. Ibid., 402, 406–7. The differences over what was found objectionable in this verse and the respective answers of "Hippolytus" and Epiphanius are canvassed in Brent, *Hippolytus*, 162–64; Manor, "Epiphanius' *Alogi*," 238–39.

bar Salibi's "Gaius" on Revelation included the accusation that it was forged by Cerinthus or that he rejected the Fourth Gospel was still forthcoming.[86] In 1895, J. Rendel Harris publicized a Latin translation of an excerpt from bar Salibi's *Commentary on the Four Gospels* where "Gaius" griped about how the wedding of Cana followed Jesus' baptism (*Bodleian Fell* 6 and 7), another similarity to Epiphanius's *Alogi*.[87] However, there were text-critical signs that the name "Gaius" was interpolated into the manuscript tradition that had a nameless heretic as the mouthpiece of this complaint.[88] Lastly, in 1906, Theodore Robinson recovered the preface to bar Salibi's *Commentary on the Apocalypse*, which made it clear that "Hippolytus" opposed "Gaius" for his indictment of Revelation and the Fourth Gospel as Cerinthian counterfeits.[89]

Bar Salibi's dialogue between Hippolytus and Gaius was correlated with the titles *Heads against Gaius* (*kephalaia kata Gaiou*) and *Defense on behalf of the Apocalypse and the Gospel of John* (*apologia hyper tēs apokalypseōs kai tou euaggeliou Iōannou*) listed in a catalogue of Hippolytan works compiled by Ebed-Jesu (ca. 1298 CE). This was either a single work, if the *Defense on behalf of the Apocalypse and the Gospel of John* was the subtitle for *Heads against Gaius*, or were two closely related apologetic tracts.[90] The antiquity of the text(s) seemed to be confirmed

---

86. Gwynn ("Heads against Gaius," 406, 408–9) assumed Hippolytus and Gaius were of one accord on the truthfulness and authority of the Fourth Gospel.

87. Harris, "Presbyter Gaius," 47–48, 54–55.

88. See Ibid., 48–49; cf. Brent, *Hippolytus*, 145; Hill, *Johannine Corpus*, 181; Manor, "Epiphanius Alogi," 24–25, 199, 236; Manor, "Papias, Origen, and Eusebius," 16–17. Although conceding that it was a scribal correction, Harris ("Presbyter Gaius," 49–50) argues that the dialogue between Gaius and Hippolytus in Gwynn's fragments from the *Commentary on the Apocalypse* show that the scribe rightly clarified that the "certain heretic" was Gaius.

89. Robinson, "Muratorian Canon," 487.

90. Gwynn, "Heads against Caius," 404–5; Harris, "Presbyter Gaius," 45–46, 56; Robinson, "Muratorian Canon," 491. I agree with Brent (*Hippolytus*, 170) that the best reading is that *kephalaia kata Gaiou* and *apologia hyper tēs apokalypseōs kai tou euaggeliou Iōannou* were two discrete texts separated by *kai* ("and") and that Ebed-Jesu would have used a different conjunction if he

by the title *Concerning the Gospel according to John and the Apocalypse* (*hyper tou kata Iōannen euaggeliou kai apokalypseōs*, among the Hippolytan writings etched on the plinth of a marble statue re-dedicated to Hippolytus.[91] The import of this evidence seemed to be that the portrait of Gaius as the obdurate opponent of Montanism who demeaned the authorship of the Fourth Gospel and Revelation dated as far back as Hippolytus of Rome in the third century and Hippolytus's *Heads against Gaius* might have been Epiphanius's source.[92]

The counterproposal of Brent and Manor is that bar Salibi did not possess a Hippolytan work, the *Heads against Gaius*, but his fragments were abstracted from a *florilegium* that was re-edited into a fictitious dialogue between Hippolytus and Gaius.[93] There was no lost source underlying bar Salibi's fragments and Epiphanius's *Panarion*: the overlap between the two was limited to two instances where influence stemming from Epiphanius on bar Salibi cannot be ruled out.[94] This was not out of step with the unceasing production of Eastern Hippolytan pseudepigrapha.[95] The "criticism-response" formula that pitted one scripture against another was also a regular fixture of bar Salibi's literary output.[96] Why were Hippolytus and Gaius cast as dialogue partners? For Brent, the standing of Hippolytus as a standard bearer of orthodoxy and the commonality of "Gaius" as a Roman *praenomen* facilitated

---

wanted to indicate that the latter was a subtitle.

91. For the details about how Pirro Ligorio unearthed a mutilated statue of the originally feminine figure of Themista of Lampsacus from the cemetery of the Via Tiburtina in 1551 and why the statue had been appropriated by a Hippolytan school in antiquity, see Brent, *Hippolytus*, 3–114.

92. Smith, "Gaius," 206–62, 264; Culpepper, *Life of a Legend*, 121–22.

93. Brent, *Hippolytus*, 150–61; Manor, "Epiphanius' *Alogi*," 207–11. One of Brent's points is that, if bar Salibi had an actual writing of Hippolytus in his possession, its author had a rather inflated ego in referring to himself in the third person as the "blessed" (*beatus*) Hippolytus of Rome in "saintly proportions" (*Hippolytus*, 176).

94. Brent, *Hippolytus*, 162–69; Manor, "Epiphanius' *Alogi*," 235–36.

95. Brent, *Hippolytus*, 178–79.

96. Manor, "Epiphanius' *Alogi*," 218–21.

their selection as types signifying orthodox and heterodox Christians.⁹⁷ For Manor, bar Salibi cast Hippolytus and Gaius as debaters sparring over Revelation since he had a catena with genuine Hippolytan extracts on the one hand and Eusebius's portrayal of Gaius as a vocal detractor of chiliasm on the other.⁹⁸ Finally, bar Salibi's preface summed up Eusebius's compilation of what Patristic luminaries had to say about Revelation's authorship (*Hist. Eccl.* 3.18.2–3; 3.39.5–7; 7.25.7–27), including Gaius's antagonism towards Cerinthus's forged apocalypse (3.28.2), and his placement of Gaius in the same literary context as Hippolytus (6.20.2–3). Its portrayal of Cerinthus as a Judaizer and the suspected forger of the Johannine corpus was indebted to Epiphanius (*Pan.* 28.4.1–2, 6; 51.3.6).⁹⁹ Thus, bar Salibi's preface may stand at the tail end of a long process of legendary accretions and may conflict with some of his fragments that presumed that the Fourth Gospel was a mutual authority for the disputants "Hippolytus" and "Gaius."¹⁰⁰

To consent to Brent's and Manor's counter-arguments, Ebed-Jesu and the Hippolytan statue must be sidelined. Brent argues that Ebed-Jesu conjured up the existence of the *Heads against Gaius* and the *Defense on behalf of the Apocalypse and the Gospel of John* after reading the exchange between "Hippolytus" and "Gaius" that bar Salibi jotted down, and roped the Fourth Gospel into their clash over Revelation.¹⁰¹ While Francis Watson questioned whether Ebed-Jesu was in the habit of manufacturing fictional literary

---

97. Brent, *Hippolytus*, 176–78, 182–83.

98. Manor, "Epiphanius' *Alogi*," 227–29, 234–35.

99. Ibid., 221–28, 230; cf. Brent, *Hippolytus*, 176; Hill, *Johannine Corpus*, 186. Manor ("Epiphanius' *Alogi*," 224–25) points out another piece of evidence in that bar Salibi's reference to "Hippolytus of Bostra" is based on how Eusebius names Hippolytus after Beryllus, the bishop of Bostra. Yet Myllykoski ("Cerinthus," 217) insists that the one sentence defending the Johannine corpus in bar Salibi's preface derives from Hippolytus, not Epiphanius.

100. See Gwynn, "Heads against Caius," 406, 408; Brent, *Hippolytus*, 145; Hill, *Johannine Corpus*, 193–94; Manor, "Epiphanius' *Alogi*," 23. Bar Salibi's "Hippolytus" answered the first and the fifth critiques of "Gaius" with allusions to John 11:10, 12:35–36, and 14:30 (*Comm. Apoc.* 8, 19).

101. Brent, *Hippolytus*, 171–73.

titles and was acquainted with bar Salibi's commentaries,[102] Manor has exposed the quirks of Ebed Jesu's catalogue from the lack of corroboration for the literary works listed on it to its omissions of well-known Hippolytan works.[103] Ebed-Jesu's *Defense on behalf of the Apocalypse and the Gospel of John* is not exactly identical to what was transcribed on the statue. The title on the statue has the "Gospel according to John" and the "Apocalypse" in the reverse order and, while the letter *alpha* is barely visible before the preposition *hyper* on it, there is slightly enough room for the article *ta* ("the") to have preceded the *hyper* rather than the noun *apologia* ("defense").[104] *The Matters concerning the Gospel according to John and the Apocalypse* engraved on the statue may not have been an apologetic piece, let alone a counterattack against Gaius, but Watson responds that these are miniscule variations and that it was not an ancient convention to fix titles accurately.[105]

The data is sparse, complex, and separated over centuries, so we can wrap up this section with some provisional conclusions. As part of his hostility against the New Prophecy, Gaius of Rome implicated Cerinthus in forging Revelation in the name of an apostle to prop up his carnal millennium. This was a popular tactic for discrediting Revelation and re-surfaced in the schism in Alexandria over Nepos's millennial worldview. Gaius may not have extended this charge to the authorship of the Fourth Gospel, a matter that Eusebius would not have taken lightly, but someone evidently did out of fear that the Fourth Gospel had dangerous affinities with Cerinthus's theology. According to the Syriac evidence, Hippolytus of Rome was the first to defend the Johannine literature from this assault on its authenticity. If this data is unreliable, the accusation of Cerinthian authorship cannot be traced back before Epiphanius. Epiphanius did not bother refuting this charge since it was self-evidently preposterous to him.

102. Watson, *Gospel Writing*, 482n128.

103. Manor, "Epiphanius' *Alogi*," 212–16.

104. Brent, *Hippolytus*, 172; Hill, *Johannine Corpus*, 184; Manor, "Epiphanius' *Alogi*," 54–55, 210.

105. Watson, *Gospel Writing*, 482n28

Conclusion: The Authorial Function

The attributions of the Fourth Gospel to the "Apostle John" or the "heretic Cerinthus" may seem to be on opposite ends of the spectrum, but they are really mirror images of each other and they exemplify the authorial function marvellously. If the aim was to sanction the reading of a text for a Christian interpretive community and to ensure that the interpretive strategies do not veer too far off from the normative ideals of the community, a text was assigned to one of their illustrious founders. If the text was perceived to be detrimental to the objectives of the community, it had to derive from an apostate who had transgressed the social boundaries that guarded their beliefs and practices. If grapes cannot be picked from thorn-bushes nor figs from thistles (Matthew 7:16–17; Luke 6:43–44), orthodox truth cannot originate with false prophets. Sound doctrines descended from the apostles and their tried-and-true successors.

Conclusion

The Historical and Theological Implications

JOHN, THE SON OF Zebedee, was transformed into an exemplary disciple who had a close bond with Jesus, an exile languishing on the island of Patmos, an aging patron who shepherded a Christian assembly in Asia Minor, an instructor of influential bishops in Hierapolis and Smyrna, and an author of five writings within the New Testament. This is an impressive dossier for a hard-working Galilean fisherman who could not have afforded the luxury of a formal education to become literate! If we are at the point where we can deconstruct the Patristic edifice, this does not mean that we cannot sympathize with the intentions behind it. They were searching for adequate criteria to sort out the wealth of Gospel literature that was being churned out in the first few centuries that had clashing visions about who Jesus was and what he came to do. They were also threatened by rival groups who boasted that Jesus had secretly transmitted to them the keys to unlocking the mysteries of the Gospels, apart from the publicly approved channels by which doctrine was to be imparted from one bishop to the next.

The apostolicity of the Fourth Gospel ensured that it would find a home in the canon of Christian Scripture. The hermeneutical lens that the Church Fathers and Mothers supposedly inherited from the apostles regulated the permissible interpretations of the Fourth Gospel's contents. Without the second-century Christian scribes and intellectuals who shaped the literary and theological import of the Fourth Gospel, its eventual canonization was by no means assured in the second century. The slander that the fourth evangelist was the maligned Cerinthus was calculated to prevent this outcome. What a loss it would have been if the Fourth Gospel had been consigned to the dustbin of history! The rich iconography and catacomb art inspired by Johannine scenes from the wedding at Cana to the resurrection of Lazarus testify to the Fourth Gospel's popularity for the masses.[1] The terminology and conceptual categories in the Fourth Gospel had a marked impact upon the dogmatic formulations about the dual nature of Christ established in the post-Constantinian ecumenical councils. Today, millions of Christians hear the Fourth Gospel's words in their devotions, music, liturgies, and sermons. A word-for-word, film adaptation of the *Good News Bible* translation of the Fourth Gospel was even released in 2003. It is fortunate for scholars and laypersons alike that the Fourth Gospel survived for posterity, albeit with an overlay of scribal redactions and ecclesiastical lore.

It does a disservice to the Fourth Gospel to make its truthfulness contingent on the insecure Patristic traditions about its apostolic, Johannine authorship. I have argued that these traditions did not start picking up steam until sometime after Justin Martyr, when subscriptions were affixed to the four canonical Gospels and Ptolemy and Irenaeus were singing the praises of the disciple John. Truth be told, authorship was never the absolute criterion for inclusion in the canon, but this criterion was applied in concert with the requirements about a text's catholicity, antiquity, and conformity to the rule of faith. Even with that admission, the criteria worked out by fourth-century Christians do not have to dictate what Christians affirm about the canon today. And while we stand on the shoulders of these Patristic giants and benefit from their great learning, we do not face the same issues nor implement the same interpretive procedures. Each generation returns to the text with their contextually-bound interpretive frameworks and discovers new treasures from the Fourth Gospel along with the old.

---

1. On this iconography, see Braun, *Jean Le Théologien*, 149–60; Hill, *Johannine Corpus*, 155–66.

Conclusion

For some Christian readers, if the evangelist was not an apostle, the next best thing might be that the evangelist conferred with a real flesh-and-blood eyewitness in the person of an elite Judean follower of Jesus (i.e., the beloved disciple) and that the representation of the topography and culture of first-century Judea in the Fourth Gospel was generally accurate. The final redaction of this text seems to have happened in the early second century since the editorial addition of the Johannine Epilogue did not leave an imprint on the manuscript tradition; the Patristic and manuscript witnesses (e.g., the Ryland's Library Papyrus P52) help to set a more precise *terminus ad quem* ("limit to which") for dating the text. Yet the authorship and antiquity of the Fourth Gospel do not have to be the grounds for its canonicity among communities of faith. Its scriptural status continues to be confessed by the Christian flock throughout history who have listened the voice of the "Good Shepherd" within its pages.

Bibliography

Abramowski, Luise. "The 'Memoirs of the Apostles' in Justin." In *The Gospel and The Gospels*, edited by Peter Stuhlmacher, 323–35. Grand Rapids: Eerdmans, 1991.
Annand, Rupert. "Papias and the Four Gospels." *Scottish Journal of Theology* 9 (1956) 46–62.
Attridge, Harold W. "The Acts of John and the Fourth Gospel." In *From Judaism to Christianity: Tradition and Transition. A Festschrift for Thomas H. Tobin, S.J., on the Occasion of His Sixty-fifth Birthday*, edited by Patricia Walters, 255–66. Leiden: Brill, 2010.
Bacon, B. W. "The Elder John, Papias, Irenaeus, Eusebius and the Syriac Translator." *Journal of Biblical Literature* 27 (1908) 1–23.
Barker, James W. *John's Use of Matthew*. Minneapolis: Fortress, 2015.
———. "Written Gospel or Oral Tradition? Patristic Parallels to John 3:3, 5." *Early Christianity* 6 (2015) 543–58.
Barnes, Timothy D. "'Another Shall Gird Thee': Probative Evidence for the Death of Peter." In *Peter in Early Christianity*, edited by Helen K. Bond and Larry W. Hurtado, 76–98. Grand Rapids: Eerdmans, 2015.
Barrett, C. K. *The Gospel According to St. John*. 2nd ed. Philadelphia: Westminster, 1978.
Barthes, Roland. "The Death of the Author." In *Image-Music-Text*. Translated by Stephen Heath, 142–48. New York: Hill and Wang, 1977.
Bartlet Vernon. "Papias's 'Exposition': Its Date and Contents." In *Amicitiae Corolla: A Volume of Essays Presented to James Rendel Harris, D. Litt. on the Occasion of his Eightieth Birthday*, edited by H. G. Wood, 15–44. London: University of London Press, 1933.
Batovici, Dan. "The Second Century Reception of John: A Survey of Methodologies." *Currents in Biblical Research* 10 (2012) 396–409.
Bauckham, Richard. *Jesus and the Eyewitnesses: The Gospels as Eyewitness Testimony*. Grand Rapids: Eerdmans, 2006.
———. *The Testimony of the Beloved Disciple: Narrative, History, and Theology in the Gospel of John*. Grand Rapids: Baker Academic, 2007.

Bibliography

Bauer, Walter. *Orthodoxy and Heresy in Earliest Christianity*. Edited by Robert A. Kraft and Gerhard Krodel. Translated by Paul J. Achtemeier. Philadelphia: Fortress, 1971.

Baum, Armin Daniel. "The Anonymity of the New Testament History Books: A Stylistic Device in the Context of Greco-Roman and Ancient Near Eastern Literature." *Novum Testamentum* 50 (2008) 120–42.

―――. "The Original Epilogue (John 20:30-31), the Secondary Appendix (21:1-23), and the Editorial Epilogues (21:24-25) of John's Gospel. Observations against the Background of Ancient Literary Conventions." In *Earliest Christian History: History, Literature, and Theology. Essays from the Tyndale Fellowship in Honor of Martin Hengel*, edited by Michael F. Bird and Jason Maston, 227–70. Wissenschaftliche Untersuchungen zum Neuen Testament 2.320. Tübingen: Mohr Siebeck, 2012.

Beasley-Murray, George R. *John*. Word Biblical Commentary 36. Waco: Word, 1987.

Beck, David R. "'Whom Jesus Loved': Anonymity and Identity, Belief and Witness in the Fourth Gospel." In *Characters and Characterization in the Gospel of John*, edited by Christopher W. Skinner, 221–239. Library of New Testament Studies 461. London: Bloomsbury, 2013.

Bellinzoni, A. J. *The Sayings of Jesus in the Writings of Justin Martyr*. Novum Testamentum Supplementary Series 17. Leiden: Brill, 1967.

Bennema, Cornelius. *Encountering Jesus: Character Studies in the Gospel of John*. Minneapolis: Fortress, 2014.

Bernier, Jonathan. *Aposynagōgos and the Historical Jesus in John: Rethinking the Historicity of the Johannine Expulsion Passages*. Leiden: Brill, 2013.

Blomberg, Craig. *The Historical Reliability of John's Gospel: Issues and Commentary*. Downers Grove, IL: InterVarsity, 2001.

Bockmuehl, Markus. *The Remembered Peter: In Ancient Reception and Modern Debate*. Wissenschaftliche Untersuchungen zum Neuen Testament 1.262. Tübingen: Mohr Siebeck, 2010.

―――. *Seeing the Word: Refocusing New Testament Study*. Grand Rapids: Eerdmans, 2006.

Boer, Esther de. *The Gospel of Mary: Beyond a Gnostic and a Biblical Mary Magdalene*. London: T. & T. Clark, 2004.

Bokedal, Tomas. *The Formation and Significance of the Christian Biblical Canon: A Study in Text, Ritual and Interpretation*. New York: Bloomsbury T. & T. Clark, 2014.

Bourdieu, Pierre. "The Forms of Capital." In *Handbook of Theory and Research for the Sociology of Education*, 46–58. New York: Greenwood, 1986.

Braun, F. M. *Jean le Théologien et son Évangile dans l'Église Ancienne*. Paris: Gabalda, 1959.

Braun, Willi. "Resisting John: Ambivalent Redactor and Defensive Reader of the Fourth Gospel." *Studies in Religion* 19 (1990) 59–71.

Breck, John. "John 21: Appendix, Epilogue or Conclusion?" *St. Vladimir's Theological Quarterly* 36 (1992) 27–49.

Bibliography

Brent, Allen. *Hippolytus and the Roman Church in the Third Century. Communities in Tension before the Emergence of a Monarch-Bishop.* Supplements to Vigiliae Christianae 31. Leiden: Brill, 1995.

Brodie, Thomas L. *The Gospel According to John: A Literary and Theological Commentary.* New York: Oxford University Press, 1993.

Brown, Raymond. *The Community of the Beloved Disciple.* London: Geoffrey Chapman, 1979.

———. *The Gospel According to John I-XII.* Anchor Bible 29. New York: Doubleday, 1966.

———. *The Gospel According to John XIII-XXI.* Anchor Bible 29. New York: Doubleday, 1984.

Bruce, F. F. *The Canon of Scripture.* Downers Grove, IL: InterVarsity, 1988.

Bruyne, Donatien de. "Les plus anciens prologues Latines des Evangiles." *Revue Bénédictine* 40 (1928) 193–214.

Bultmann, Rudolf. *The Gospel of John: A Commentary.* Translated by George R. Beasley-Murray. Philadelphia: Westminster, 1971.

Campenhausen, Hans von. *The Formation of the Christian Bible.* Translated by J. A. Baker. Philadelphia: Fortress, 1972.

Carlson, Stephen. "Clement of Alexandria on the 'Order' of the Gospels." *New Testament Studies* 47 (2001) 118–125.

Carson, D. A. *The Gospel According to John.* Grand Rapids: Eerdmans, 1991.

Casey, Maurice. *Is John's Gospel True?* London and New York: Routledge, 1996.

Charlesworth, James H. *The Beloved Disciple: Whose Witness Validates the Gospel of John?* Valley Forge, PA: Trinity, 1995.

Collins, Raymond F. *These Things have been Written: Studies on the Fourth Gospel.* Louvain Theological and Pastoral Monologues, 2. Grand Rapids: Eerdmans, 1990.

Cook, John Granger. *Crucifixion in the Mediterranean World.* Wissenschaftliche Untersuchungen zum Neuen Testament 327. Tübingen: Mohr Siebeck, 2014.

Cullmann, Oscar. *The Johannine Circle: Its Place in Judaism, Among the Disciples of Jesus, and in Early Christianity.* Bloomsbury: SCM, 1976.

Culpepper, R. Alan. *John, the Son of Zebedee: The Life of a Legend.* Minneapolis: Fortress, 2000.

Czachesz, István. "The Gospel of the Acts of John: Its Relation to the Fourth Gospel." In *The Legacy of John: Second-Century Reception of the Fourth Gospel,* edited by Tuomas Raisimus, 49–72. Leiden: Brill, 2010.

DeConick, April D. "Why are the Heavens Closed? The Johannine Revelation of the Father in the Catholic-Gnostic Debate." In *John's Gospel and Intimations of Apocalyptic,* edited by Catrin H. Williams and Christopher Rowland, 147–79. London: T. & T. Clark, 2013.

Deeks, David G. "Papias Revisited (Part 1)." *Expository Times* 88 (1977) 296–301.

———. "Papias Revisited (Part 2)." *Expository Times* 88 (1977) 324–29.

Bibliography

Dunderberg, Ismo. *The Beloved Disciple in Conflict: Revisiting the Gospels of John and Thomas*. Oxford: Oxford University Press, 2006.

Ehrman, Bart D. *Forgery and Counter-forgery: The Use of Literary Deceit in Early Christian Polemics*. Oxford: Oxford University Press, 2013.

———. *The Orthodox Corruption of Scripture: The Effect of Early Christological Controversies on the Text of the New Testament*. New York: Oxford University Press, 1993.

Ellis, Peter F. "The Authenticity of John 21." *St. Vladimir's Theological Quarterly* 36 (1992) 17–25.

Elowsky, Joel C., ed. *John 1-10. Ancient Christian Commentary on Scripture New Testament IVa*. Downers Grove, IL: InterVarsity, 2006.

Farmer, William R., and Denis M. Farkasfalvy. *The Formation of the New Testament Canon: An Ecumenical Approach*. Ramsey, NJ: Paulist, 1983.

Fish, Stanley. *Is There a Text in this Class? The Authority of Interpretive Communities*. Cambridge, MA: Harvard University Press, 1980.

Foster, Paul. "The Writings of Justin Martyr and the so-called Gospel of Peter." In *Justin Martyr and His Worlds*, edited by Sarah Parvis and Paul Foster, 104–12. Minneapolis: Fortress, 2007.

Foucault, Michael. "What is an Author?" In *Aesthetics, Method and Epistemology: Volume 2*, edited by James Faubion. Translated by Robert Hurley et al, 205-222. London: Penguin, 2000.

Franzmann, Majella, and Michael Lattke. "Gnostic Jesuses and the Gnostic Jesus of John." In *Gnosisforschung und Religionsgeschichte: Festschrift für Kurt Rudolph zum 65. Geburtstag*, edited by H. Preißler and H. Siewert, 143–54. Marburg: Diagonal-Verlag, 1994.

Gadamer, Hans-Georg. *Truth and Method*. London: Sheed and Ward, 1975.

Gamble, Henry Y. *The New Testament Canon: Its Making and Meaning*. Philadelphia: Fortress, 1985.

Gathercole, S. J. "The Titles of the Gospels in the Earliest New Testament Manuscripts." *Zeitschrift für die Neutestamentliche Wissenschaft* 104 (2013): 33-76.

Gaventa, Beverly Roberts. "The Archive of Excess: John 21 and the Problem of Narrative Closure." In *Exploring the Gospel of John*, edited by R. Alan Culpepper and C. Clifton Black, 240–52. Louisville, KY: Westminster John Knox, 1996.

Goodacre, Mark. *Thomas and the Gospels: The Case for Thomas's Familiarity with the Synoptics*. Grand Rapids: Eerdmans/SPCK, 2012.

Goulder, Michael W. "Did Peter Ever Go to Rome?" *Scottish Journal of Theology* 57.4 (2004) 377–96.

Grant, Robert M. *The Formation of the New Testament*. London: Hutchinson University Library, 1965.

———. *Irenaeus of Lyons*. New York: Routledge, 1997.

Grassi, J. A. *The Secret Identity of the Beloved Disciple*. New York: Paulist, 1992.

Bibliography

Gregory, Andrew. *The Reception of Luke and Acts in the Period before Irenaeus.* Wissenschaftliche Untersuchungen zum Neuen Testament 2.169. Tübingen: Mohr Siebeck, 2003.

Gregory, Andrew, and Christopher M. Tuckett, eds. *The Reception of the New Testament in the Apostolic Fathers.* Oxford: Oxford University Press, 2005.

———. "Reflections on Method: What Constitutes the Use of Writings that later formed the New Testament in the Apostolic Fathers." In *The Reception of the New Testament in the Apostolic Fathers*, edited by Andrew Gregory and Christopher Tuckett, 61–82. Oxford: Oxford University Press, 2005.

Gundry, Robert H. "The Apostolically Johannine Pre-Papian Tradition Concerning the Gospels of Mark and Matthew." In *The Old is Better. New Testament Essays in Support of Traditional Interpretations*, 49–73. Wissenschaftliche Untersuchungen zum Neuen Testament 178. Tübingen: Mohr Siebeck, 2005.

Gutwenger, Engelbert. "The Anti-Marcionite Prologues." *Theological Studies* 7 (1946) 393–409.

Gwynn, John. "Hippolytus and his 'Heads against Caius.'" *Hermathena* 6 (1888) 397–418.

Haenchen, Ernst. *John.* 2 vols. Translated by Robert W. Funk. Edited by Robert W. Funk and Ulrich Busse. Hermeneia. Philadelphia: Fortress, 1984.

Hanson, K. C. "The Galilean Fishing Economy." *Biblical Theology Bulletin* 27 (1997) 99–111.

Harris, J. Rendel. "Presbyter Gaius and the Fourth Gospel." In *Hermas in Arcadia and Other Essays*, 43–57. Cambridge: Cambridge University Press, 1896.

Head, Peter M. "On the Christology of the Gospel of Peter." *Vigiliae Christianae* 46 (1992) 209–24.

Heard, Richard. "APOMNĒMONEUMATA in Papias, Justin and Irenaeus." *New Testament Studies* 1 (1954) 122–29.

———. "The Old Gospel Prologues." *Journal of Theological Studies* 6 (1955) 1–16.

Hengel, Martin. *The Johannine Question.* Translated by J. Bowden. London: SCM, 1989.

———. *Die Johanneische Frage: Ein Lösungsversuch mit einem Beitrag zur Apokalypse von Jörg Frey.* Tübingen: Mohr Siebeck, 1993.

———. *The Four Gospels and the One Gospel of Jesus Christ.* London: SCM, 2000.

Hezser, Catherine. *Jewish Literacy in Roman Palestine.* Tübingen: Mohr Siebeck, 2001.

Hill, Charles E. "Cerinthus, Gnostic or Chiliast: A New Solution to an Old Problem." *Journal of Early Christian Studies* 8 (2000) 135–72.

———. *The Johannine Corpus in the Early Church.* Oxford: Oxford University Press, 2004

———. "The 'Orthodox Gospel': The Reception of John in the Great Church Prior to Irenaeus." In *The Legacy of John: Second-Century Reception of the Fourth Gospel*, edited by Tuomas Rasimus, 233–300. Leiden: Brill, 2010.

Bibliography

———. "Papias of Hierapolis." *The Expository Times* 117 (2006) 309–15.
———. "What Papias Said about John (and Luke): A New 'Papian' Fragment." *The Journal of Theological Studies* 49 (1998) 582–629.
Hillmer, Melvyn Raymond. "The Gospel of John in the Second Century." ThD diss., Harvard University, 1966.
Hirsch, E. D. *Validity in Interpretation*. New Haven, CT: Yale University Press, 1967.
Holmes, Michael W. *The Apostolic Fathers: Greek Texts and English Translations*. 3rd ed. Grand Rapids: Baker Academic, 2007.
———. "Polycarp's Letter to the Philippians and the Writings that Later Formed the New Testament." In *The Reception of the New Testament in the Apostolic Fathers*, edited by Andrew F. Gregory and Christopher M. Tuckett, 187–227. Oxford: Oxford University Press, 2005.
Hoskyns, Edwyn. *The Fourth Gospel*. London: Faber and Faber, 1947.
Jackson, H. M. "Ancient Self-referential Conventions and their Implications for the Authorship and Integrity of the Gospel of John." *Journal of Theological Studies* 50 (1999) 1–34.
Jauss, Hans Robert. *Towards an Aesthetic of Reception*. Translated by Timothy Bahti. Brighton: Harvester, 1982.
Keefer, Kyle. *The Branches of the Gospel of John: The Reception of the Fourth Gospel in the Early Church*. Library of New Testament Studies. London: Bloomsbury T. & T. Clark, 2006.
Keener, Craig S. *The Gospel of John: A Commentary*. 2 vols. Peabody: Hendrickson, 2003.
Keith, Chris. "The Competitive Textualization of the Jesus Tradition in John 20:30–31 and 21:24–25." *Catholic Biblical Quarterly* 78 (2016) 321–37.
Kelhoffer, James A. "'How Soon a Book' Revisited: EUAGGELION as a Reference to 'Gospel' Materials in the First Half of the Second Century." *Zeitschrift für die neutestamentliche Wissenschaft* 95 (2004) 1–34.
Koester, Helmut. *Ancient Christian Gospels: Their History and Development*. Philadelphia: Continnuum, 1990.
Kok, Michael J. *The Gospel on the Margins: The Reception of Mark in the Second Century*. Minneapolis: Fortress, 2015.
Körtner, Ulrich H. J. *Papias von Hierapolis: Ein Beitrag zur Geschichte des frühen Christentums*. Forschung zur Religion und Literatur des Alten und Neuen Testaments 1303. Göttingen: Vandenhoek & Ruprecht, 1983.
Köstenberger, Andreas J. "Early Doubts of the Apostolic Authorship of the Fourth Gospel in the History of Modern Biblical Criticism." In *Studies on John and Gender: A Decade of Scholarship*, 17–47. Stuttgarter Biblische Beiträge 38. New York: Peter Lang, 2001.
———. *John*. Baker Exegetical Commentary on the New Testament. Grand Rapids: Baker Academic, 2004.
Köstenberger, Andreas J. and Stephen O. Snout. "'The Disciple Jesus Loved': Witness, Author, Apostle—A Response to Richard Bauckham's *Jesus and the Eyewitnesses*." *Bulletin for Biblical Research* 18 (2008) 209–31.

Bibliography

Kraus, Thomas J. "'Uneducated,' 'Ignorant,' or even 'Illiterate'? Aspects and Background for an Understanding of ΑΓΡΑΜΜΑΤΟΙ (and ΙΔΙΩΤΑΙ) in Acts 4:13." *New Testament Studies* 45 (1999) 434–49.
Kügler, J. *Der Jünger, den Jesus liebte: Literarische, theologische und historische Untersuchungen zu einer Schlüsselgestalt johanneischer Theologie und Geschichte.* Stuttgarter Biblische Beiträge 16. Stuttgart: Katholisches Bibelwerk, 1988.
Lagrange, M. J. *L'Evangile selon S. Jean.* 8th ed. Paris: Gabalda, 1948.
Lalleman, Pieter J. *The Acts of John. A Two-Stage Initiation into Johannine Gnosticism.* Leuven: Peeters, 1998.
Lattke, M. "John 20,30f. als Buchschluß." *Zeitschrift für die Neutestamentliche Wissenschaft und die Kunde der Älteren Kirche* 78 (1987) 288–92.
Lightfoot, R. H. *Essays on the Work Entitled Supernatural Religion.* London: Macmillan, 1889.
Lincoln, Andrew T. "The Beloved Disciple as Eyewitness and the Fourth Gospel as Witness." *Journal for the Study of the New Testament* 85 (2002) 3–26.
Lindars, Barnabas. *The Gospel of John.* New Century Bible Commentary. London: Marshall, Morgan and Scott, 1972.
MacDonald, Dennis. *Two Shipwrecked Gospels: The Logoi of Jesus and Papias's Exposition of Logia about the Lord.* Atlanta: Society of Biblical Literature, 2012.
MacDonald, Lee Martin. *The Biblical Canon: Its Origin, Transmission, and Authority.* Peabody: Hendrickson, 2007.
Malina, Bruce J. and Richard L. Rohrbaugh. *Social-Science Commentary on the Gospel of John.* Minneapolis: Fortress, 1998.
Manor, T. Scott. "Epiphanius' Alogi and the Question of Early Ecclesiastical Opposition to the Johannine Corpus." PhD diss., University of Edinburgh, 2012.
———. "Papias, Origen, and Eusebius: The Criticisms and Defense of the Gospel of John." *Vigiliae Christianae* 67 (2013) 1–21.
Massaux, Édouard. *The Influence of the Gospel of Saint Matthew on Christian Literature Before Saint Irenaeus.* 3 Vols. Translated by Norman Belval and Suzanne Hecht. Edited by A. J. Bellinzoni. Macon, GA: Mercer University Press, 1990.
McGrath, James. "Mark's Missing Ending: Clues from the Gospel of John and the Gospel of Peter." *Bible and Interpretation* (February 2010). (http://www.bibleinterp.com/articles/mcg.shtml).
Metzger, Bruce M. *The Canon of the New Testament: Its Origin, Development, and Significance.* Oxford: Clarendon, 1987.
———. *A Textual Commentary on the Greek New Testament.* 2nd ed. Stuttgart: United Bible Societies, 1994.
Meyer, Marvin. "Whom Did Jesus Love Most? Beloved Disciples in John and Other Gospels." In *The Legacy of John: Second-Century Reception of the Fourth Gospel*, edited by Tuomas Rasimus, 73–92. Leiden: Brill, 2010.

Bibliography

Michaels, J. Ramsay. *The Gospel of John.* New International Commentary on the New Testament. Grand Rapids: Eerdmans, 2010.
Minear, Paul. "The Original Functions of John 21." *Journal of Biblical Literature* 102 (1983) 85-98.
Minns, Denis. *Irenaeus: An Introduction.* New York: T. & T. Clark, 2010.
Mitchell, Margaret M. "Patristic Counter-Evidence to the Claim that 'The Gospels were Written for All Christians." *New Testament Studies* 51 (2005) 36-79.
Moloney, Francis J. *The Gospel of John.* Sacra Pagina 4. Collegeville, MN: Liturgical, 1998.
Mommsen, Theodor. "Papianisches." *Zeitschrift für die Neutestamentliche Wissenschaft* 3 (1902) 156-59.
Morris, Leon. *The Gospel According to John.* Grand Rapids: Eerdmans, 1995.
Munck, Johannes. "Presbyters and Disciples of the Lord in Papias." *Harvard Theological Review* 52 (1959) 223-43.
Mutschler, Bernhard. "John and His Gospel in the Mirror of Irenaeus of Lyons: Perspectives of Recent Research." In *The Legacy of John: Second-Century Reception of the Fourth Gospel,* edited by Tuomas Rasimus, 319-43. Leiden: Brill, 2010.
Myllykoski, Matti. "Cerinthus." In *A Companion to Second-Century Christian "Heretics,"* edited by Antti Marjanen and Petri Luomanen, 213-46. Vigiliae Christianae Supplements 76. Boston: Brill, 2005.
Nagel, Titus. *Die Rezeption des Johannesevangeliums im 2. Jahrhundert: Studien zur vorirenäischen Auslegung des vierten Evangeliums in christlicher und christlich-gnostischer Literatur.* Arbeiten zur Bibel und ihrer Geschichte 2. Leipzig: Evangelische Verlagsanstalt, 2000.
Neirynck, Frans. "The Other Disciple in John 18, 15-16." *Ephemerides Theologicae Lovanienses* 51 (1975) 113-41.
Norelli, Enrico. *Papia di Hierapolis: Esposizione degli Oracoli del signore: I Frammenti.* Milan: Paoline, 2005.
Osborn, Eric. *Irenaeus of Lyons.* Cambridge: Cambridge University Press, 2001.
———. *Justin Martyr.* Tübingen: Mohr Siebeck, 1973.
Pagels, Elaine H. *The Johannine Gospel in Gnostic Exegesis: Heracleon's Commentary on John.* SBLMS 17. Nashville: Abingdon, 1973.
Parker, Pierson. "John the Son of Zebedee and the Fourth Gospel." *Journal of Biblical Literature* 81 (1962) 35-43.
Parvis, Paul. "Justin Martyr." *Expository Times* 120 (2008) 53-61.
Perumalil, A. C. "Are Not Papias and Irenaeus Competent to Report on the Gospels?" *Expository Times* 91 (1980) 332-37.
Pervo, Richard. *The Acts of John.* Salem, OR: Polebridge, 2016.
Pesch, Rudolf. *Der reiche Fischfang.* Düsseldorf: Patmos-Verlag, 1969.
Pilhofer, Peter. "Justin und das Petrusevangelium." *Zeitschrift für die neutestamentliche Wissenschaft* 81 (1990) 60-78.
Pollard, T. E. *Johannine Christology and the Early Church.* Cambridge: Cambridge University Press, 1970.

BIBLIOGRAPHY

Porter, Stanley E. "The Ending of John's Gospel." In *From Biblical Criticism to Biblical Faith: Essays in Honor of Lee Martin McDonald*, edited by William H. Brackney and Craig A. Evans, 55–73. Macon, GA: Mercer University Press, 2007.
Pryor, John W. "Justin Martyr and the Fourth Gospel." *Second Century* 9 (1992) 153–69.
Quast, Kevin. *Peter and the Beloved Disciple: Figures for a Community in Crisis*. Journal for the Study of the New Testament Supplement Series 32. Sheffield: Journal for the Study of the Old Testament, 1989.
Rasimus, Tuomas, ed. *The Legacy of John: Second-Century Reception of the Fourth Gospel*. Leiden: Brill, 2010.
———. "Ptolemaeus and the Valentinian Exegesis of John's Prologue." In *The Legacy of John: Second-Century Reception of the Fourth Gospel*, edited by Tuomas Rasimus, 145–72. Leiden: Brill, 2010.
Reader, W. "The Twelve Jewels of Revelation 21:19–20: Tradition History and Modern Interpretations." *Journal of Biblical Literature* 100 (1981) 433–57.
Regul, Jürgen. *Die antimarcionitischen Evangelienprologe*. Vetus Latina 6. Freiburg, DE: Herder, 1969.
Resseguie, James L. "The Beloved Disciple: The Ideal Point of View." In *Character Studies in the Fourth Gospel: Narrative Approaches to Seventy Figures in John*, edited by Steven A. Hunt, D. Francois Tolmie, and Ruben Zimmermann, 537–49 in. Wissenschaftliche Untersuchungen zum Neuen Testament 314. Tübingen: Mohr Siebeck, 2013.
Ridderbos, Hermann. *The Gospel of John: A Theological Commentary*. Translated by John Vriend. Grand Rapids: Eerdmans, 1997.
Robinson, Theodore H. "The Authorship of the Muratorian Canon." *The Expositor* 7 (1906) 481–95.
Ruckstuhl, Eugen. "Zur Aussage und Botschaft von Johannes 21." In *Jesus im Horizont der Evangelien*, 327–53. Stuttgarter Biblische Aufsatzbände 3 Stuttgart: Katholisches Bibelwerk, 1988.
Sanders, J. N. *The Fourth Gospel in the Early Church: Its Origin and Influence on Christian Theology up to Irenaeus*. Cambridge: Cambridge University Press, 1943.
Schäferdiek, Knut. "The Acts of John." In *New Testament Apocrypha: Volume 2. Writings Related to the Apostles; Apocalypses and Related Subjects* translated by R. Mcl. Wilson. Edited by Wilhelm Schneemelcher, 152–209 Louisville, KY: Westminster/John Knox Press, 2003.
Schenke, Gesa. "Das Erscheinen Jesu vor den Jüngern und der ungläubige Thomas: Johannes 20,19–31." In *Coptica—Gnostica—Manichaica Mélanges offerts à Wolf-Peter Funk*, edited by Louis Painchaud and Paul-Hubert Poirier, 893–904. Paris: Les presses de l'Université Laval/Peeters, 2006.
Schenke, Hans-Martin. "The Function and Background of the Beloved Disciple in the Gospel of John." In *Nag Hammadi, Gnosticism, and Early*

Bibliography

Christianity, edited by C. W. Hendrick and R. Hodgson, 111–25. Peabody: Hendrickson, 1986.

Schnabel, Eckhard J. "The Muratorian Fragment: The State of Research." *Journal of the Evangelical Theological Society* 57 (2014) 231–64.

Schnackenburg, Rudolf. *The Gospel According to St. John*. 3 vols. Translated by Devin Smyth et al. 1.75–104. New York: Seabury and Crossroad, 1980.

Schnelle, Udo. *Antidocetic Christology in the Gospel of John: An Investigation of the Place of the Fourth Gospel in the Johannine School*. Translated by Linda Maloney. Minneapolis: Fortress, 1992.

Schoedel, William R. "Papias." In *Aufstieg und Niedergang der römischen Welt* 2.27.1, edited by Wolfgang Haase. 235–70. Berlin: de Gruyter, 1993.

Shanks, Monte A. *Papias and the New Testament*. Eugene, OR: Pickwick, 2013.

Siegert, F. "Unbeachtete Papiaszitate bei armenischen Schriftstellern." *New Testament Studies* 27 (1981) 605–14.

Sim, David C. "The Gospel of Matthew, John the Elder and the Papias Tradition: A Response to R.H. Gundry." *Harvard Theological Review* 63 (2007) 283–99.

Skinner, Christopher. *John and Thomas—Gospels in Conflict?* Princeton Theological Monograph Series 115. Eugene, OR: Pickwick, 2009.

———. *Reading John: Cascade Companions*. Eugene, OR: Cascade, 2015.

Sloyan, G. S. "The Gnostic Adoption of John's Gospel and Its Canonization by the Church Catholic." *Biblical Theology Bulletin*, 26 (1996) 125–32.

Smith, Dwight Moody. *The Composition and Order of the Fourth Gospel: Bultmann's Literary Theory*. New Haven, CT: Yale University Press, 1965.

———. *John among the Gospels*. Columbia: University of Carolina Press, 2001.

Smith, Joseph Daniel. "Gaius and the Controversy over the Johannine Literature." PhD diss., Yale University, 1979.

Stanton, Graham N. *Jesus and Gospel*. Cambridge: Cambridge University Press, 2004.

Stewart, Alistair C. *The Original Bishops: Office and Order in the First Christian Communities*. Grand Rapids: Baker Academic, 2014.

Tabor, James D. *The Jesus Dynasty*. New York: Simon and Schuster, 2006.

Theobald, Michael. "Der Jünger, den Jesus liebte Beobachtungen zum narrativen Konzept der johanneischen Redaktion." In *Studien zum Corpus Iohanneum*, 493–530. WUNT 267. Tübingen: Mohr Siebeck, 2010.

Thiselton, Anthony C. *New Horizons in Hermeneutics*. Grand Rapids: Zondervan, 1992.

Thompson, Marianne Meye. *John: A Commentary*. Louisville, KY: Westminster John Knox, 2015.

Thyen, Hartwig. "Entwicklungen innerhalb der johanneischen Theologie und Kirche im Spiegel von Joh 21 und der Lieblingsjüngertexte des Evangeliums." In *L'Evangile de Jean: Sources, redaction, théologie*, edited by M. de Jonge, 259–99. Bibliothecca Ephemeridum Theologicarum Lovaniensium 44. Leuven: Leuven University Press, 1977.

Bibliography

Trobisch, David. *The First Edition of the New Testament*. New York: Oxford University Press, 2000.
Vanhoozer, Kevin J. *Is There a Meaning in this Text?: The Bible, The Reader, and the Morality of Literary Knowledge*. Grand Rapids: Zondervan, 1998.
Von Wahlde, Urban C. *The Gospel and Letters of John*. 3 vols. Eerdmans Critical Commentary. Grand Rapids: Eerdmans, 2010.
Waetjen, Herman C. *The Gospel of the Beloved Disciple: A Work in Two Editions*. London: T. & T. Clark, 2005.
Watson, Francis. *Gospel Writing: A Canonical Perspective*. Grand Rapids: Eerdmans, 2013.
Westcott, Brook Foss. *The Gospel According to St. John*. Thornapple Commentaries. Grand Rapids: Baker Academic, 1980.
Wiles, Maurice F. *The Spiritual Gospel: The Interpretation of the Fourth Gospel in the Early Church*. Cambridge: Cambridge University Press, 1960.
Williams, P. J. "The John Manuscript 'Without John 21.'" http://evangelicaltextualcriticism.blogspot.ca/2006/09/john-manuscript-without-john-21.html.
Wimsatt, W. K., and Monroe C. Beardsley. "The Intentional Fallacy." In *The Verbal Icon: Studies in the Meaning of Poetry*, 3–19. Lexington: University of Kentucky Press, 1954.
Witherington, Ben. *John's Wisdom: A Commentary on the Fourth Gospel*. Louisville, KY: Westminster John Konx, 1995.
Yarbrough, R. W. "The Date of Papias: A Reassessment." *Journal of the Evangelical Theological Society* 2 (1983) 181–91.
Zelyck, Lorne. "Irenaeus and the Authorship of the Fourth Gospel." In *The Origins of John's Gospel*, edited by Stanley E. Porter and Hughson T. Ong 239–258. Leiden: Brill, 2016.
Zumstein, Jean. *Kreative Erinnerung: Relecture und Auslegung im Johannesevangelium*. Zürich: Theologischer Verlag, 2004.
Zwierlein, Otto *Petrus in Rom, die literarischen Zeugnisse: Mit einer kritischer Edition der Martyrien des Petrus und Paulus auf neuer handschriflicher Grundlage*. Untersuchungen zur antiken Literatur und Geschichte, Bd. 96 Berlin: De Gruyter, 2009.

Author Index

Abramowski, Luise, 65n19, 81nn82–84
Annand, Rupert, 61n3, 62n7, 67n30, 69n38, 92n125
Attridge, Harold, 99–100, 99n152, 100n154, 100n156, 100n161

Bacon, B. W., 62n8, 65nn19–20, 66n24, 96n141
Barker, James W., ix, 9n28, 86n102, 86nn103–4, 87n106, 97n145, 101n166
Barnes, Timothy D., 52–53, 53nn91–92, 54n98, 55n103
Barrett, C. K., xivn11, xvin17, 1n3, 2n8, 4n14, 5n16, 5–6n17, 6n18, 7n20, 9n27, 10n32, 11n38, 13n46, 21n75, 22n78, 24, 24n89, 26n95, 34n16, 35, 35nn17–19, 36n24, 39n40, 41n45, 45, 45n57, 45n58, 52, 52n86, 52n89, 61n5, 66n22, 67n29, 70n42, 72n51, 77n68, 83n93, 91n118, 92n124, 94n133, 95n136, 96–97, 96n142, 97nn143–44
Barthes, Roland, 104–5, 105n5, 106–7n13, 107, 107nn20–21, 108, 108n30, 109n32
Bartlet, Vernon, 51n4, 62n9, 67n30, 77n70
Batovici, Dan, 83n94, 84, 84nn96–97, 87n106

Bauckham, Richard, xvin18, 2n5, 4–5n15, 12n44, 13n46, 15nn51–52, 16n56, 18–19, 18n61, 19n64, 20n73, 23, 23nn84–85, 30n2, 32n8, 36, 36n22, 37, 37n27, 37n29, 38–39, 38n32, 38n35, 39n36, 41–42, 41n45, 41n49, 44, 44n56, 45–46, 45n59, 46n61, 47n70, 49n75, 66n24, 67n29, 70, 70n46, 71n50, 73n55, 74n61, 74–75n62, 76, 76n64, 76n66, 78nn71–72, 91n117, 92, 92n122, 92n125, 93–94, 93n129, 94n131, 97, 97n146, 98, 98n150, 100n159, 119n76
Bauer, Walter, xivn11
Baum, Armin Daniel, 31n7, 32n8, 34n16, 37n28, 39, 39nn38–39, 43n51, 46–47, 46n62, 46n65, 47n67, 47n69
Beardsley, Monroe C., 106, 106n18
Beasley-Murray, George R., 4n15, 7n20, 9n27, 10n32, 15n51, 16n56, 18nn60–61, 22n79, 23n85, 26n94, 35n19, 39n40, 45n57, 48n71, 52n86, 91n118
Beck, David R., xin2, 1n4, 4–5n15, 12n43, 16n56, 19n67
Bellinzoni, A. J., 83n92, 86, 86nn101–2

143

Author Index

Bennema, Cornelius, 1n4, 4–5n15, 12n43, 16n56, 19nn65–66, 20n70, 21n75, 27, 27n99, 45n59

Bernier, Jonathan, *ix*, 18n61

Blomberg, Craig, *xvi*n15, 2n6, 3n9, 3n11, 5n16, 5–6n17, 6nn18–19, 7n21, 8n25, 10n30, 11nn33–34,11n37, 12n39, 12n41, 13n48, 15n54, 18n63, 20n70, 26n94, 37nn26–27, 38n33, 41nn45–46, 41n48, 45n59, 47n68, 48n71, 49n75, 51n83, 52n87, 69n40, 72n51, 77n70, 82n87, 98n149

Bockmuehl, Markus, 56n106, 70, 70nn43–44,106n14, 107, 107n19

de Boer, Esther A., *xi*n3, *xii*n4

Bokedal, Tomas, 109–10, 110n38, 111, 111nn45–46

Bourdieu, Pierre, 109n33

Braun, F. M., *xv*n13, 82, 82–83n90, 83n91, 84n98, 85n100, 87nn104–5, 87n107, 98n150, 100n162, 128n1

Braun, Willi, *ix*, 35–36, 35n19, 36n20, 39n40, 50n80

Breck, John, 36n21, 37–38, 37n26, 37–38n30, 41nn45–46

Brent, Allen, 116, 116n62, 116–117n63, 117n66, 117n68, 118nn70–71, 119n74, 119n77, 120nn79–80, 121nn82–83, 121n85, 122n88, 122n90, 123–24, 123n91, 123nn93–95, 124n97, 124nn99–101, 125n104

Brodie, Thomas L., 8n24, 38n31, 41, 41n44, 41nn47–48, 45n57

Brown, Raymond, *i*, *xiv*n11, *xvi*, *xvi*n16, *xvii*n19, 4n15, 5n16, 5–6n17, 7nn20–21, 9n27,
11n34, 11n37, 12n39, 12n43, 16nn55–56, 18n61, 19n66, 20n70, 21n74, 21nn77–78, 23n85, 26n94, 35, 35nn18–19, 36n24, 38n34, 39n40, 45n57, 48n71, 49, 49n75, 50n80, 51n82, 52n86, 67n29, 71n49, 72n51, 92n124

Bruce, F. F., 110n39, 110n42, 111n47

de Bruyne, Donatien, 73–74, 73n56, 74n57

Bultmann, Rudolf, *xvii*n19, 8n23, 21n77, 22–23, 22nn81–82, 25n91, 27n101, 31, 31n4, 34n16, 35n17, 35n19, 39n40, 50–51, 50n78, 51–52, 52n85, 72n52

von Campenhausen, Hans, *xiv*n11, 81n85, 109n37, 110nn41–42, 111n47

Carlson, Stephen, *ix*, 79n77

Carson, D. A., *xvi*15, 2n6, 3n9, 3n11, 4n14, 5n16, 6nn18–19, 7n20, 8n25, 10n30, 11n33, 11n37, 12n39, 18n63, 21n74, 22nn78–79, 26n94, 34n16, 36n24, 38n33, 39n37, 41n45, 41n48, 45n59, 46n63, 47n70, 51n83, 52n86, 63n14, 67n30, 68n34, 69nn39–40, 74n58, 91n117

Casey, Maurice, 2n8, 3n10, 12n44, 20n69, 21nn76–77, 22, 22n80, 25n92, 35n19, 48n72, 49n77, 79n80, 94n133, 96n138

Charlesworth, James H., xi–xii, *xii*nn4–5, *xvi*n18, 2n5, 3n11, 4–5n15, 6n18, 8, 8nn23–24, 10n29, 12n43, 14, 14n50, 21nn77–79, 23n85, 27, 27n100, 27n103, 28n104,

Author Index

45n57, 48n71, 72n52, 103n1, 104n2
Collins, Raymond F., 1n4, 16n56
Cook, John Granger., 53, 53n93, 53n94
Cullmann, Oscar, 4n15, 11n34, 12n44, 15n51, 16nn55–56, 18n61, 20n70, 23n85, 48n71
Culpepper, R. Alan, xiin4, xivn11, 1n3, 7n22, 12–13, 12n44, 13nn45–46, 14n49, 15n51, 15n53, 16n56, 17n57, 18nn60–51, 21n75, 22n79, 23n85, 23n57, 48n71, 51n82, 67n29, 72n51, 74n57, 79n80, 92n122, 92n124, 116n59, 117n64, 123n92
Czachesz, István, 100, 100n155, 100n157, 100n159

DeConick, April D., xivn11, 115n58
Deeks, David G., 62n8, 67n30, 68n33, 69n41, 74–75n62
Dunderberg, Ismo, 1n3, 20, 20n69, 20n71, 23, 23n84, 23n87, 43–44, 44n54, 48n72

Ehrman, Bart D., 11n37, 12n42, 43n53, 49n73, 82n88, 85n100, 88n109, 96, 96n139
Ellis, Peter F., 36n21, 37–38, 37n27, 41n45, 41n48
Elowsky, Joel C., xvin15

Farmer, William R., 81n86, 110n38, 110n41, 111nn44–45, 111n47
Farkasfalvy, Denis M., 81n86, 109–10, 110n38, 110n41, 111nn44–45, 111n47
Fish, Stanley, 107–8, 107nn22–24, 113n50
Foster, Paul, 82n88, 85n100

Foucault, Michael, 108–9, 108n31, 109nn32–36
Franzmann, Majella, xiv–xv, xivn11, xvn12, 115n58

Gadamer, Hans-Georg, 108n25
Gamble, Henry Y., 81n85, 83n92, 109n37, 110n39, 103nn41–42, 111n45, 111n47
Gaventa, Beverly Roberts, 32n8, 39n40, 40, 40nn41–42
Goodacre, Mark, 44, 44n55
Goulder, Michael W., 53–54, 54nn95–96, 54n99, 55n104
Grant, Robert M., 63nn13–14, 74–75n62, 79n80, 90n115, 91n116, 110n39, 111n45, 111n47
Grassi, J. A., xiiin4, 1n2, 4–5n15, 7n20, 10nn29–30, 16n56, 18nn60–61, 20n70, 22n78, 23n85, 48n71
Gregory, Andrew, xivn10, 9n28, 51n84, 55, 55n105, 76n65, 79n75, 83n94, 84n95, 84n96
Gundry, Robert H., 61n4, 62n9, 63n11, 63n14, 64n15, 67n30, 68n34, 69n9, 42n70, 71, 71n47
Gutwenger, Engelbert, 74nn57–58
Gwynn, John, 121–22, 121nn84–85, 122n86, 122n88, 122n90, 124n100

Haenchen, Ernst, xivn11, 1n3, 5–6n17, 14n49, 16n56, 18n60, 20n70, 21n74, 22n79, 23n85, 24n88, 26n95, 34n16, 35n19, 39n40, 48n71, 52n90, 67n29, 72n52, 74n57, 74n59, 83n92, 92n124, 95n136
Hanson, K. C., 17–18, 17n58, 18n59,

145

Author Index

Harris, J. Rendel, 122, 122nn87–88, 122n90
Head, Peter M., 111n47
Heard, Richard, 74n57, 74n59, 81n83, 82n88
Hengel, Martin, *xiii–xiv*, *xiv*n10, *xv*n13, *xvi–xvii*, *xvi*n18, 4n15, 12n44, 16n56, 18n61, 23n85, 45n59, 48n71, 52n86, 59n1, 62n8, 71n50, 72n52, 73n55, 74–75n62, 82n87, 84n98, 87nn104–5, 87nn107–8, 89n112, 92n124, 95n134, 101n166, 114n54, 119n76
Hezser, Catherine, 11n37
Hill, Charles E., *xiii*n9, *xiv*n11, *xv*n13, 61n3, 61n5, 67n29, 68n33, 70n45, 74–75n62, 76–77, 77nn69–72, 79nn75–76, 81n85, 81–82n86, 82n87, 83n94, 84n98, 85nn99–100, 87n104, 87nn107–8, 88, 88n111, 89–90, 89n112, 89n114, 94n132, 95, 95nn134–35, 99, 99nn152–53, 100n162, 101n166, 114nn53–54, 115nn55–56, 116, 116n59, 116nn62–63, 117, 117nn66–67, 117n69, 118n70, 118n72, 119n74, 119n77, 121nn82–83, 122n88, 124nn99–100, 124n104, 128n1
Hillmer, Melvyn Raymond, *xiv*n11, 83n92, 83n94
Hirsch Jr., E. D., 105, 105nn8–9, 106, 106nn15–16, 108, 108nn28–29, 108n29
Holmes, Michael W., 60n2, 65n18, 95n136
Hoskyns, Edwyn, *xvi*n15, 2nn5–6, 4nn14–15, 6n19, 8n25, 16n56, 21n75, 21n77, 22n78, 36n21, 36n23, 41n43, 41n45, 46n63, 47n70, 49n75, 52n86, 104n2

Jackson, H. M., 30n2, 45n59, 46–47, 46n61, 46n64, 47n66, 47n70, 49n75
Jauss, Hans Robert, 108, 108nn26–27

Keefer, Kyle, *xv*n13, 105, 105n13, 108n27, 114n52
Keener, Craig S., *xvi*n15, 2n6, 3n9, 3n11, 5n16, 5–6n17, 6nn18–19, 8n23, 12n41, 12n43, 14n49, 15n54, 17n58, 21n75, 22n78, 30n2, 34n16, 36, 36n25, 38n34, 41n44, 46n63, 47n70, 49n75, 51n83, 52n86, 104n3
Keith, Chris, 34n15, 45, 45n60
Kelhoffer, James A., *xiii*n7
Koester, Helmut, *xiii*n7, *xiii*n8, *xiv*n11, 43n52, 50n80, 61n5, 75n63, 81n83, 81n85, 83n92, 83n94, 85n100, 86, 86nn101–2, 89, 89n113, 109n37
Kok, Michael J., 61nn3–4, 67n29, 68–69n37, 70n42, 71n48, 75n63, 78n72, 78n74, 79n77, 79n80, 81n83, 82n88, 87n104, 88n109, 96n138, 98n148, 119n76
Körtner, Ulrich H. J., 60n2, 61n4, 62n9, 66n24, 70n42, 71n48, 75n63, 79, 79n79
Köstenberger, Andreas J., *xv*n15, 2n6, 3n9, 3n11, 4n14, 4–5n15, 6nn18–19, 7n20, 7n21, 8n25, 11n33, 13n48, 16n56, 21n74, 22nn78–79, 37n27, 45n59, 46n61, 52n87, 67n30, 68n34, 69nn39–40,

Author Index

71, 71n47, 76n67, 92n124,
94n131, 98n149, 103, 103n1
Kügler, J., *xii*n4, 1n3, 8n23, 9n27,
12n44, 14n49, 20n69, 21n77,
22n78, 23, 23n86

Lagrange, M. J., 39n38, 47n68
Lalleman, Pieter J., 99, 99nn152–
53, 100n158, 100n161,
101nn165–66
Lattke, Michael, *xiv–xv*, *xiv*n11,
*xv*n12, 32, 32nn9–10,
115n58
Lightfoot, R. H., 61n5, 67n30,
68n33, 74, 74n58, 74n60,
74–75n62
Lincoln, Andrew T., 20, 20nn72–73,
22n78, 23n85, 28n107, 30n3
Lindars, Barnabas, *xiv*n11, 1n1,
5–6n17, 6n18, 8n23, 10n32,
12n43, 12n44, 14n49, 15n53,
20n70, 21nn75–76, 22nn78–
79, 26n94, 35n19, 48n72,
72n51, 75n63, 92n124

MacDonald, Dennis, 61nn3–4,
62n9, 73n54, 75n63
MacDonald, Lee Martin,
110nn39–41, 110–11n42,
111, 111nn43–45, 111n47,
112n48
Manor, T. Scott, 78n71, 78n73,
79n76, 115n55, 116, 116n60,
116nn62–63, 117nn65–66,
117n68, 118nn70–71,
119nn74–75, 119n77,
120n78, 120n80, 121nn82–
83, 121n85, 122n88, 123,
123nn93–94, 123n96,
124–25, 124nn98–100,
125nn103–4
Massaux, Édouard, 82–83, 83n91,
83n94, 84n98, 87n105,
87n107

McGrath, James, 51n82
Metzger, Bruce M., 25–26n93,
33nn13–14, 81–82n86,
110, 110nn39–40, 110n42,
111n47
Meyer, Marvin, 20n71
Michaels, J. Ramsay, 1n1, 3–4,
4n12, 8n23, 12n43, 14n49,
15nn51–52, 21n74, 21n76,
22n79, 26n94, 28n104,
36n21, 38n33, 41n46, 63n14,
64n15, 69n39, 92n124,
97–98, 98n147
Minear, Paul, 36n21, 41n48
Minns, Denis, 90n115, 91n120,
95n137, 112n49, 114n52
Mitchell, Margaret M., 79, 79n78
Moloney, Francis J., 4–5n15, 11n34,
16n56, 21n75, 23n85, 35n19,
45n57, 48n71, 52n86
Mommsen, Theodor, 65n19
Morris, Leon, *xv*, *xv*n14, *xvi*n15,
2n6, 3n9, 3n11, 4nn14–15,
5–6n17, 6nn18–19, 7nn20–
21, 8n25, 11n33, 15n54,
21n74, 22nn78–79, 36n123,
37n26, 38n33, 39n37,
45n59, 47n70, 52n87, 65n15,
91n117
Munck, Johannes, 65n21, 66n23,
67n30, 68n33
Mutschler, Bernhard, 91n116,
91n121, 92n122, 92n124,
93n128
Myllykoski, Matti, 95n135,
114nn53–54, 115n55,
115n57, 124n99

Nagel, Titus, *xiii*n9, *xv*n13,
74–75n62, 83n94, 87n104,
87n107, 89n112, 100n156
Neirynck, Frans, 16n56, 20n69,
50n81

147

Author Index

Norelli, Enrico, 60n2, 61n3, 62n8, 72n52, 75n63

Osborn, Eric, 90n115, 91nn116–17, 92n124, 112n49, 113n51, 114n52

Pagels, Elaine H., 115n58
Parker, Pierson, 10, 10nn29–30, 11, 11nn35–36, 13n47, 15n53, 18nn60–62, 28–29, 29n108
Parvis, Paul, 80n81
Perumalil, A. C., 62n7, 63, 63nn12–14, 71n49, 91, 91n117, 91n119, 91n121
Pervo, Richard, 99–100, 99n152, 100n154, 100n163, 101, 101n167
Pesch, Rudolf, 50n81
Pilhofer, Peter, 85n100
Pollard, T. E., xivn11
Porter, Stanley E., 33n12, 35n17, 39n37
Pryor, John W., 82n89, 84n98, 88n110

Quast, Kevin, 4n14, 4n15, 7n20, 15n51, 16n55, 16n56, 18n61, 19n66, 20n70, 21n75, 22n79, 23n85, 25–26n93, 36n24, 41n45, 48n71, 50, 50n79, 50n80

Rasimus, Tuomas, xvn13, 115n58
Reader, W., 99n151
Regul, Jürgen, 74n57
Resseguie, James L., 1n4, 4–5n15, 16n56, 21n75, 22n78, 26n96, 46n61
Ridderbos, Hermann, xvin15, 3n9, 4n14, 4–5n15, 5n16, 5–6n17, 6n18, 7n20, 8n25, 16n56, 21n75

Robinson, Theodore H., 122, 122nn89–90
Ruckstuhl, Eugen, 34n16

Sanders, J. N., xivn11, 83n93, 92n124, 95n136
Schäferdiek, Knut, 99n152, 100n160, 100n164, 101nn165–66
Schenke, Gesa, 32–33n11
Schenke, Hans-Martin, xiin5, 20n69
Schnabel, Eckhard J., xii–xiiin6
Schnackenburg, Rudolf, xivn11, xvi, xvin16, 3n9, 5n16, 8n23, 10nn31–32, 11n37, 12n39, 12nn43–44, 14n49, 15n54, 16n55, 18n61, 19, 19n66, 19n68, 20n70, 21n75, 22n78, 23n85, 25nn90–91, 27n102, 35n19, 39n40, 45n57, 48n71, 66n22, 66n24, 67n29, 70n42, 72n51, 74n59, 77n68, 91n118, 92n124, 98n150, 104n2
Schnelle, Udo, 4–5n15, 16n56, 21n77, 22n79, 30n1, 35n19, 39n40, 45n59, 48n71, 114n54
Schoedel, William R., 60n2, 61n4, 62n9, 64n17, 66n24, 68n33, 72n51
Shanks, Monte A., 60n2, 61n4, 62, 62n10, 63n14, 64, 64nn15–16, 67–68, 67n28, 67nn30–31, 68n32, 68n34, 68n37, 71, 71n47, 72–73, 72n51, 72n53, 73n54, 74–75n62, 91n117, 91n121, 92n122, 96n140
Siegert, F., 60n2
Sim, David C., 61n6, 63n11, 66n24, 67n29, 70n42, 71n48
Skinner, Christopher, ix, 1nn3–4, 14n49, 16n56, 21n75, 26–27, 27n98, 35n19

148

Author Index

Sloyan, G. S., *xiv*n11, 115n58
Smith, Dwight Moody, 9n28, 31, 31n6
Smith, Joseph Daniel, 116, 116nn60–62, 117, 117n64, 118–19, 118n71, 119n73, 119n76, 120, 120n81, 123n92
Snout, Stephen O., 2n6, 3n9, 3n11, 4n14, 6nn18–19, 45n59, 46n61, 68n34, 69nn39–40, 92n124, 94n131
Stanton, Graham N., 81n83, 81–82n86, 82, 82nn87–88, 84n98, 88n109, 89n112
Stewart, Alistair C., 66–67, 66nn25–26, 67n27, 68n33, 68nn35–36

Tabor, James D., *xiii*n4, 8n26
Theobald, Michael, 1n3, 4–5n15, 16n56, 21n75, 24n88, 25n90, 31n5, 45n59, 49n74, 49n76
Thiselton, Anthony C., 107–8, 108n25, 114n52
Thompson, Marianne Meye, *xvi*n18, 12nn43–44, 16n56, 18n61, 19, 19n68, 21n75, 22nn78–79, 28n104, 35–36n19, 39n40, 45n57, 48n71, 52n86, 73n55, 84n98
Thyen, Hartwig, 1n3, 4n15, 10n32, 16n56, 22n79, 23n85, 24n88, 25n90, 31n5, 37n27, 45n59, 48n71, 49n74
Trobisch, David, 34, 34n15, 45n59
Tuckett, Christopher M., 83n94, 84nn95–96

Vanhoozer, Kevin J., 104n4, 105, 105nn6–7, 105nn10–12, 106, 106n17, 108n28

Waetjen, Herman C., *xvii*n19, 3n11, 4, 4n13, 16n56, 22n78, 39n40, 50n80, 52n86, 72n52
Watson, Francis, 75n63, 76n64, 79n80, 82n89, 83n93, 85n100, 94n131, 96n133, 119n76, 124–25, 125n102, 125n105
Westcott, Brook Foss, *xvi*n15, 2–3, 2nn6–7, 3n9, 3n11, 4nn14–15, 6nn18–19, 8n25, 11n33, 11n37, 12n39, 16n56, 21n74, 25n93, 35n19, 39n37, 47, 47n68, 47n70, 82n87, 84n98, 91n117, 121n83
Wiles, Maurice F., *xiv*n11, 92n124
Williams, P. J., 32–33n11
Wimsatt Jr., W. K., 106, 106n18
Witherington III, Ben, 4–5n15, 11n34, 15nn51–53, 16n56, 18nn60–61, 21n75, 22nn78–79, 28n104, 39n40, 40n42, 48n71, 51n83, 52n86

Von Wahlde, Urban C., 5–6n17, 10n32, 12nn43–44, 14n49, 15n51, 16n56, 20n70, 21n74, 22n78, 23n85, 25n90, 26–27n97, 28, 28n105, 31n5, 39n40, 41n45, 48n71, 52n88, 68n33, 69n38, 71n50, 73n55, 74–75n62, 92n124

Yarbrough, R. W., 61n4, 62n7, 63n14

Zelyck, Lorne, 92–93, 92n124, 93nn126–28, 93n130, 94n131, 95n137
Zumstein, Jean, *xiv*n11, 21n75, 21n77, 22n79, 35n19, 39nn39–40, 45n59
Zwierlein, Otto, 54n97, 54nn100–101, 54n104, 55n10

Ancient Document Index

Old Testament

Numbers
21:8–9   87

Deuteronomy
19:15   47
32:8   121

Ruth
4:15   xin3

2 Kings
10:11   7

Nehemiah
3:3   7

Esther
8:8–10   45

Psalms
22   81
22:16   85
55:14   7
66:13   7

Isaiah
11:1–3   88
40:4   89
58:2   85

Ezekiel
47:10   38

Zephaniah
1:10   7

Zechariah
12:10–14   83n91

New Testament

Matthew
3:4   89
3:16–17   89
4:1–11   120
4:18–22   50
5:20   86
7:16–17   126
7:21   86
9:9–10   49

Ancient Document Index

Matthew *(continued)*

10:2	76
10:2–4	65n19
10:3	49
11:9	94
18:3	86
19:23–24	86
20:20	8
20:20–22	93
26:20	6
26:21–25	24
26:69	18
27:56	8, 98
28:16–20	36
28:17	41

Mark

1:6	89
1:9–10	89
1:12–13	120
1:15–20	4
1:16–20	17, 50
1:19–20	xviii, 7, 11
1:20	92
1:29	6
1:29–31	15
2:14–15	49
3:13–19	112
3:16–19	65n19, 76
3:17	10, 87
3:18	96
3:33–35	26
5:37	6
5:37–43	15
6:3	8
9:1	23, 48
9:2	6
9:2–9	15
9:47	86
10:35–41	10
10:39	72
13:3	6
13:3–4	15
14:17	6
14:18–21	24
14:33	6, 15
14:51–52	1
14:70	18
15:40	8
16:5–7	1
16:8	33
16:9–20	33

Luke

1:1–2	83
1:1–4	43n53, 60
1:2	5
1:5	98
1:36	98
2:42	7
2:44	7
3:15	89
3:21–22	89
4:1–13	120
5:1–11	3, 50, 51
5:10	13
5:27–29	49
6:14–16	65
6:43–44	126
7:26	94
7:36–50	51, 60
9:53	10
10:1	71
10:1–20	93
10:18	60n2
10:38–42	51
16:19–31	51
18:17	86
18:25	86
22:14	6
22:59	18
24:1–11	51
24:12	25, 25–26n93, 51, 51n84
24:13–51	33
24:15–32	41
24:24	25n93, 26
24:33–53	51

Ancient Document Index

24:50–53	36

John

1—20	34, 35
1:1	82n90, 83n91, 95n135
1:1–18	37
1:1—20:31	12, 13
1:3	83n91
1:4–5	116
1:6	39n36
1:9	82n90
1:12	39n36
1:13	82–83n90, 83n91, 85
1:14	37, 45, 82n90, 83n91, 85, 113, 116
1:17	82–83n90
1:18	26, 37, 83n91, 85, 115
1:20	82–83n90, 89
1:23	82–83n90
1:29	82–83n90
1:31	40n42
1:32–33	89
1:32–34	89, 116
1:35–36	14
1:35–40	1, 4, 5, 13, 14, 15, 18
1:35–42	4
1:36	82–83n90
1:37–39	5
1:38	35n17
1:40–44	75, 76
1:42	50
1:43–46	96
1:45–49	35
1:50–51	86
2:1	120
2:3–4	21
2:11	36, 40n42
2:23	39n36
3:1	39n36
3:1–21	87
3:2	46
3:3	82n90, 85–86, 86n102
3:3–5	83n91
3:4	85, 87
3:5	86, 86n102
3:11	46
3:13	115
3:14	52, 87, 87n105
3:14–15	83n91
3:14–17	82–83n90
3:17	82–83n90
3:18	39n36
3:19–21	116
3:22—4:1	3
3:24	78
4:10	83n91
4:24	83n91
4:34	82n90
4:54	36
5:22–26	82–83n90
5:23	82n90, 83n91
5:25	23
5:28–29	23
5:37	115
5:43	39n36
5:46	33n91
6:5–7	96
6:5–9	5
6:38	82n90
6:39–40	23
6:40	95n135
6:44	23, 95n135
6:46	115
6:53	82n90
6:54	23, 95n135
6:55	82n90
6:67	15, 16
6:67–71	112
6:68	24
6:68–69	50
6:70	6, 15
6:70–71	42

153

Ancient Document Index

John (continued)

6:71	15	13:23—20:10	48
7:5	8n26	13:23–25	*xi, xiv, xviii,*
7:37–39	38		1, 5, 18, 22,
7:38	22, 83n91		24, 29
7:52	33	13:23–27	24
7:53—8:11	33, 60	13:23–28	24
8:12	33, 116	13:26–27	25
8:44	115	13:28	25, 27
8:56	95n135	13:28–29	24
8:57	75	13:33	35
9:15	116	13:34	11, 95n135
10:1–18	16	13:34–35	14
10:3	39n36	13:36–38	24, 41
10:11	42	14:2	75
10:18	83n91	14:3	23
10:25	39n36	14:8–9	96
10:29	82–83n90	14:13	39n36
11:1–44	51	14:14	39n36
11:5	28	14:15	14
11:9	82–83n90	14:16	117
11:9–10	116	14:16–17	113
11:10	124n100	14:21	28
11:16	35, 75	14:23–24	14
11:36	28	14:26	39n36, 113
12:1–8	51	14:28	27
12:13	39n36	14:29	83n91
12:20–22	5	14:30	124n100
12:21–22	96	14:31	37
12:23	52	14:34	82–83n90
12:27	15	15:2–10	14
12:28	39n36	15:9	11
12:32	52	15:10	28
12:35–36	116, 124n100	15:12–17	14
12:36	37	15:14	28
12:40	35n17	15:15	82–83n90
12:42	8	15:16	6, 39n36
12:42–43	17	15:19	6
13—20	42, 44	15:21	39n36
13:1	11, 21, 22	15:27	6, 14
13:3	82–83n90	15:27	5
13:6–10	24	16:4	5, 6, 14
13:18	6	16:23	39n36
13:23	26, 30, 73, 100	16:24	39n36
		16:26	39n36

Ancient Document Index

16:28	27	20:2–4	16
17:1	21, 53	20:2–9	6, 18, 22, 51
17:2	82–83n90	20:2–10	1, 24, 25, 29
17:6	39n36, 82–83n90	20:3–4	11
		20:3–10	*xviii*, 51n84
17:11	39n36	20:7	73
17:12	39n36	20:8	11, 16, 27
17:24	82–83n90	20:8–10	28
17:26	39n36	20:9	27, 28, 42
18:9	17	20:10	42
18:10	39n36	20:11	25
18:15	97, 98	20:11–18	25
18:15–16	*xviii*, 1, 6, 7n22, 11, 16, 17, 18, 29	20:11–23	33
		20:14	35n17
		20:14–16	41
18:17	16	20:14–17	36, 40n42
18:17–18	50	20:19–23	36, 40
18:25–27	16, 50	20:19–31	32
19:3	113	20:22–23	36, 36n24
19:13	82n90, 83n91, 85	20:24	15, 35, 42
		20:25	14, 85
19:19	44, 45	20:27	85
19:25	4, 8, 98	20:29	42
19:25–27	6, 18, 22	20:26–29	36, 40, 40n42
19:26	*xi*n3, 73	20:30–31	21, 35, 36, 37, 38, 39, 42, 56, 107
19:26–27	*xviii*, 1, 8, 26, 29, 99		
19:27	21	20:31	31, 32, 33, 39n36
19:29	5		
19:33–35	5	20:31—21:1	40
19:34	14	21	41
19:34–35	95n135, 99	21:1	32
19:35	*xviii*, 1, 6, 18, 20n73, 21, 22, 29, 30, 31	21:1–11	50, 51
		21:1–23	37, 47
		21:1–25	13, 18, 31, 34, 39, 42, 47
19:35–37	38		
19:37	83n91, 83n91	21:2	*xii*n4, *xviii*, 1, 3, 3n11, 12, 35, 71, 75, 76
19:38–42	40		
20:1	25		
20:1–10	24	21:7	*xviii*, 1, 53
20:1–23	40n42	21:11	38
20:1–29	51	21:12	57
20:2	16, 46, 73	21:15–17	40, 50
20:2–29	51	21:15–19	50

155

John *(continued)*

21:18–19	42, 51–53, 56
21:18–24	32
21:20	73
21:20–22	5
21:20–24	*xviii*, 1, 15
21:22	48
21:22–23	40, 47
21:23	6, 22, 23, 48
21:24	9, 22, 29, 30, 36, 40n42, 43, 44–46, 49, 56–57, 77
21:24–25	37, 38, 42, 47
21:25	*xviii*, 34
30:31	22

Acts of the Apostles

1:1	43n53
1:13	96
1:13–26	*xviii*, 112
1:14	26
1:18	60
1:21–22	5
1:23	60, 96n140
1:25	56
2:1–4	36n24
3	93
3:1	6
3:3	6
3:4	6
3:11	6
4	93
4:1	6
4:1–21	55
4:5–21	97
4:6	6, 97, 98
4:13	6, 10, 18
4:19	6
4:36	98
5:17–40	55
6:5	96
8:5–6	96
8:14	6
8:14–25	10
8:17	6
8:25	6
8:26–40	96
8:38–39	55
9:1	66n23
11:30	66
12:2	6, 60, 72–73
12:3–6	55
12:12	60
12:17	53
14:23	66
15:2	66
15:4	66
15:6	66
15:23	66
15:37	98
16:4	66
16:10–17	43
20:5–15	43
20:17	66
20:17–38	60
21:1–18	43
21:8–9	60, 96, 96n140
21:18	66
27:1–37	43
28:1–16	43

Romans

1:1	94
11:3	94
16:1–23	53

1 Corinthians

1:1	94
4:9	94
9:2	94
12:28	94
15:5	*xviii*, 112
15:9	94
15:35–49	41

Ancient Document Index

2 Corinthians
1:1   94
12:11–12   94

Galatians
1:1   94
2:6–10   112
2:7–10   53
2:9   xviii, 7, 18
2:13–14   xv
2:20   11

Colossians
4:10   98

1 Thessalonians
4:13–17   48
4:15–17   23
4:17   48

1 Timothy
4:14   66
5:17   66

Titus
1:5   66

Philemon
1:10   68

James
5:14   66

1 Peter
1:1   54
1:3   86
1:23   86
2:5   98
2:9   98
2:11   54

2:17   95n135
5:1   54n96, 68
5:1–5   68
5:13   54, 56, 60

2 Peter
1:18   83–84

1 John
1:2   46
1:4   46
1:5   46
1:6   46
1:7   46
2:2   113
2:7   95n135
2:24   95n135
3:11   95n135
4:2   113
4:2–3   95
5:6   113
5:6–8   95, 95n135
5:13   37

2 John
1:1   58, 73, 79, 97
7   95, 95n135, 113

3 John
1:1   58, 73, 79, 97
12   46

Revelation
1:1   59
1:2   72
1:4   59
1:6   98
1:9   59
2–3   101
2:18   120, 120n80
5:10   98
9:15   121

Ancient Document Index

Revelation *(continued)*

12:9	60n2
17	54
19:9	118
20:1–6	59, 63, 81, 115, 118, 119
20:6	98
21:14	59
21:19–20	98, 99
22:5	37
22:8	59

Apocrypha

Sirach

50:27–29	39
51:1–12	39
51:13–30	39

2 Maccabees

1:1–9	39
1:10—2:18	39

Pseudepigrapha

Ascension of Isaiah

4.1–4	54

Second Baruch

29:5	59

Early Christian Writings

Acts of John by Leucius   xiv, 97–101

18–86	99
56.1	101
87–105	99
88.5–9	99
89.5–6	100
97.1—101.14	99
97.3	99
98–101	99
101.7–8	99
101.11	99
106–115	99
56.1	101
89.5–6	xiv

Acts of John by Prochorus   7

Acts of Peter

35	56
36–39	53

Andrew of Caesarea, Commentary on Revelation

12.9	60n2
34.12	59–60

Anti-Marcionite Prologue to John   73–74, 98n148

Apocalypse of Peter

14.4–6	54

Ancient Document Index

Apollinarius of Laodicea,
Fragments on Matthew
27.5   60

Apostolic Constitutions
6.15.5   86

Epistle of Barnabas
12.2   52
12.4   52
12.5–7   87

1 Clement
4–6   55
5.4   54, 55, 56
5.6–7   55
5.7   56
6.1–2   55

Clement of Alexandria,
Excerpts of Theodotus
7.3   xiv
35.1   xiv
41.3   xiv

Cyprian, *Testimonies against the Jews*
2.20   52

Didache
13.3   98

Didascalia Apostolorum
7   33

Didymus the Blind,
Commentary on Ecclesiastes
223.6–13   33

Dionysius bar Salibi,
Commentary on the Apocalypse
Preface   122, 124
1–2   114
8   124n106
9   124n106
10   121

Dionysius bar Salibi,
Commentary on the Four Gospels   122

Epiphanius, *Panarion*   119, 125
28.2   115
28.4   115
28.4.1–2   124
28.4.6   124
28.5   115
30.24.6   70, 72
33.3.6   xiv
51.3.1–3   120
51.3.6   114, 119, 124
51.4.1–2   114, 121
51.4.9–10   120
51.8.1   121
51.21.15–16   120
51.22.1   120
51.32.2   120
51.33.1–3   120
51.34.2–3   120
51.34.2–8   121

Epiphanius the Monk,
Life of the Virgin   7

Eusebius,
Ecclesiastical History
2.14.1–6   55
2.15.1–2   77, 78
2.15.2   78, 78n72
2.25.6–7   117

Ancient Document Index

Eusebius,
Ecclesiastical History
(continued)

2.25.8	54
3.3.5	110, 119
3.18.2–3	124
3.23.1	*xii*
3.23.4	72
3.34.5	77
3.24.5–7	77
3.24.5–8	77, 78, 79
3.24.5–13	78n72
3.24.6–7	79
3.24.7	77
3.24.8	77
3.23.8–13	78
3.24.11	77
3.24.11–13	77
3.25.1–7	110
3.25.2	119
3.25.4	119
3.25.6	101
3.28.2	114, 117
3.28.4–5	114
3.31.3	70, 72, 96, 97
3.31.4	117
3.34.1	61
3.36.1–2	61
3.39.2	62
3.39.3–4	60, 61, 73, 75, 81
3.39.4	58, 61, 65, 65n18, 84
3.39.5–7	62, 124
3.39.6	73
3.39.9	60, 61, 62, 96n140
3.39.13	61n6
3.39.14	69
3.39.15	58, 60, 74, 75, 77, 81, 82
3.39.15–16	*xiii*, 75, 77, 80
3.39.15–17	62, 73
3.39.16	74, 76n64
3.39.17	33, 60
4.3.2	62, 70
4.5.3	96n141
4.16.7–9	80
5.1	90
5.4.1–2	90
5.5.8	70
5.8.4	*xii*
5.20.4–8	90
5.20.5–6	91, 112
5.20.6	91
5.24.2	7, 96, 97
5.24.2–3	70
5.24.3	72
5.24.7	70
5.24.16	91, 92n123, 112
6.12.2	111
6.14.5	9, 79
6.14.5–7	78
6.14.7	*xii*, 9
6.20.2–3	124
6.20.3	117, 119
6.25.6	*xii*
6.25.11–14	110
6.25.14	110
7.12	78n71
7.25	113
7.25.3	114
7.25.7–27	124
17.1	55

Eusebius, *Gospel Problems and Solutions, To Marinus*

I.1—II.1	33

George the "Sinner,"
Chronicle

3.134.1	71, 72, 73n54

Gospel of Peter

3:6–7	85
6:21	85

160

Ancient Document Index

Gospel of Philip

62.32—64.9   20

Gospel of Mary

10.1–6   20
18.14–15   20

Hippolytus, *Refutation of all Heresies*

1.proeum.6   98
6.15   55
7.18   98
7.33.1–2   114
8.10   86
10.21.1–3   114
10.34.1   117n66

Hippolytus of Thebes, *Syntagmate chronologico*   7

Historia passionis Domini   7

Ignatius, *Epistle to the Magnesians*

5.1   56
6.1   66

Ignatius, *Epistle to the Romans*

4.3   54

Ignatius, *Epistle to the Smyrneans*

8.1   66

Ignatius, *Epistle to the Tralians*

3.1   66

Irenaeus, *Against Heresies*

1.4.4   113
1.8.5   *xiv*, 92n123, 113
1.9.4   113
1.10.1   95
1.11.4   113
1.16.3   92n123
1.23.1–4   55
1.26.1   114
1.26.2   114
2.2.5   92n123
2.9.1   95
2.22.3   92n123
2.22.5   63n12, 66, 70, 72, 75, 92n123
2.22.5–6   75
2.24.4   92
3.1.1   *xii*, 54, 92n123
3.2.2   66
3.3.2   54
3.3.2–3   112
3.3.4   70, 72, 91, 92n123, 112
3.11.1   92n123, 95
3.11.3   92n123
3.11.9   117
3.12.3–5   92
3.12.14   93
3.12.15   92
3.16.5   92n123
3.16.8   92n123
3.22.2   92n123
4.20.11   92n123
4.21.3   114
4.26.2   114
4.28.1   66
4.30.4   92n123
4.31.1   95n135
4.33.2   95n135
5.5.1   66, 75
5.18.2   92n123
5.21.1   92n123
5.30.1   66, 75

Ancient Document Index

Irenaeus, *Against Heresies* (continued)

5.30.3	xviii–xix
5.33.3	59, 62, 75, 92n123
5.33.4	62, 63, 73, 91, 112
5.35.2	92n123
5.36.1	66
5.36.1–2	75
5.36.2	75
6.33.3	66

Irenaeus, *Demonstration of the Apostolic Preaching*

79	52

Jerome, *On Illustrious Men*

1	55
9	70, 72, 73
18	113

Jerome, *Epistle 120, To Hedibia*

	33

Jerome, *Epistle 129, To Dardanus*

	110

Justin Martyr, *Dialogue with Trypho the Jew*

1.2	80
2.3—8.1	80
10.2	xiii, 81
14.1	83n91
17	82n90
32.2	83n91
54.2	83n91, 85
61.1	83n91, 84, 85
61.1—62.5	88
62.3	83n91
63	82–83n90
63.2	85
66	82–83n90
69.6	83n91
76.1	83n91, 85
78.3	88
81.4	59, 63, 81, 118
84.2	83n91, 84
87.2	88–89
87.3	89
87.3–5	89
88	82–83n90
88.3	89
88.4	89
87.5	89
88.3	89, 89–90
88.6	89
88.7	89
91	82–83n90
90.4–5	52
91.4	87n105
94.5	83n91, 87n105
98–107	81
100.1	xiii, 81, 83n91
100.2	84
100.4	xiii, 87, 88
101.3	xiii, 87
101.7	xiii, 87
102.5	xiii, 87
103.6	xiii, 87
103.8	xiii, 82, 87
104.1	xiii, 87
105.1	xiii, 83n91, 87, 88
105.5	xiii
105.6	xiii, 87
106	82–83n90
106.1	xiii, 87
106.3	82, 88
106.4	xiii, 87
111	82–83n90
112.1–2	87n105
117.4	83n91
118.1	83n91
121	82–83n90
136.3	83n91

Ancient Document Index

Justin Martyr, *First Apology*

1.1	80
5.4	84
6.2	83n91
10.6	84
21.1	84
22.2	84
23.2	84, 85
26	55
32.9–10	84
32.10	83n91
32.11	83n91, 85
33.2	83n91
33.5	81
35	52, 81n85
35.4	85
35.7	85
35.8	83n91
35.9	81
48.3	81
52.12	83n91
56	55
60.2–3	87
60.7	84
61	82–83n90
61.4–5	83n91, 85, 87
61.5	87, 87n105, 87n106
63.2	84
63.15	83n91, 84
66.1–3	xiii, 87
66.2	84
66.3	xiii, 81
67.3	xiii, 81, 87, 109n37

Justin Martyr, *Second Apology*

6.3	83n91, 84

Martyrdom of Polycarp

16.2	94

The Muratorian Canon

	xii, xii–xiiin6
9–16	xiii, 76, 79
33	76
19–26	77

Origen, *Commentary on Matthew*

16.6	72

Origen, *Commentary on John*

6.3.3	xiv
10.2	78

Philip of Side, *Christian History*   60, 62, 71, 72, 73n54

Photios I, *Bibliotheca*

48	117

Pionius, *Life of Polycarp*

20–23	94

Polycarp, *Letter to the Philippians*

5.2	95n135
7.1	95
7.2	95n135

Pseudo-Clement, *Homilies*

11.26.2	86

Second Apocalypse of James

56.16–23	2c

Tatian, *Address to the Greeks*

19	8c

Ancient Document Index

Tertullian, *Against Marcion*

3.4	115
3.21	115
3.24	115
4.2	111
4.3	xv
4.5	xii
4.6	115

Tertullian, *Against Praxeas*

1	113
25.4	32
30	113

Tertullian, *On the Soul*

50.5	32

Tertullian, *Scorpion's Sting*

15.3	32, 53

Tertullian, *On Fasting*

1	113
12	113

Tertullian, *On Monogamy*

14	113

Tertullian, *On the Prescription of the Heretics*

33.10	118

Theodoret of Cyus, *Compendium of Heretical Fables*

3.3	118

Theophilus of Antioch, *Apology to Autolycus*

2.9	xiii
2.22	xiii
3.12	xiii

Jewish and Greco-Roman Writings

Aeschines, *Against Timarchus*

177	36n25

Artemidorus, *Interpretation of Dreams*

1.76	52

Cornelius Nepos, *The Lives of Illustrious Men*

25.9.1	39n38

Dionysius of Halicarnassus, *Roman Antiquities*

1.80.1	53

Epictetus, *Discourses*

3.26.22	52

Josephus, *Jewish War*

3.202	46

Plautus, *The Braggart Soldier*

2.4.7	52

Polybius, *Histories*

39.8.4–6	36–37n25

Ancient Document Index

Tacitus, *Annals*
15.44.4   52

Thucydides, *Histories*
1.1.1   30n2
270.4   30n2
4.104.4   30n2
5.26.1   30n2

Xenophon, *Hellenica*
3.2.25   36–37n25
4.8.19   36–37n25

www.ingramcontent.com/pod-product-compliance
Lightning Source LLC
Chambersburg PA
CBHW020851160426
43192CB00007B/882